REVELATIONS & REFERENCES

My Revelations, My References

with your bible

by REVBON

ISBN: 978-87-93084-37-7
Published by Piffz
www.piffz.com

CONTENTS

Foreword 8

Testimonials 10

    Bonnie's Testimony 10

    The Perfect Storm 12

    A Short Story On Chaplain Al Kolades 13

Visions 16

    Map Of The World 16

    A Clean Slate 17

I Beg Your Pardon! I Didn't Promise You A Rose Garden 20

The Healer 22

The Miracle Of Jesus On The Cross 24

Who Will Testify? 25

Three Components Of Faith 26

The Confession Seat 27

Get Right, Go Right 28

Daredevils Daring God 30

Communion 32

Believe In God 33

The Great Designer 34

Go With God 'Vaya Con Dios' 35

Unwrap Him And Let Him Loose 36

Midnight, God's Finest Hour 38

Are You Connected With The Belt Of Truth?..41

Are You Having A Bad Day..43

Under His Mighty Hand..45

Change Of Heart..46

Wonderful To Me 48

To See Into The Distance 50

Delight In The Lord..51

Delivery Only...54

Meaningless Faith..55

How To Take And How To Give Corrections In Ministry...............................58

Good Christian Conduct...60

Golden Years 2009...62

Good Citizenship..64

Passing The Buck..66

Holy Spirit Let Us Pray 69

His Arms Are Open 72

Heavy Burdens..73

Heavenly Worship Or Earthly Pride...75

Is Your House In Order?...78

It Is Not The Length Or The Width, It Is The Depth And The Weight.............79

Immutable God...81

Get The Hell Out! 83

Great Is Thy Faithfulness..86

God Can...88

Grace 89

'I Am' With You Always..91

Hope Is Gone, Grab Your Harp 93

God's Will 97

God Moves 100

God Bless You 103

God And Your Finances 104

Heads And Tails..109

Human Sacrifice 111

Glory From The Tongue 115

Heavenly Words..118

God's Treasures Our Trash 121

Intercessory Prayer 124

Intimate Relationship 125

It Is All About Love 128

God's Calling, Our Comfort 130

God's Faithfulness And Man's Failures 133

Go Into The Closet And Shut The Door! 136

Glory Came Down 137

God Closed The Door 140

In God's Way 141

On Top Of It 143

Out Of The Belly 145

Proud Heart 148

Is It A Religion Or A Relationship? 151

Relationships Without Compromises 154

Respecting Authority 156

Regret Or Rejoice 160

Refreshing 163

Rebirth 165

Rebellion 167

Heart Change 171

Good Luck, Bad Luck, And No Luck 173

In His Name 174

Prosperity 176

Light And Darkness 179

Promises 181

Perseverance 182

Passed Away Or Passed On 183

No Barrier, No Detours 186

Lost And Found 188

Repent And Receive 189

Longevity Is What We Wish For 190

Is It Possible To Be A Good Christian And Not Go To Church? 193

Our Advocate 196

Old Habits Die Hard 197

Good Example 199

Get Naked 203

Be Not Afraid 204

A Hardened Heart 206

Expectations 209

Fear Causes Failure 211

Emotions Etc 214

Eccentrics 216

Distored Anger 218

Molech The False God 221

Anticipation 224

Breathing In And Breathing Out 227

Good, Bad And The Ugly 228

Keeping Things In Order 233

Is Not An Easy Task 233

Marriage A Holy Covenant 235

Beleivers In Bondage 238

Controlling Spirit 240

Love Your Neighbour As Yourself 243

Micah's House 245

Matchmaker 247

Anger Is Like An Allergy 248

It Does Not Help To Complain 251

King Of Kings "Was First A Seed" 252

Lose Your Temper 253

Is Your Desire To Obey God? 255

Deliverance 258

Dieting 259

FOREWORD

Dear reader, this book is my revelations that I have gotten from the Holy Spirit over the years I have been saved, and I wanted to keep a record of them, so I wrote this book. The Bible references that you can read with your Bible will help you with your own revelations. You are quite welcome to use this book in your own ministry.

I believe that for you to have a good understanding of God's Word, the Bible, as well as this book, you need to be committed to Jesus and be saved.

That is a condition that is required of all of us, to understand and enjoy the Bible as well as giving our life to Christ so we can be with Him forever. Most of us know the verses from John chapter 3:16-17 (KJV)

"For God so loved the world that he gave his only begotten Son, that whosoever believeth in him should not perish, but have everlasting life. For God sent not his Son into the world to condemn the world; but that the world through him might be saved."

You can open your heart to Jesus and be with Him forever.

This is the prayer we have all said to Jesus, from our hearts.

'The Sinner's Prayer.' (Pray it out loud.)

"Father God, I come to You, in the name of Jesus and through the Holy Spirit. I have broken your laws and my sins have separated me from You.

Forgive me Lord Jesus, I am sorry and now I want to turn away from my past and sinful life. Please forgive me.

I believe that You, Lord Jesus, died on the cross for my sin. You rose from the dead and are alive to hear my prayers.

I invite You, Lord Jesus, to be the Lord of my life, to rule and reign in my heart forever. Please send Your Holy Spirit to help me obey You.

I want to do Your will for the rest of my life. In the precious Name of Jesus, I pray.

Amen and amen."

Congratulations now you are born-again and saved. We are all now family in Christ, and citizens of the Kingdom of Heaven. I hope these revelations and references help you in your new life with Jesus.

REVBON

TESTIMONIALS

BONNIE'S TESTIMONY
(My testimony 2006)

My name is Bonnie I was raised in the Christian Science church. When I was 11 years old to my mother sent me a Christian Science home were there were a lot of handicap children and adults. I lived and worked in the home for six years. My mother came and got me from there when the owners wanted to adopt me and send me to private school. My mother said "no". My mother and I could not live together. She did not do any thing to help me go to school; she wanted me to be a model. I had a hard time forgiving her for sending me away.

I left home when I was 18; I married and lived in Galveston. . We were only together 3 years, separated and finally got a divorce.. I then worked as a fashion and photo model for the next 6 years in Galveston, Houston and Dallas, which pleased my mother. I had a lot of boyfriends and went to a lot of parties always on the weekends, so it was then I learned to smoke and drink and gamble. I never had enough money and I was always trying different things to get more money ,moving around a lot a taking a lot of extra jobs, I found no happiness any where or with any one.

One Sunday at lunch I met a Norwegian seaman, 6 weeks later I married him and moved to Norway. My mother was shocked and angry that I could do such a thing. I was quite happy in Norway and we had two sons.

In 1977 we were spending the summer in our cabin on the fjord. We met a couple and as customary in Norway they invited us to their tent for waffles and coffee. They told us they were street preachers and invited us to come to hear them preach and sing. We went with them and became the best of friends.

We stayed good friends after we had left our cabin for the winter.

One Saturday they called and asked us to dinner. After dinner we found out they were also having a home group meeting with lots of singing and a good witness. That night I felt the pull of the Holy Spirit like a rush going through me and with a lot of tears of shame, because I needed to forgive my mother because of the jealously I had inside me. I was jealous of my sister and how my mother favored her over me.

On the sofa in their living room I gave my life to Christ ,I repented for my feelings about my mother and my sister that evening and there , with all my new Christian family I also became a Christian. That night I was born-again. My husband and I found more joy in our relationship and with our sons after that evening with our dear friends. Two weeks later my husband had a miracle at sea and fell on his knees and got saved there in a storm on the fjord. My three sons are saved.

Also I learned a new song that evening" Min Konge og Jeg" My King and I we walk hand in hand along life's rugged path. That has been my daily goal to stay focused on Him from that night in Norway. Since then I have lived in Spain and back here to the States. In all those years I have not let go of the King of Kings hand, but what is even more wonderful for me is that He has not let go of me.

Jesus can do the same for you. He can change your life forever, for the better. No matter what problem you have or are facing God can overcome the problem and set you free. Pray this prayer with me.

> *"Dear Heavenly Father, I come to you through the Spirit in the name of Jesus Christ, your Son. I believe He died on the cross for my sin. I repent of my sin, and ask you to forgive me. I believe You raised Jesus from the dead, and I receive Him now as my personal Savior and Lord. Amen"*

~

THE PERFECT STORM

(My Norwegian husband's testimony 1975)

Dear reader, there was a very tragic film some years ago and I found it on one of my videos, "The Perfect Storm." Perhaps you remember it? The Lord reminded me of a storm in the Bible. There were several storms in the Bible. The one He was referring to was when Jesus was sleeping in the boat. I am going to take these verses slowly and use them as I am directed by the Spirit.

Reference: Mark 4: 35-38

I must admit I have had many days when I felt darkness setting in around me (verses 37, 38). In Norway my husband got saved in 1977. The miracle was that he was out on the fjord and was hauling in the net. The wind came up, to the point that waves were coming into the boat. The week before a friend had drowned because he couldn't remove his rubber overalls and boots to swim to shore. My husband had been a seaman for 40 years, so he decided he would cut off his clothes in the boat and try to swim to shore. But he was not able to stand still enough to do it. The storm was picking up and he was sitting in a half water filled boat, holding on. He was very fearful and shouted to the Lord, "If You are up there Jesus help me now?"

Reference: Mark 4: 39

At once the waves stopped coming over the boat, the wind lied down and my husband continued hauling the net and started up the motor. The strange thing was he could see the waves and the wind at the back of the boat, but in front the water was calm so he got back to the harbour and saw many people standing at pier watching him come in, the storm was following him from the back of his boat and as he arrived with cases of fish to his boat slip, the storm was raging again. There were pictures in the local newspaper, from that day he was called, "The big Fisherman" in our community. My husband gave thanks and gave his life to Jesus, and he served Jesus until that very day the Lord took him home in 1996. That was the perfect storm in my husband's life because he did not have to weather it alone and knew from that day that Jesus is Lord. How about you, how do you weather the storms in your life?

Reference: Mark 4: 40, 41

Are you fearful or do you have faith in the Master? If you have faith in Him and hear His voice say, "Peace, be still," you have also weathered the perfect storm. Amen and amen.

~

A SHORT STORY ON CHAPLAIN AL KOLADES
(Pastor Al's testimony 1939-2016)

Allen Julius Kolodziejczyk was born to his Polish parents.

Isabella and Julian. They raised their only child in a Catholic Church environment in Allegheny Pennsylvania until he was 20.

At the age of 20 he served in the Air Force in Japan decoding enemy codes then returning to his home he married Lillian his school sweetheart and changed his name to Kolades. Allen wanted to make his own way my working for himself selling various products and putting together a band playing his trumpet and his xylophone.

He with wife Lillian and the band traveled from coast to coast, selling his wares and playing his music for several years, at last coming to Miami where they all settled down Allen got steady work selling cookware and his band got a full time gig at a club in the city.

It was one day Allen was selling in his assigned area in the city that he was challenged by an elderly lady. She told him she would buy his cookware if he would come to her church on Sunday. Well Allen thinking this will be a good sale he attended her church that Sunday and there he fell to his knees and excepted Jesus as his Savior that very morning .The same Sunday evening he took Lillian with him for his baptism and she excepted Christ and was baptized there also.

This new found life with Christ slowly changed their lifestyle .No more clubs no more band and now Allen was playing his music in their new church.

After a few years he felt he must go further in his faith so he and Lillian sold their home, their boat and one car in Miami. In the other car they drove to Dothan Alabama where Allen attended and studied at Bethany Bible College. Lillian in great support ,worked at the telephone company and in the college library. As Allen was still studying he also was offered a position leading music and a choir in the local church.

When he was finished with his studies and had a completed his certificate as a minister and Chaplain he was still serving in many churches from 1994 to 2000. When offered a position as a minister to a church in Lakeland, they returned in 2000 and settled in central Florida. He wanted to be a minister and to set up his own business .So he and Lillian sold on the markets and he ministered on the weekend.

Time had passed selling on diffident markets ,when they decided to settle in one place, Market World Auburndale ..Also Chaplain Al had always desired to have his own church. So in Market World he started Christian Community Mission which held a Sunday service at 8AM and is still holding that service every Sunday with our new Pastor Gene Miller..

Sadly Lillian was taken to heaven after suffering four years with Alzheimer's decease. We still have her angel on our prayer page..

Allen remarried in Sept 25, 2006 to Bonnie. Together they had a mission shop and the church. There was as many as 300 that gave their lives to Christ in their church and in their mission shop. Some of them have gone on to begin their own ministries in Florida, up North and. California.

Chaplain Al and Bonnie decided to sell the shop in 2015 when he was diagnosed with lung cancer; sadly Chaplain Al went to be with the Lord Aug 21, 2016.

Bonnie sold their home and returned to Spain and with the family, where Allen had always desired to minister and serve Christ.

AMEN & AMEN.

VISIONS

These are a couple of visions I received prior to writing my revelations.

MAP OF THE WORLD

It was in Norway in Sjeberg after Helge and I had been baptised and we had moved into the Betania (on the 2nd floor) with little Tommy and Eddie.

We were the newest arrivals in the church and we were also the new caretakers of the church. We were so new we were only on 'milk' and getting lots of personal feeding; the 'ins and outs' of being a good Christian in a Pentecostal Church.

Then one Tuesday evening at a prayer meeting where we were always on our knees I had my eyes closed and praying in a childlike manner as we didn't know how to pray. It was then, there on my knees, I received a vision.

I saw a map of the world; it was dark with very little light on it. I could see that there were scattered bright lights, all in different places, on the map. One person asked me if I was alright and I told them that I could see a picture in front of me. They told me to tell everyone what it was and I did. The map kept changing; all the bright lights that were scattered over the map started to breakup and smaller lights began to move in all directions. When the smaller lights stopped moving the whole map was lighted up and everything on the map could be seen. The borders of the counties and continents, rivers, seas and oceans were easily identified. The minister explained that the bright lights were the large churches in the world and that the world map was only visible where those large churches were located. The wonderful thing was in my picture the way the bright lights broke up and the smaller lights scattered in all directions over the whole face of the world map and all the dark area were gone, all the dark areas were now full of light.

Then the minister read two passages, Matthew 5: 14-16, *"Ye are the light of the world. A city that is set on a hill cannot be hid. Neither do men light a candle and put it under a bush, but on a candlestick; and giveth light unto all that are in the house. Let your light so shine before men, that they may see your good works and glorify your Father which is in heaven."*

Next he read out Mark 15: 14-16, *"Go ye into all the world and preach the gospel to every creature."*

Everyone was saying that this was such a blessing that I had seen that picture and \I had to repeat what I had seen at the Sunday evening meeting. Because of that first vision I still believe that God has some special place He wants my light to shine and light up darkness for others. Thank You Jesus. Amen and amen.

~

A CLEAN SLATE

I remember this vision as though it were yesterday even though it was in 1982. I was saved in 1977, but the enemy had been telling me for quite a while that I must not be too sure that all my sins were forgiven. So, I was having second thoughts about my salvation, and if God had really forgiven me my sinful past.

Then, one night my husband was sleeping and I thought I was as well, but I don't know if I was dreaming or awake, I do know that my husband never woke up or knew anything about what I saw that night. This is my vision:

I saw a large scroll up and down and across my bedroom wall. My name was at the top and listed and numbered below were my past sins and a lot I didn't remember, they were all written in black letters on this large scroll on my bedroom wall. Then while I reading and in tears at what I was seeing suddenly there was a red liquid I recognised as blood, was running down the scroll and the black letters were moving and they were running down the scroll with the blood.

All this was going on for quite a while as I was watching the blood wash away the black letters, and in time I saw the blood stop running and I saw that there were only six black letters left at the top of the scroll, it was my name, there was not one black letter left that had been written under my name. All the letters, all my past sins that had been written and listed there were gone. The scroll was there, my name at the top was there, but under my name the parchment was snow white, my sins were definitely forgiven.

I slept like a baby after that and in the morning I was a new person, no question about it, I was a wonderful new person and I had a 'clean slate' to prove it, praise the Lord. Amen and amen.

After reading this can I suggest that you say this prayer:

"Jesus I repent of my sins and I want to serve You from this day for the rest of my life. Because Your word is truth. Jesus I believe that You died on the cross and rose up from the dead so that I can be saved and have eternal life in Heaven with You. I confess with my mouth that I am new born again and cleansed by the Blood of Christ. Jesus hear my prayer for Your precious name sake. Amen."

I BEG YOUR PARDON!
I DIDN'T PROMISE YOU A ROSE GARDEN

Dear reader, this is my first revelation back in 2002 and this song has great memories for me. But I have not thought about it in years until this morning. It was number one on charts in 1970 when I left the States to marry my husband and live in Norway. My husband liked to sing it in his broken English. I woke up this morning with this song on my mind. I knew the Lord was telling me something. I keep notes on things I heard, but I never thought to write for a blog or sermon. But this morning a door opened in my life, and all I wanted to do is write what the Spirit was telling me. Fortunately, all the mistakes I was making on the computer were corrected. So, I started to write. I spent the whole morning listening and writing.

I think this started with my visitor yesterday; a friend that had helped me put the roof on my conservatory. It was incredible that we even tried to do it, but we did it, a man's job. We were so pleased we treated ourselves to cake and ice cream. She knows I am Christian, and we were talking a little about the Bible. She told me that she did not believe in the Devil, and I told her that is what the Devil wants you to think, so you won't rebuke him. He has deceived her.

I think I am getting a message from the Lord, and I want to write it all. The rose garden is beautiful to look at, all the different colours and lovely fragrances. Roses are of very special significance to love and romance. Everything about a rose garden is so perfect that most gardeners pride themselves on them. The rose is always the star performer in the flower show. Yes, the rose is very special: of all the most beautiful pieces of art in God's creation roses stand out among them all. But one can be deceived by the beauty of the rose.

If you stand back and look at the garden or the bush, then you are very happy with what your eyes are beholding. But you may see a sign that says, "Please Do Not TOUCH." That sign is there for a very good reason. Protection: for the rose and the visitor. When we think we can take our dominion over the rose, we start to touch it. Ouch! The beauty of the rose has deceived us; we have been pricked by its thorns. That is the way it fights back, wanting to be left alone. Also, it wants to get back at us trying to take dominion over it.

Like the enemy, the devil, he wants to be left alone to spin his web of destruction and hurt God's children. Or he fights back when he is confronted, that is when we take advantage of our God given dominion over him. In the world all his games, treats, and pleasures are very deceiving. As long as we, "The body of Christ," let him alone and don't face him or challenge him, he looks very attractive. But when we move in closer and speak the 'Name of Jesus' he shows his true colours and, in some cases, his harmful thorns.

The only way to live in the world that is round us is as our Lord Jesus told us; "He the Devil," or, "the prince of the air," will try to take control. We must stand firm and always face him and speak to him in Jesus Name. The moment we turn our backs on him, he has an advantage over us. We must not turn our backs, but keep him behind us, the Lord Jesus said, "Get thee behind Me Satan," and this should be our first utterance in the morning; and our last reply in the evening: as well as repeated throughout the day. The very second he shows himself in conversation with others, on the TV, radio, or newspaper, even on the Net. WHAM! Put him back in his place in Jesus Name.

When he tries to attack our body with sickness, or disease or even death, we must shout aloud, "In Jesus Name get thee behind me Satan." When he tries to inflict uneasy feelings in our relationships with others; jealousy, pride, prejudices, hate, and different offences, whatever weapon he tries to use against our love, our peace our happiness, our joy and our fulfilment, we must be armed and armoured in the 'Blood of Christ' to meet him face to face, 'full steam ahead' and tell Satan to get out and go away as Jesus is Lord.

The one thing Satan has most success in is telling us how inefficient we are. That he does by keeping us down in our communities, down in our workplaces, and down in our finances. Oh yes, he really makes his mark in these areas. Next to our health he hits our wealth. How do we attack him, when he is attacking our finances, our sowing, planting, and harvesting. He tries to plunge his dirty fingers in all three of them. How do we survive? Help is on the way. We have the Word. We meet him head on, as Jesus did with the Word.

Reference: Mathew 4: 10

In others, I sadly see that my friend is being deceived by Satan. She needs to have her eyes on Jesus, her ears listening to the Word and her mind on a 24-7 watch schedule, 'Watch and pray.'

Reference: Mathew 26; 41

My faith is 'mustard seed size' and the Lord said, "That will do," it is enough to win over the enemy. Although I have it, is it enough to win over the enemy deceiving my friend? She is looking at the roses; I need to put up a sign. "Take care they can hurt you." Wow, what a wonderful morning we have had Lord, I like writing. This is like a revelation. Thank You, Lord. Amen and amen.

~

THE HEALER

Dear reader, I have a friend that is very doubtful of Christians. She will not accept spiritual healing in the Name of Jesus. She said there are some tricks to this healing in churches. I have seen many healing in our church and other churches where we visited when I was in the choir. I know that the Pastors are truly men of God, and I was always excited to visit some of our Pastor friends.

Reference: 1 Corinthians 12: 28

I know that I know and therefore I know, I believe in the touch of Jesus in our lives, and I can stand on it.

Reference: Isaiah 53: 5

I asked the Lord to show me more. I started to cry, and I did as I heard the Lord say, "Love overflowing love." We want love in our lives. First from our parents, our brothers or sisters, from our church, from our friends; yes even from our spouses, grandchildren and on and on. We all want to be loved and want somebody to love. But the love we want, and the love we get, and the love we give, is seldom the 'agape love,' the love of Christ.

When I examine myself, how often do I show Christ's Love? Not like I should. All the people that are healed have a similar experience. They say they feel like a warm fire is building up inside them and from this warming they receive and become aware of their healing and deliverance. The love of Christ is that fire. Jesus loved us to the point of giving up His life for us. He was obedient to His Heavenly Father. Our Heavenly Father wanted to open a relationship between Him and us, "Father and child."

Jesus' death on the Cross opened up that relationship for ever. I was half asleep one day, but I remember a program my husband and I watched years ago about the 'Shroud of Turin.' The scientists said that the print of the Lord's body and face was made by heat. After examining the burned patches that were made by a fire in the monastery in the 14th century the scientists concluded that the prints were also made by fire. In other words, when the dead body of Jesus lay in the tomb, God the Father sent fire and resurrected Him to life. I don't know about the shroud, but I believe that Jesus died and was resurrected by the Father.

This is what I want my friend who is so doubtful of healings to understand. How many times did God say, "This is my Son in whom I am well pleased?" The Father's love restored life to His Son Jesus, and He crowned Him King of kings and Lord of lord's. The fire of God, the love of Christ applied by the Holy Spirit is what heals mankind today. No tricks, no magicians, no actors, only Jesus love heals; only Jesus name heals; only Jesus heals.

Reference: Luke 9: 2

Jesus is the only Healer. Amen and amen.

THE MIRACLE OF JESUS ON THE CROSS

Dear reader, why did salvation have to be so painful?

Reference: Isaiah 53: 5-12

The Holy Spirit answered, "Because there is so much sin that has to be paid for." How true it is that when sin is to be redeemed it is done with physical pain. In verse 12 the Devil thought that Jesus was dead for good, but no, that was not the case, Jesus was holding a 'wildcard.' He had paid the price with death and lived and that was the miracle.

Reference: Romans 6: 10

Jesus died on the cross, was laid in a tomb, and arose from the dead taking all power away from the Devil.

Reference: Revelation 1: 18

Jesus took the keys to Hell from the Devil and opened the portal, freeing all those that were imprisoned even though they were classed as righteous. He set them free and that was a miracle.

Reference: 1 Corinthians 15: 54, 55

Jesus won life over death for eternity, for that and us all started on Easter morning.

Reference: 1 Peter 1:3, 4

For us sinners that are so unworthy of Jesus' sacrifice, we have been given redemption, restoration, and He has renewed us for our new life. That is a miracle.

For you and me the miracle of the cross is salvation and that is the greatest miracle that we will ever need. Amen and amen.

~

WHO WILL TESTIFY?

Dear reader, I have always written the messages I have received from the Holy Spirit; in the exact manner it was given me. I use the Word to confirm my message. But this time it is more than a message, it is a warning.

Reference: Hebrews 9: 27

Everyone until the Lord comes is going to die; everyone is going to be judged. It is a fact and nothing you have, nothing you say, or nothing you can do can change that fact.

Reference: Luke 16: 19-28

Here the rubber hits the road. How many family members, co-workers, neighbours, do we have that are not saved? Why? Don't we love them? Don't we care? Yes, we love them, yes we care, but they don't want to know. So, do we give up? My message from the Holy Spirit is clear, who will testify to them that Jesus is Lord if we don't?

References: Mathew 28: 19, 20; Isaiah 6: 8

"Also I heard the voice of the Lord, saying, whom shall I send, and who will go for us? Then said I, here am I; send me." (KJV) Amen and amen.

THREE COMPONENTS OF FAITH

Dear reader, I heard a sermon the other day that touched me and made a big impact on my spirit. When Jesus was born, there was a very big star in the sky. I believe the theory is that three planets got so close to each other that they caused a very bright star.

Reference: Mathew 2:1, 2, 9, 10

They saw a bright star that nobody else saw. How could that be? Well, let us close our eyes and pray for a person that is heavy on our heart. What did you see when you had your eyes closed, did you see that person? Yes, you did, you saw that person in your spirit that revealed a picture in your mind.

Reference: Hebrews 11: 1

My message today is that faith holds three components, the first is audio, and the second is vocal, the third is optical. We receive our salvation when we hear (audio) about our Saviour and receive Him and get saved, the seed of faith is planted within us. Our faith grows and we become a witness and a worshiper, and we speak (vocal) of our faith and our Saviour. But where does the optical appear, it appears when we hope or pray, when we hope we follow it with prayer and when we pray, we see in our spirit what we have hoped for manifested in our minds vision. Then we have faith that it will be manifested for all to see. What we see encourages our faith, in the same way as to what we hear, and what we speak. Faith is definitely made up of all three.

If your faith is faint, and you want to encourage it, you must ask yourself, is what am I listening to, to encourage my faith? Is what I am talking about encouraging my faith? Is what I am hoping for and can see for myself in the future in the will of God and, is it also encouraging my faith? We all must examine ourselves with these questions. I for one should be the first to make some changes to what am I listening to? What is my conversation about, my prayer time and what am I hoping for? Are these His will? When we are willing to make some adjustments in our life, starting from the heart we will increase our faith and nourish it. And our faith will grow and be strong. Amen and amen.

~

THE CONFESSION SEAT

Dear reader, I was watching a film yesterday and there was a woman in a small village. All the villagers went to church to confess, but it was the woman's confession that was in the film that was so moving. I have heard many confessions on TV before I was born-again. I always thought that those people would surely go to Heaven, they were so sincere. But then I learned more about confessions, when Jesus came into my life.

I learned that confessions that count for anything are given at the foot of the cross. A confession seat in a grand church being visited everyday of the year does not pay the price to come to Heaven. The cross is the only way. I heard confessions and, in some cases, hard self-inflicted sufferings during the Easter week we have just finished. Before I understood salvation through the 'Blood of Christ' I believed that these people were surely saved and would go to Heaven, because of their sufferings and regrets. But I say, "Hallelujah," now because I truly understand that it was Jesus' suffering that paid for my salvation and has given me the opportunity to be with Him in Heaven for eternity.

I am a sinner and before I met Jesus, I was a big one. Praise God I am only a little one now. Hallelujah. I still come to the cross and ask my dear Saviour Jesus for His forgiveness every day and I take communion with Him in the way Paul has taught us. I know that Jesus has paid for my sins, but He likes to hear my voice and talk with me. Food for thought, did you know that miracles begin with a conversation with the Lord. There are so many sinners out in the world that have been deceived by the 'confession seat.' They need to know the truth, they need to come to the cross, and they need to be saved. Amen and amen.

GET RIGHT, GO RIGHT

Dear reader, this is so important to me to say, "Get right with God." We would ask our visitors and our customers in our mission shop that we used to have; "Do you have a relationship with Jesus?" or, "Are they right with God?"

Reference: Romans 10: 6-9

In our mission shop we had approximately 300 confessions of faith over the ten years I was in Florida.

Our customers knew we were connected to a church, and they humoured us by saying that they knew Jesus; the truth is when they said that we knew that they do not know Him. Oh, yes, they knew of Him, but they have no relationship with Him.

Reference: Romans 10: 9-11

We are now retired from our shop, but not our ministry. Sales are necessary in any business, but in a mission shop under the church, salvation is more important than income. Leading our customers to Christ and giving them the opportunity to have eternal life was the true work of our successful business.

Reference: Romans 10: 13, 14

There was no doubt in our minds that the customer who, "Get's right with God," and gets saved in our church or our little shop will have every chance to turn their lives around and, "go right with God."

Reference: Romans 10: 15

Praise God, we all have the Word to preach and the gospel to share. We are not in need of a church or mission shop to 'bring glad tidings of good things!' After we prayed the 'Sinner's Prayer' with those blessed customers (I say blessed because what a great blessing can one receive than to meet and to have Jesus in your life), we very seldom got to see those new saved Christians in our shop again, they were in transit, 'snowbirds,' in Florida.

Reference: Ephesians 4: 13-15

Although we may never see them again, we must pray for them. We took their names and wrote them on the 'prayer board' and put them on our church bulletin.

Reference: Philippians 1: 9 -11

Here in these verses, we see where after getting right with God, we must dedicate our lives to going right with God and walking with Christ.

Reference: 2 Timothy 3: 16, 17

When we are moving in the right direction with God, we can use the Scriptures as our GPS. Only through the word of God can we direct our lives closer to Christ. In the same way you would begin a trip by going to your GPS for directions; you begin your day going to the Bible for directions for that day.

Reference: Colossians 2: 6, 7

Here you have the purpose of our witness in the church and in the shop. We prayed with and we prayed for them that this very seed of Christ Jesus will build up faith within them to strengthen them and others around them.

Reference: Romans 8: 1, 2

When we have the privilege of leading a person to Christ, sometimes we also have the privilege of being there for a while with them on their new journey, that privilege comes with an altar call in church. That is where we can see on a daily or weekly basis that they are stepping out and taking baby steps in the Spirit.

Question, is there a reward for "Get right and Go right" life for Christ?

Reference: Hebrews 10: 35-39

Yes, there is a reward, there is Jesus, there is Heaven and there is eternal life, so I encourage you to be a good witness. The path is straight, and the path is long, this is the path we must stay on to walk with Jesus. There are many paths, and there are many out there that are on the way to Hell. Do you believe that the Lord will hold you guilty for the salvation of someone you neglected to witness to?

Reference: Ezekiel 3: 18, 19

Ouch! Now we have retired and left the mission shop, I hope we have not lost souls in the years we have been there. We are retiring from this business, so we will be able to get down to business and win souls for Christ in 2013, in Spain. You too, let's all spread the gospel to our fellow man, so they can, "Get right and go right with God." Amen and amen.

~

DAREDEVILS DARING GOD

Dear reader, last Sunday there was a man that took little respect for God and His gift of life when he walked a tight wire over the Grand Canyon without any safety precautions. I did not watch his attempt or triumph, but I heard the next day he had a new goal, to walk over Manhattan, again without safety precautions. I was then and now in the same state of mind over this foolish risk, thrill, entertainment, and big buck's adventure. I walked my doggie an hour before his famous walk, I prayed for his life to be spared, but that he would experience fear, so as not to continue with this type of foolishness in the future. Surely the Devil is joyful now this young man is tempting God.

Reference: Luke 4: 9-12

When the Devil spoke to Jesus, he addressed Him as the Son of God. First he tempted Him, then he quoted the words from Psalm 91: 11, 12. At that time Jesus answered him strongly, "Thou shalt not tempt the Lord thy God." The young daredevil is doing just that. How precious is his life? Why is he risking his life? Who is leading him and who is tempting God?

Reference: Exodus 20: 13

This foolish man has no right to recklessly put his life in danger.

Reference: Psalm 143:3

Verse 3 says, "For the enemy has persecuted my soul," and the Devil is leading this young man into a life of danger. "He has smitten my life down to ground." The devil leads him to heights of danger and with only one mistake he will fall to the ground and to his death.

Reference: 1 Timothy 6: 7

The desires of this young man, the thrills, and the risks, the fame and the fortune are all foolish and he will find himself in darkness and, if he continues in this lifestyle tempting God, he will see destruction and death.

Reference: John 15: 12

In this verse our Lord tells us to love one another, and only for our family and friends do we risk our lives. Not for fame and fortune or the thrill of it. "If thou be the Son of God, cast thy self-down from hence," that was one of the Devil's temptation for Jesus. He rebuked him with the word of God. You can make it across the wire over the canyon without safety precautions, no belt, no wire. That was the Devil's temptation for the young man walking the tight wire. He has not rebuked the Devil; he is still tempting God.

Reference: 1 peter 4: 7

Only prayer can help this young man. Only Jesus can keep him alive and saved for eternal life. Amen and amen.

~

COMMUNION

Dear Lord, how could You have so much peace?

Reference: 1 Corinthians 11:23

If it was me or any of us, we would not be able to sit down and have a quiet meal. No sir, we would be trying to think of a way out of the horrible things that were going to happen to us in only a few hours. We would be praying, fasting, and reading and calling out to Father God for help. But You Lord Jesus; You sat down with Your friends and one enemy and had a calm, and peaceful meal.

Reference: 1 Corinthians 11: 24, 25

How can we have that calm, that peace, and that faith when we are facing all our troubles?

Reference: 2 Corinthians 1: 4

Thank You Jesus for sharing that last meal with us also. Thank You that today we share that meal with You, as You Lord break the bread, 'Your Body,' and You give thanks. You Lord also take the cup, 'Your Blood,' and You give thanksgiving to God for it for the 'New Testament of Salvation' for us to live by. In memory of 'that same night' we can share that meal with You every day. Blessed be the Lord our Saviour Jesus Christ. Amen and amen.

~

BELIEVE IN GOD

Dear reader, have you ever felt that God has let you down? I felt so strongly that He did not heal my husband and just let him die. He left me with our Care Home, Elim, full of people which was our business. My sons were not being very helpful, because they too were hurting from the loss of their dad. So, I was really put out with my Heavenly Father, He had surely let me down. Perhaps you remember a day you felt the same about God. Well, we got through it and in that walk, perhaps I should refer to it as a crawl, I did learn more about God. PTL (Praise the Lord). I think of Abraham, God playing a not so amusing joke on him, giving him the name, 'Father of many.' When he was 113 years old with one legitimate son and God waking him up in the middle of the night, telling him He wants Isaac back. Me I would have said something like, "What is going on? You give a son in my old age, so people are not laughing at me anymore. And now, You say you want him back."

Reference: Hebrews 11: 17, 18

Abraham was amazing with his faith in God. When God said something, Abraham believed it. What great faith he had in God.

Reference: Galatians 3: 6

Well, you may say, "O I have faith," me too, although I believe mine is still 'mustard seed size' and I hold on to it hoping that 'in good ground it will grow.' But Abraham had more than faith; he knew God was not going to let him down. Abraham believed God, and that is where we let God down.

Reference: Hebrews 11: 1-3

So here lies our faith, and our hope, but where lies our belief? We would never think of God letting us down if we believed in Him. Amen and amen.

$\sim$

THE GREAT DESIGNER

My dear friend asked me to pray for her grandson this morning as she and he were on the way to the doctor. Apparently something was wrong. He cannot lose weight. Something is physically wrong with him, so he is taking some tests. I was being reminded of my son that has trouble with his weight. I called on the Lord as I put down the phone. There was like a large screen in front of me in the day room. The Lord was showing me a large flower. It had three dimensions. I saw all the dimensions 'The Great Designer' had put together. First a stem like a pillar holding up a sculpture of art. Then three leaves growing up the stem. A precise distance was between each one of them. The leaves were coloured dark green and looked like they had been cut out with pinking shears around the edges. The stem ended in a flower that had a white, priestly collar of three layers of petals lying gracefully one on top of each other. The bottom layer shows a pinch of yellow on the ends. Each petal is just barely to the side of the layer below. A golden crown of little seeds is set in the very centre of the collar of petals. These seeds are for sowing. Seeds for sowing, 'The Great Designer wants His beauties to flourish and to carpet the 'Earth.' The Lord was showing me how man is so perfectly designed. How my dear friend's grandson and my son are so perfectly designed. How their bodies are so perfectly designed for us to behold the flowers and all their beauty we must follow certain laws of nature. We must cultivate the ground. We must see to it that our flowers have enough water.

Reference: Romans 12: 1

We must cut and prune our flowers, to keep them disciplined in their place. As for us, to behold our bodies and all our beauty we must follow certain laws of nature. We must cultivate our bodies; we must nourish our bodies and we must discipline our bodies.

Reference: 1 Corinthians 6: 19-20

Praise the Lord for His love. Thank You Jesus for the price You paid on the Cross, so that these two can go on and flourish. They can live in good health and glorify 'The Great Designer' in the way that He designed them. Amen and amen.

GO WITH GOD 'VAYA CON DIOS'

Dear reader, I have always used that phase in Spain when someone was leaving. But now here in the States when I use it, without thinking they don't speak Spanish. I must tell them its meaning. In Spain it was more accepted as, "God go with you." Perhaps you think it is the same. I am here to tell you it is not the same. God going with you is like saying, "God wasn't with you before and now at the time of you leaving you are blessed with His presence." That is very nice, but not as nice as, "Go with God." God is Spirit and the Spirit can go where we might not think ourselves to be. When a person is getting ready to travel, it is nice to say, "God go with you." You are showing that person that you are concerned for their being and protection.

Reference: Psalm 139: 9, 10

This is a precious Psalm to me and, "Oh, yes," we definitely want to see those we love protected, and who do we believers ask to protect them? God, of course, is not a gold medallion on the neck representing a Heavenly being.

Reference: Joshua 1:9

That is all well and good and faithful blessings for our loved ones. But now let's get to the meat.

Psalm 103: 8, 9

Now picture this, we are getting into the car and making our way into the world, perhaps we are going to work, or to school, or we have errands, perhaps we are going to church. Whatever we must do, we are going to meet other people and how is our meeting them going to go? If God is going with us, then He is following us to protect us, in most cases, I believe He would have His angels doing that for Him. Although, if we are going with Him, we would be following Him, and He would always be ahead of us for our protection and to smooth out whatever is there to greet us, may it be pleasant or unpleasant. It would be His compassion and grace that others would see in us, and no matter what we meet that is unpleasant we would be slow to anger and full of love for our fellow man. Oh, I know, you are saying she doesn't have a clue of what my day is like. I do have a clue, and so does God.

Reference: Jeremiah 29: 11-13

Aren't those wonderful verses? There we have our answer, so the next time someone says, "God go with you" pause, say thank you but I would rather, "Go with God." Now do you still think they are the same? Amen and amen.

~

UNWRAP HIM AND LET HIM LOOSE

Dear reader, Jesus never touched Lazarus; He did not even touch his tomb stone. Jesus was there at the tomb, to call Lazarus from death to life. Then He commanded that Lazarus be loosed from his grave clothes. Grave clothes were long strips of fine cloth wrapped around the dead body. I want this revelation to be about our salvation, about how Jesus called us one day from darkness to light, from death to life. I am about to take each verse and reveal what the Holy Spirit is saying to us.

Reference: John 11: 40-44

How beautiful is this verse 40 as He is about to save a dead man by calling him by his name, commanding him to come out of the tomb, and this dead man Lazarus obeyed the command. How often do you see the glory of God in your church or your home or in your life? Jesus made it very clear and very simple, and how can we do that? Although there is one problem, when the grave clothes are still binding you, you will find it very hard to believe, because although you are saved you are still prepared for the grave. You are still in your grave clothes. In verse 41 we read, "So they took away the stone." We don't know how many people were present at this place. We do know there were believers and non-believers. Who do you think took away the stone? The believers took it away and they were the ones that were standing close to the tomb, they were participating with what was about to happen. The non-believers were standing back and observing, doubting, and judging; what a sorry group of people they were. But Jesus had the believers on His side, so His work could continue, and a miracle would happen.

In verse 42 Jesus knew amongst those who heard Him pray were believers. He wanted to encourage them and to teach them. He also knew they would be the ones, who would be giving thanks and doing great miracles. The prayer Jesus prayed to His Heavenly Father is also our prayer. We thank Him daily that He hears us, He is our Father, and we are His children. That is the relationship we have, and He always hears us, which is our witness to others.

Verse 43 and 44 says that Lazarus came on his own out of the tomb, but he could not help himself out of the grave clothes, he was bound from head to foot with long strips of cloth. When Jesus called us we were wrapped in rags, we came dirty and full of sin. When Jesus called us, we came to life; we stumbled out of our dark past in need of shedding our grave clothes.

Lastly in verse 45 Jesus said, "Take off the grave clothes and let him go." Now we are getting to the second miracle, the miracle of love. When the brothers began to unwrap the grave clothes around Lazarus, they know that this time it was not a dead body they were caring for, but their living brother. When Jesus saved us and loosed us from our past sin, to be born -again, to be brought out of darkness into light and to be brought from death to life, that for us was the same miracle of God's love that Lazarus experienced. Jesus gives us hope for the future and increases our faith for today.

Reference: Revelation 3: 5

Praise God, Jesus has set us free. He has our grave clothes loosed, unwrapped, and removed to be replaced with a new, refreshing, and beautiful snow-white raiment, with our name written in the book of life, so we are accepted into Heaven with Him forever. Amen and amen.

~

MIDNIGHT, GOD'S FINEST HOUR

Dear reader midnight is when many people are sleeping. Although there are those that work at night, I would say they make up a small proportion compared to day workers. We all need our rest, and the doctors say that eight hours is good for everyone. How about you, do you get your eight hours? Some people can't sleep. They have worries and problems that they think about all night and they can't sleep.

In the Bible there are many accounts written where God's finest hour was at midnight. I do believe God rests; we know He rested on the seventh day after creation. I believed that since God invented sleep, He may also enjoy it, but the Holy Spirit does not sleep. He is always awake and on watch. Also, there are angels that are on watch. I heard a preacher say there are 40,000 angels assigned to each saved person, praise God, I like that. Like knowing that at midnight, I am not being neglected or forgotten. Midnight situations can occur night or day; our darkest hours can come night or day. God has made these times in our lives some of His finest handiwork. There are many in the Bible that have experienced His handiwork at midnight. Moses was not doing very well convincing the Israelites that God was going to deliver them from the Egyptians. God had done some miracles, which to me were incredible, but the Israelites were in bondage, physically, and spiritually they could not see the light, because they were in the dark. Their only light was hope that one day God would send a deliverer to free them. All that was going on around them to the Egyptians, yet they didn't believe what Moses and Aaron were telling them. At last, at midnight, they encountered salvation.

Reference: Exodus 11: 4-7

Inside their homes where their door lintels were covered with the blood of a lamb they could hear the moaning of the Egyptian mothers whilst holding their first born dead in their arms. Now at midnight God had changed Pharaoh's mind.

Reference: Exodus 12: 30, 31

God told Moses that He would free his people. Every time a glint of freedom was in sight because of God's miracles. Pharaoh would make the people suffer even more. Moses was almost ready to give up when God mentioned midnight; the hour He planned for a great miracle. God delivered the nation of Israel at midnight.

One of the greatest love stories told in the Bible is the story of Ruth and Boaz. Their humble courtship was conducted in a wheat field. Ruth was a widow, who gleaned after the reapers in the wheat field, so she had food for herself and Naomi, her mother-in – law. Boaz, the wealthy landowner of the wheat fields, was single and waiting for a blessed bride. God knew their hearts and I believe He had it all planned when Ruth arrived in that field. Although the enemy always was robbing the farmers, God used the 'threshing floor' at midnight to bring them together to be man and wife. God blessed them in the darkest hour of the day.

Reference: Ruth 3: 6- 11

When we see Jesus' family tree, we find Ruth and Boaz are on it. They were the parents of Obed, who fathered Jesse, the father of King David. So in another midnight God was sealing a relationship that would in the future be a part of His Son Jesus. So, what about a visitation at midnight? When things are the worst and everything looks very dark in our lives, we need a visitation from God. For us our midnight hour seems hopeless, for God it is an opportunity.

Reference: Acts 16: 25, 26

Paul and Silas were in the worst conditions that you or I could hardly imagine.

Most of the prisoners wanted to die quickly; they were in such agony. In the physical realm these two men would not want to go on suffering this kind of torture. They turned their feelings to worshiping God. They were probably going to be put to some horrible death for preaching the Gospel and their belief in Christ. They believed God for their deliverance. Whether it be death or their freedom, they were giving thanks to God. What happened at midnight? Looking at verse 25 have you ever heard of an earthquake, shaking only one building? How precise God is. What I love is that at the midnight hour, not only the two that were singing were freed but each one's bands were loosed. We have no idea how many were in that prison. What we do know is at midnight a great revival took place.

Reference: Acts 16: 27-29

Paul and Silas were arrested for preaching in the city. There were not many that listened and believed in the city. Their most fruitful sermon was in prison and all that heard them got saved. Outside the prison walls it was dark and still no one heard the earthquake. No one heard the worship service. Those in the city were not aware of God's visitation at midnight.

Reference: Mathew 25: 1-12

Jesus tells the parable of the ten virgins with their lamps. As you know only five had extra oil with them. They were all there in the place they knew the bridegroom would come. They all fell asleep waiting for him. But they were not all prepared for his coming. Although they all waited until midnight, only five were blessed and the other five were turned away. For the five that were prepared the midnight hour was a joyful time for them, they would be enjoying the company of the bridegroom and the festivities of the wedding. For the other five midnight was their darkest hour, they lost their opportunity to see the bridegroom and to join in with the wedding party. Midnight comes every 24 hours, and we cannot change that. What we do have control over is our feelings, and thoughts that are involved around our midnight experiences. If we can give God thanks and worship Him in the middle of our circumstances, we will bring light into the dark areas of our lives. If we can give over our families, our relationships, our finances, and our health to God, at that midnight hour He will bring light into the darkness. We know what it is like when we carry a lighted candle into a dark room. After a few seconds everything in the room is exposed to the light.

Reference: Psalm 119: 62

Let us also approach midnight with thanksgiving and worship God. Let us give God our midnight to be His finest hour. Amen and amen.

~

ARE YOU CONNECTED WITH THE BELT OF TRUTH?

When I drew a soldier for my children, I thought every piece was separated, but I was wrong.

Reference: Ephesians 6: 10-18

First Paul tells us to be strong in the Lord. When we look outside our houses, we feel safe and protected; we see the world where we feel completely different. Paul was concerned about his fellow Christians; he knew there was little chance for the Church to survive without daily preparation of strong believers. Paul tells us that the enemy is a schemer; he is the power of spiritual forces of evil, of darkness concealed in the rulers and authorities of Rome. We face those same threats when we step out of our homes, for that reason we too must be daily prepared to meet the enemy. It is one thing to say, "Be strong," but it is another thing to know how to be strong. Paul says we must follow the example of a Roman soldier and dress ourselves in full armour. The soldier knew what each piece was to protect him and to give him advantage over his enemy. Each piece had been carefully crafted to the soldier's physic. The helmet had been measured to his exact head size and the strap would fit precisely on his chin. The full armour was made up of six pieces. From top to bottom; 1) The helmet of salvation, 2) The breastplate of righteousness, 3) The belt of truth, 4) The shoes of the Gospel of Peace, 5) The sword of the Spirit, 6) The shield of faith. However we are only looking at a couple of these pieces of armour.

Reference: Ephesians 6: 13-18

Jesus spoke of faith twenty-three times in the Gospels. He referred to 'little faith and great faith.'

Reference: Mathew 8

This is a great chapter to read and in verse 26 we find 'little faith,' but before that in verse 10 we find 'great faith.' He questioned others if they had any faith.

Reference: Mark 4: 40, 41; 5: 34

In verse 40 Jesus asks, "How is it that ye have no faith?" and in Mathew 8:10 'Jesus had marvelled at their faith.' In chapter 5: 5 Jesus says, "Thy faith has made thee whole." Little was mentioned about faith in the Old Testament, we find a great deal about faith mentioned in the New Testament. I believe that in the Old Testament they had only laws that were almost impossible to keep. In the New Testament they had hope, they had a Messiah, a Saviour. In other words they had something they could believe in. After His death and resurrection, He stayed with his followers, so there were many that always had faith in Him. In fact, about five hundred persons saw Him, later others saw Him ascend to his Father in Heaven. For some years their faith blossomed, but later for many it withered. It was that time Paul was called by the Lord to spread the 'Good News.' He was called to encourage those that still had faith and to those that had lost it.

Reference: Acts 20: 21, 20

Truth and righteousness are compatible and depend on each other. The belt is carrying the sword which is the word of God. The Word of God is truth. Once you, dear reader, are fully covered with the breastplate and fastened tightly by the belt. You can take hold of your shield of faith. (Ephesians 6: 16) After that the servant would place on the soldier's head the helmet of salvation. At last, he would give his master the shield of faith. Are you getting this dear reader? The proper way to put on your armour each day is in this order: 1) Shoes of the Gospel of Peace, 2) The breastplate of righteousness, 3) The belt of truth, 4) The helmet of salvation, 5) The sword of the Spirit and 6) The shield of faith.

Reference: Ephesians 6: 18

Back to the question, "Are you connected to the belt of truth?" I want so to encourage your faith, and this is the way the Holy Spirit has shown me to do so, with these verses from the Bible on faith and the importance of being connected to the belt of truth.

Reference: John 8: 32

And for this very reason that John has said, we need to be connected to the belt of truth and all the rest will be ours also. Amen and amen.

~

ARE YOU HAVING A BAD DAY

Dear reader, we all have had bad days. I have been reading about Paul and Silas having a bad day. The day started out very well, they were walking on a country road praying and they met up with Lydia. She was a good Christian woman and so was her whole family and she invited them to stay in her house. They had free room and board. After breakfast they went to the marketplace to pray and teach, and they met another woman, a fortune teller that made a living telling fortunes in the market.

Reference: Acts 16: 16, 17

When her masters saw their 'meal ticket' was gone, no longer able to make money, they had Paul and Silas arrested, whipped and thrown into a prison cell then put in stocks. The day started off so well and now instead of having a good meal and a warm bed, they were suffering in a cold prison cell. What to do?

Reference: Acts 16: 25, 26

Happiness is from the outside and joy is from the inside. The day started great, they were happy, and they were happy also when in the name of Jesus they delivered this one woman and she got saved. They were not happy sitting in prison because their day had turned bad, but they were still in love with Jesus and still had faith in God, so they were joyful, they were full of joy with the love of Christ in a bad situation. When they prayed, possibly in tongues and sang praises, perhaps they sang in tongues also. They translated for the other prisoners to understand because they were so full of joy. During the day one woman got saved, but that night their great revival was in the prison where everyone got saved and baptized. When we find ourselves having a bad day it is good to remember what Joseph said to his brothers.

Reference: Genesis 50: 19, 20

How great was that, that Joseph's brothers gave him a lot of bad days, but God turned it around and blessed Joseph and his brothers. I just wanted to encourage you, to keep your joy, to keep your faith, when you are having a bad day. Amen and amen.

〜

UNDER HIS MIGHTY HAND

Dear reader, I learned a lesson yesterday. I have been having the most unusual trouble with my computer. The poor man that has been helping me with it has to drive half an hour to get to my house in the mountains. He drives up from the coast. He has a lot of customers, but he has been back and forth three times. Tomorrow, we hope to get it right. Last night while I was praying my eye caught a glimpse of the 'stay in prayer mode' sticker I had placed on the screen 3 days ago. I became aware as I was praying that I had pointed myself out to the enemy and he had pinpointed me for his attacks.

Reference: 1Peter 5: 8

Well, that was my problem. I was not sober and vigilant; I was not on watch when it concerned my computer. I thought I was 'under the blood' in my home and that would include everything in my home. We do get negligent. We take advantage of the Word. We forget that our material goods are targeted for enemy attacks as well as our person. Let me give you an example, our automobiles, yes, our cars. Do we honestly believe that because we have a 'Fish' sticker on the back window that we are safe in traffic? Well, you are not, unless you take time to speak to your Heavenly Father and ask Him to take the ride with you. How about parking places? Yes, even in parking places God reigns.

Reference: 1 Peter 5: 7

Are you sure when you put on your 'I love Jesus' t-shirt you are protected from all the controversy outside your home? I don't think so. The only protection we have is the presence of Christ with us and we only get that as we dress every morning in the 'armour of God.' (Ephesians 6: 10-18)

Reference: 1 Peter 5: 6

We pursue God constantly to be under His Mighty Hand. Whatever you pursue becomes your purpose. God's purpose is to have you pursue that purpose with

Him. Once you do, He will exalt you. We pray for family and friends, for the sick and for the unsaved. Not to forget Israel. Pray for them and give a daily thanksgiving for them. When we get in the car we should pray and if possible, in tongues. The Holy Spirit knows what lies ahead and He brings to God all the right words. My boys remember we always prayed for a parking space, and we still do. You never grow out of good prayer habits (1 Thessalonians 5: 17). Needless to say, when that computer comes tomorrow, I will lay my hands on it and pray that it be safe under the Mighty Hand. I will thank Him for His protection on my house, my car, my health and my material goods (Joshua 24: 15). Amen and amen.

∾

CHANGE OF HEART

Dear reader, sadly we lose blessings that are only for us to take. How this comes about is because we always believe ourselves to be right all the time and in everything. We think if we are not that good, (meaning we are not right all the time) then others do not think well about us or want to be with us, they agree with our boldness, but condemn us for our weakness. We are judged by our intelligence, our wisdom, or our kindness. But others have no right to judge us, for our mistakes or being wrong about a few things. The way others think about us or judge us fills us with fear, anxiety, and lack of confidence. So, all our concepts of how great we are diminish with fear. Therefore, where we may be assigned a blessing from the Lord, we can lose it because of our fear. We can build our confidence, when we pray about any problem that comes up for us or for others, that is the right move. While attending church we are so quick to question something, or anything said from the pulpit.

Reference: 1 Corinthians 8: 2, 3

We may find we gain a wealth of knowledge from the speaker and therefore we also gain our blessings. The attitude of always being right is the first step in losing our blessings.

Reference: Revelation 2: 16

Reading from the last book in the Bible, we are instructed to change our attitude. That change cannot come about without one more things, our mind, or our thinking. A stubborn mind has no room for new ideas and blessings. In verse 16, John tells us the Lord will fight against us and our attitudes. He will use a, "Sword of God;" in other words, "the Word of God."

Reference: Isaiah 31: 8

Through the Bible we read of many instances where God has shown His wrath. Isaiah tells us that, "The Word of God," will smite our attitudes. Paul also speaks of the 'sword, Spirit of God' or the 'Word of God' will smite His enemies, in other words our attitude and thinking that does not please God. Our wrong thinking is God's enemy. I am sure we do not want to be God's enemy. Paul speaks in the book of Ephesians.

Reference: Ephesians 4: 23, 24

In this verse Paul says, "Change and better yourself." We all want to better ourselves. The question is, "Do we want to better ourselves by a complete inventory of our minds, what are we thinking?" How do we get our blessings when we don't want to lose them? The answer is resigning to the Holy Spirit and listening to Him, this is our first step in gaining new blessings. The Holy Spirit may convict us, and we may have to go back in our 'mind inventory' selecting something in our attitudes that must be cast out, and then we will grow closer to the Lord.

Three things will bring us closer to the Lord; each one will bring us a blessing. First we need 'conviction' from the Holy Spirit; secondly we need 'correction' from the Holy Spirit; thirdly we need 'change' from the Holy Spirit. Some of our churches are not listening to the Holy Spirit. The congregation in these churches are waiting for their blessings, but there is none. When you are in a church that compromises with the world and has a 'deaf ear' to the truth, to the Gospel and to the message of the cross, you will lose what blessings the Lord has for you. Compromising does not always mean that evil is let in the door, but it does mean the truth has been twisted, so God's laws are bent out of order. Instead of spending all our time trying to prove how right we are, we should open our ears and listen to gain knowledge that will strengthen our life with Christ.

Reference: 1 Peter 4: 10, 11

In verse 10 Peter says, "We need to take all our blessings and pass them on." Our blessings are manifested in our special abilities. Our blessings increase as we share them with others. Our boasting about how right we are will be changed, Paul tells us, "We will not lose our blessings by sharing them." How many do you have that you can share with others today? Let us begin our mornings with, "Bless the Lord Oh my soul and all that is in me." Amen and amen.

~

WONDERFUL TO ME

Dear reader, I am sure sometimes you hear a song of Praise; your breath is taken away and tears fill your eyes. Well yesterday this is what happened to me. I started singing, "Here I am to worship, here I am to bow down, here I am to say that you are my God." The first thing that touched me was, "Here I am." Where have I been, why was I not here before, have I just arrived?

It doesn't make any difference where I have been or where I was, or if I just arrived. What is important is that I am here now, worshipping Jesus. Hallelujah. The next sentence is, "Here I am to bow down." I don't know about you, but I have been guilty of bowing down to other people. I found myself being easily dominated by other people; they dominated my mind, my home, my time, and my money.

I have discovered that I can live without these people in my life, and I do not have to bow down to them any longer. Jesus is the only one I bow down to. Praise the Lord. Then the song continues, "Here I am to say that You're my God." After being saved and baptised in 1977 I still find it hard at times to witness to others. But praise the Lord I am learning to open my mouth and say, "You're my God."

Oh, I like what comes next, "You're altogether lovely." How nice it is to be around lovely people, there are so many nasty people in this world, we want to have lovely people in our lives and in our homes and families. Is there anyone you know more lovely than Jesus? He is, "Altogether lovely." Hallelujah. Then comes, "You're altogether worthy." We look at ourselves, at what we own and how much we do, and we think we are really worth something. We are something all right, but we are not worthy. Jesus is the only one that is worthy. Jesus is the only one that died for you and me. Jesus is the only one that rose from the grave and lives again. Therefore, Jesus is the only one that is worthy. Praise His Holy Name. And so, we come to the last words, "You're altogether wonderful to me."

I was in the wrong place, doing the wrong things, living the wrong kind of life, and Jesus came into my life, and now here I am worshipping and bowing down and calling Him my God. He is the most lovely person in my life and He is the only worthy person in my life, so He and He alone is, "Altogether wonderful to me." Let's sing it if you know the tune.

"Here I am to worship, here I am to bow down, here I am to say that you're my God. You're altogether lovely, You're altogether worthy, You're altogether wonderful to me." Amen and amen.

TO SEE INTO THE DISTANCE

I like the story of the Shunammite woman. I wrote a revelation the other day, 'Great is Thy Faithfulness.' So, I am still in 2 Kings 4. I was so moved by the faith of that woman. But this is the verse that touched me today.

Reference: 2 Kings 4: 25

Elisha saw the woman afar off. I looked up on the web about Mount Carmel. The mountain range faces the area of where the battle of Armageddon may take place. Are you getting this dear reader? Mount Carmel is a prayer mount of Israel, and this prayer mountain faces Armageddon? Elisha was praying and God was giving the prophet instructions to revive her son, and he saw the woman afar off. He saw the woman before she left the house, he was there praying and waiting to greet her. God had shown him she was on her way, and he sent his servant to greet her. The servant had not seen her; it was the man of God that saw her coming. He let the woman tell him what had happened and to ask for him to return with her. But he didn't go with her right away; he sent his staff with his servant. The woman would not leave the mountain or the prophet, she was holding onto what she knew was her blessing, her son that was dead was returned to her alive. This is a very good story to read.

This story brings me to another story, the one Jesus told about the Prodigal Son. The lad did everything wrong, he probably was very lazy. He spent his life thinking of what he was going to get from his parents. Don't you think his father knew that he was going to get into trouble; he also knew his son would not listen to him. So, what choice did he have? He must let his son go. He didn't stop praying for his son. So, when his son came to his senses and was on the road back to his father his father saw him afar off. There are those you prayer for. And we get downhearted and think our prayers will never be answered. Our children that we pray for may never return, they are out there in the world doing the things that they know they should not be doing. This is for us and who we are praying for that they will come to their senses, and they will be on the road back again. We will see them afar off and we can run to meet them, I don't know about you, but this excites me.

Reference: Luke 15: 22-24

What a wonderful story. Amen and amen.

~

DELIGHT IN THE LORD

Dear reader, what a beautiful word, "delight," I like the word, it's heart-warming. I like to know that I can always declare, "I delight in the Lord." Our goal here on earth is to delight in the Lord, and more importantly that He delights in me. Praise God we can go to the word and find so many beautiful verses that state His delight in us. Although it is in the Word there are specifications that God puts there also. I have some of those heart-warming verses which serve as big hugs from our Heavenly Father.

Reference: 2 Samuel 22: 20

Can you feel those strong arms of our Heavenly Father around you in this verse? David is speaking in this verse. King Saul wanted to kill David because he was jealous of his popularity. The Lord rescued him from the wrath of the king and David is giving thanks to God. How does this verse apply to us? What did God rescue you from? What was it that God set you free from? The answer 'why' He did so is in the very next words, "Because He delighted in me." Wow, to be the pleasure of the Almighty God, what an honour. After the reward of salvation through Jesus, after deliverance through Him, we are the Lord's delight. How does that make you feel? It makes me feel Grrrrrrreeeat. Even when we make mistakes the Word reassures us of God's power and pleasure.

Reference: Psalm 37: 23, 24

I love that 'if I fail it is not fatal.' The Lord takes delight in my footsteps, even if I am wobbling and not very steady. He will support me and find pleasure in doing so. Although we all want to be as surefooted as a mountain goat, we are not; we slip and slide on rocky areas. Have you ever been slipping and sliding and called out to God. Yes, of course you have, you knew He was there to steady you and tears, perhaps, fell from your eyes as you felt Him drying them. I know I have been there. What a wonderful experience when you feel His hand holding you up. While He is holding you up and guiding every footstep, He is delighted in every step you take.

Reference: Psalm 40: 8

Now it is our turn to be so delighted. What is it we are so delighted about? We are to be delighted to do the will of God and to follow His laws that are also written in our hearts. Well perhaps I am jumping the gun. Is it your pleasure to do the will of God? Did you know that the right and the wrong will abide within your heart and reminding you of the difference is the laws God put there. Funny thing about mankind, he does know the difference between right and wrong from childhood, but how? In the verse we get the answer God put His laws within our hearts from the beginning of creation. It is up to us to follow those laws and find delight in doing that.

Reference: Psalm 119: 16, 92, 93

Doctors have proven that a clean bill of health comes with a clean lifestyle. David believes the same. He knew that only obeying God is what saved his life. Not all of us have been in a lifestyle where our lives were hanging by a thread. Some find their deepest delight in drugs, alcohol, tobacco, crime. All of these lifestyles would have caused us despair and death in the end. Changing our heart is the beginning of changing our lifestyle and finding delight in the Lord and His laws. David said he would never lay aside God's laws. Well, I am sure that all of us that love the Lord would want to say the same. Although at times unaware of our will getting in the way of God's will. It takes a whack, to get us out of the way and make way for the Lord. We have covered pleasure and delight in these three verses so far, all had to do with the Lord and us. Now we come to having delight in relationships.

Reference: Romans 12: 10

Here Paul tells us to find pleasure by honouring each other. Now he is speaking to the church. We cannot honour one that is not honouring God. It is our brothers and sisters in Christ that Jesus was referring to when He said, "Your neighbour," and those Paul is referring to when he said, "Honour each other." At the time we confess with our mouths and say within our hearts that Jesus is Lord, is when we delight in the Lord. At the time we take delight in honouring, loving, and praying for our family in Christ is when the Lord delights in us. Therefore, loving our brothers and sisters in Christ is a part of a perfect and delightful relationship with God.

Reference: Psalm 37: 4

There are many things that come about in our lives that we really do not get delighted about. Oh, no when health is bad, finances are bad, and relationships are bad, what do we do? We turn to God and ask Him to restore them. But here David who had to run for his life, first from King Saul and then from his own son Absalom who wanted his father dead. He was tempted and fell to temptation which caused him to be a murderer and an adulterer. What or who did he blame? No-one, nothing, oh no, he glorified God and found pleasure in doing so. Although David fell and was in anguish many times, he only had one answer.

Reference: Psalm 135: 3

We find it hard to give thanks and sing praise to the Lord when we are down and out. But that is the only way to get up and get going again. The Lord knows how hard it is for us, that is why He created praise, worship, and thanksgiving, because they are actions and they are physical, we have to act, we have to say, and do praise, worship and thanksgiving. When we do we are 'back on the floor' and delighted. Remember where we started? Delight means: 'something that

gives great pleasure and enjoyment.' This is my goal and I hope it is yours also
(Isaiah 58: 14, Then shall you delight thyself in the Lord. {KJV}) Amen and amen.

~

DELIVERY ONLY

Dear reader, I was reminded yesterday that I had done something I was telling
others not to do. I am the one that is guilty, in other words, I was not practising
what I was preaching. I have told the church, "When you have a problem take it
to the cross, give thanks to the Lord that you can lay it down at the cross. Well,
I got a problem and was stressing myself out with worry. This is what happens,
we bring forth our prayer to the Lord at the cross, we spend some time talking to
Him about our problem and what we are worried about, and then we go to bed.
We get up in the morning and our first thing we mention with our prayer time
is the problem we gave to Him last night, but we have picked it up again and we
are burdened with it again because we are holding on to it. We lay them down,
but don t let go.

Reference: Mathew 11: 28

When I lay down my request at the cross I start a collection of requests, I begin
to make a pile at the foot of the cross. I begin to make sure they are there and
start to remind the Lord what I brought to the cross. First, I must repent for
my lack of faith and shame. I have mentally placed a sign on the cross 'Delivery
Only' once I lay down my burden, I must let it go. I need to give thanks; I need
to trust in Him. I need to stop demonstrating to Him that I can take better care
of my collection than He can. How stupid of me. I am giving Him a direct signal
that I don't really trust Jesus with my collection. When we are cleaning out the
attic and the cellar, throwing out half the contents, two days later, I regret what I
threw out, that is the flesh. Prayer and thanksgiving are much more important.
That is the spiritual area I need to stay in. The Lord will direct my path as I focus
on Him.

We must trust in Him and His supremacy at the cross, the source of our salvation. Paul says it perfectly in Colossians 1: 20, "And, having made peace through the blood of his cross, by him to reconcile all things unto himself; by him, I say, whether they be things in earth, or things in heaven." (KJV) Thank you, Jesus. Amen and amen.

~

MEANINGLESS FAITH

Dear reader, do you know there is such a thing as meaningless faith? Yes, and it is also found in the life of Christians. First let us go to what we as Christian s define faith without meaning or perhaps, we could say without substance. Those who have idols and false gods have such faith. Oh, no they don't have it intentionally, they have it ignorantly. They sincerely and sadly put their faith into graven images or a so-called prophet or saint. They spend all their energy praying and crying out to these and get no answer. They believe that all their faith and worship move these false gods and prophets so that they will be blessed by them. Believing is not really faith because it lacks power and action. We can take a quick look at Mount Carmel where Elijah met up with the 400 prophets of Baal. The intense way in which these prophets cried out to Baal is read in the book of 1 Kings.

Reference: 1 Kings 18: 20-39

I will touch on some of the verses to make a point of what I am saying. 400 prophets and all the people were brainwashed into believing that Baal was God. Jezebel brought this false god with her when she married the king. Their sacrifices were not only animals, they were also human. God had had enough so He called Elijah to put a stop to it and get the people back to worshipping Him. As we read in verse 21 the people were given a choice but said nothing. Elijah did not mess around; he got right to the point of why he had come to Mount Carmel. As you read the verses, you see he even disgraced the worshippers of Baal. He laughed at them and made fun of all their efforts to get Baal to answer. All day had gone by and no result had come, for these false god worshippers. Elijah stepped forward and began to worship Jehovah. Now we come to the comment I made about Christians having meaningless faith. The phrase means less faith, in other words powerless faith. The image of Baal was meaningless to anyone that did not know who it was. Only those that gave him their faith made him of any importance at all. They were worshipping something they could see, and along comes Elijah worshipping something they could not see. The stone image was cold and powerless. There was no love, mercy, or grace in him. But on the other hand, God was all those things and He listened and answered with the power of the Holy Spirit. I like these verses from Jonah 2: 8, 9.

Reference: 1 Kings 36-40

Elijah believed in God, and he had faith in God, but that is not why God answer his cry. God loves His creations and although these worshippers had convinced the people that Baal was their god, He wanted them to know the truth. Not only 400 prophets were guilty of false worshipping, but so were the people. God's grace extended to the people through the faith of Elijah. Elijah's faith was not only in his own reputation of being a great believer and follower of Jehovah. Elijah's faith was in the grace of God that He had for His people. So many times, we hear a Christian question their faith or another Christian's faith, as if that was a source of answered prayer. The only source of answered prayer is God's grace given by the Holy Spirit through our faith and His grace. This is the story of Elijah at Mount Camel that was one of the great examples of one man's faith. I like to go to Paul speaking of faith.

Reference: Romans 3: 23, 24

At the beginning of where we are in this verse we are at the cross, where the grace of God was on hold. Jesus was alone for three hours suffering on the cross, because we were still sinning and worshipping false gods. He paid the price that we should have paid. Although was human, the love steadfastly carried out His divine assignment from the Father was grace.

Reference: 2 Corinthians 12: 8, 9

Paul was one who really knew what the grace of God meant in his life. He was in and out of problems everyday throughout his ministry. Here he is suffering; in fact, in the verse above, he tells the Lord that Satan is overpowering him to the point of giving up. He is suffering, he needs a strong helper. The grace of God, or in other words the Holy Spirit is a strong helper, sufficient for us also. You would think that all Paul had gone through, that in only these three days it was for him like 'a straw that broke the camel's back.' It was not so much the suffering that was getting him down, it was the need he had for the presence of God at that time. After he heard from God he got better physically and spiritually. Remember Elijah, he was facing 400 angry prophets, alone he could do nothing, his faith was in God and God spoke to him, he silenced the 400 prophets and revealed the true God. 400 prophets with 'meaningless faith' facing one prophet with 'meaningful faith.' Paul had a great deal of faith, but his faith did not relieve his anxiety, his peace came from the grace that was spoken to Elijah. The power of God's grace in Paul's life when God spoke to him, that was all he needed, he was once again strengthened and ready to serve. Each one of us needs God's grace and Paul assures us that we all have been assigned it.

Reference: Ephesians 4: 7, 8

To strengthen our faith is not done by actions, it has to be done with a humble heart. To receive our appropriate portion of God's grace that will keep our cup overflowing, we must turn off the faith works and turn on the receiving spirit. We must extend our arms to Heaven to receive His amazing grace.

Reference: Hebrews 4: 16

Like all other areas of our Christian lives, growth in His grace also will take some time. We can grow in the spirit much faster than we grow in the flesh.

Although we can try to make some quick growth by spending more time in the Word, that is why I would like for you to find these verses in your own Bible and make them your own.

In closing hope I have made it clear that through faith and by grace, prayers are answered. Our faith is not ever to stand alone, if so, it can become 'meaningless.' Have a look at 2 Peter 3: 18. Amen and amen.

~

HOW TO TAKE AND HOW TO GIVE CORRECTIONS IN MINISTRY

Dear reader, I just had a very unpleasant experience. I tried to ask someone to, "Consider their ways," after something that was said on Sunday. My church is my home; also I have always been a very 'open house' sort of person. As the Holy Spirit has moved me into someone's life or has moved someone into mine I have tried to open my heart as well as my door to anyone for a new relationship. Don't get me wrong, I have not always had a great relationship with everyone. It was only for a short time; I saw why the Holy Spirit brought us together. I take every introduction from the Holy Spirit very precious and seriously. I am sure you know it is easier to correct a non -believer, than one who is saved and living for Christ.

Well, that is what happened to me. I asked this new Christian sister not to repeat something she had said in my presence. Well, she was and still is offended. The Lord had given her a very nice singing voice, that all of us in the church were enjoyed the worship. She wanted to spend time with me and that was alright. She paid no attention to my request, in fact the bad words increased. I told my husband and we prayed about it. When I was with another sister and she heard the bad words we offered to pray to rebuke that bad habit. She stayed one more week then she left; my husband told me she said she didn't like the correction and went back to her old church. How did Jesus handle His disciples and others while correcting them? Looking to the Bible two incidents come to mind. Who better to show Christ's corrections than Peter?

Reference: Mathew 16: 17-19

First Jesus blesses Peter for his faith and his revelation from the Holy Spirit. Then what happens? When Peter is feeling 'holier than thou' he says the exact thing that gets him a hard correction from the Lord. If Jesus had said these things to me, I would have been crying my eyes out in the bathroom.

Reference: Mathew 16: 23

We all know what happened to Peter the night Jesus was arrested. Peter denied knowing Jesus three times and had a broken heart because he believed the next day that Jesus was dead. Jesus needed Peter to lead the disciples and He also needed Peter to build the church. After Peter's denial of Jesus, Peter was only good for fishing. Therefore, he led the disciples to the sea to fish. So, we know what Peter did, let us look to see what Jesus did.

Reference: John 21: 15-21

I was Biblical with my sister who used a bad word (in my opinion), I asked to not speak like that, I brought in another sister, sitting in public and using foul language was not a good testimony for our church, or for a lovely woman from our church. We loved our sister, but she wasn't about to change her bad habit. So, what could we do? We wanted to make sure she understood her well-being was important to us. Jesus did that for Peter. My husband and the other sister and I prayed with the offended sister on Sunday, and it seemed all was well. She asked the Holy Spirit to help her stop the bad language. But two days passed, and she called and told my husband she was leaving the church. To correct or make corrections must always be done in the same way, with love, with this experience that turned out unpleasant, but we had the Lord's peace about it because we applied the love of Christ that He spoke to Peter to our sister. And we wished our sister well in her ministry of music. My husband reassured me not to feel guilty about this sister's attitude. He read from Romans.

Reference: Romans 13: 8

Perhaps our experience which was unpleasant but settled with love expressed to our sister. Giving or taking corrections at times for the body and the protection of the church is always number one for the Lord. Amen and amen.

~

GOOD CHRISTIAN CONDUCT

Reference: James 1: 19-27

Dear reader, today I am interested in James, the half brother of Jesus, he was in Jerusalem and the leader of the church there. He wrote the book of James as an outreach to the 'Twelve Tribes scattered among the nations.' I would like to comment on chapter one, verse nineteen to the end of the chapter, and to take it apart to reveal my message on good Christian conduct. First James says, "Dear brothers take note of this;" he wants to be recognised and regarded as a teacher giving vital instructions to their growth. "Everyone should be quick to listen." James is jumping right in there and saying, "I want your attention;" "slow to speak;" in other words listening is gold and talking is brass. No comparison, James also says, "slow to become angry." James knew if a person was a good listener, paused, and prayed before speaking, they would also be slow to anger. James reminds them that a man's anger does not bring about the righteous life that God desires.

Then he gets hard on their case. "Therefore, get rid of all moral filth and the evil that is so prevalent, and humbly accept the word planted in you which can save you." James continues with his instructions, "Do not merely listen to the word and so deceive yourselves." Do what it says. He uses an example, "Anyone who listens to the word, but does not do what it says, is like a man who looks at his face in the mirror and after looking at himself, goes away and immediately forgets what he looks like." James continues, "But the man that looks intently into the perfect law that gives freedom and continues to do this, not forgetting what he has heard, but doing it, he will be blessed in what he does." Most people think that good conduct has to do with actions, and that is right, but the actions are usually preceded by listening and speaking.

As James continues, he has a very definite thing to say about the tongue. "If anyone considers himself religious and yet does not keep a tight rein on his tongue, he deceives himself and his religion is worthless." So, to please God and do as He desires of us; is be a good listener. Unbelievers can be good listeners, but they don't follow instructions, the saved must also be good listeners to God to practice good Christian conduct. The unsaved can still be good speakers but with deceitful tongues. The saved must be very careful what they say and think; God is listening. He is listening to what and how it is said and what is said can predict good or evil upon others as well as yourself.

James' last words in the chapter are, "Religion that God our Father accepts as pure and faultless is this;" He is saying that if we obey the word, become good listeners, careful speakers, and slow to anger, we will be pleasing God and faithful to our religion(church). There is one more thing, God requires of us, "To look after orphans and widows in their distress and to keep oneself from being polluted by world."

From this chapter in the book of James, we learn the actions of good Christian conduct, "Love, kindness and generosity." There was a young lad that stood up in Sunday School and asked, "Why do people call me a good Christian?" Nobody said a word, until his brother held up his hand and said, "Because they don't know you." We hope we can do better than that and hope that those who know us know us by our good Christian conduct. Amen and amen.

GOLDEN YEARS 2009

Reference: Genesis 5: 32

I just had a birthday; I am on the verge of belonging to the 'Senior Citizen' group. I seriously do not believe the Lord is going to leave me here on earth for another five hundred years, but one hundred will be fine with me. That Noah lived five hundred years is not what jumped out at me from this verse, oh no, it is the second part about them still having babies. I mean late in life in his 'golden years.' I know God had a very good purpose for Noah to be father of all mankind after the flood, but what I find great is that he was that old before the Lord called him to serve Him. Now what about us, if we are serving the Lord in a ministry or church, perhaps working for our community, how old will we be when we retire? Or do we ever retire from serving the Lord?

Reference: Joshua 23: 1

Joshua spent many years serving the Lord after Moses died. I mean they didn't win over all those nations in the Promised Land in a year, no it took many years, perhaps many decades. Joshua stayed healthy and strong as long as God had him winning wars. But when the wars were over, no more battles to pray about, to plan and to fight, the Lord retired Joshua. Joshua did not retire because he became a 'Senior Citizen' on one of his many birthdays. God retired him after there was peace in Israel. Joshua also had peace and was ready to be with the Lord and receive his rewards not only in his 'golden years' but in that 'Golden City.'

Reference: Psalm 71: 17, 18

David loved the Lord from his childhood. He sang praises to the Lord to soothe his sheep out in the pasture as a young shepherd. Then he went on after slaying Goliath, to soothe King Saul with his songs of praise. We could say that a music ministry was his first calling. He was a shepherd that became a warrior and later on to be King that brought peace to Israel and Judah. Although we may not serve the Lord in such a dramatic lifestyle as David, we certainly have many ways to serve Him in our lifetime. And what a wonderful age, having the time to serve the Lord. David said, "He had grey hair and was old, but he did not want to give up his life yet."

In the second part of the verse, he is telling the Lord why he is speaking. "Until I have shown Thy strength unto this generation, and Thy power to everyone that is to come." David was concerned about his children, those that would be following in his footsteps, Israel's next king. He was a famous king, but he loved his family and was concerned for their wellbeing. Whatever may happen to his children, and how would they face their problems? Would they trust in the Lord for their guidance and strength was seriously on David's heart. He had served the Lord and that made him worthy of serving his people as their king. David knew the Lord had planned that Solomon would be the next king of Israel. I would say when we read the book of Proverbs where Solomon teaches the importance of parenthood, that he might have learned from his father. Here are some verses that we should all take to heart.

References: Proverbs 17: 6; 22: 6; 23: 22

It was very common for men and women to live long lives in the Bible. If we live to a hundred, there is a letter or certificate for the Queen or the President. Those that served the Lord were remembered in the Bible. So how is the 'Senior Citizen' group remembered, we that have come to our 'golden years' should have some recognition. In the book of John, we have the answer.

Reference: John 17: 4

When does a missionary retire, when is their ministry over? There is a ministry for each one of us. Asking the Holy Spirit to show us where He wants us and what He wants us to do is our first duty. When we reach the year of retirement, we should be ready to put on the servant's garment for the Lord.

Reference: Isaiah 58: 11

In our 'golden years' this verse above is so like God encouraging us to keep going on. Here Isaiah is telling us that under no circumstances must we give up because we are dried up. Oh, no, the Lord will not allow it, if we will allow Him to be our source of refreshment. He will keep us healthy, refreshed, and renewed. Isaiah says it so beautifully as he refers to a garden and spring. The Lord is telling him and us that we will no longer be dry, but well-watered and overflowing.

Reference: Psalm 127: 5

Here David says that a man is happy if his quiver is full. Full of what, babies! I would say full of years of serving. That is what would make our 'golden years' happy ones. With our quiver full we still have many years and plenty of ammunition to carry on serving until we reach the 'golden city.' Amen and amen.

~

GOOD CITIZENSHIP

Dear reader we must read Paul's writing in Philippians.

Reference: Philippians 3:17

We all try to be good citizens and following the 10 Commandments of Moses is a good start. We obey and respect our parents. We tell the truth and don't lie. We never take the life of another person or their property. We are faithful to our spouse. We take no other gods before our God Jehovah and we worship Him, Him only. So, following the 10 Commandments should make us a good citizen. What was Paul's meaning here in speaking to the elders of the church, they had been very good to Paul, sending him things that he needed while sitting in prison. I think Paul was reminding them about their behaviour as good Christian's not just good citizens. Here comes the crunch.

Reference: Philippians 3: 18

Paul is speaking of enemies in the church among the brethren.

Reference: Philippians 3: 19

So Paul's interest was to make these 'good church goers' into good Christians and a step further.

Reference: Philippians 3:20

Our citizenship is heavenly; we are born-again citizens of the Kingdom of God, saved, and sanctified through the 'Blood of Christ' on the cross. Here on earth, we wait for the return of our Saviour, Jesus. Paul continues, "Who by the power that enables him to do anything under His control and will transform our lowly bodies, so that we will be like Him in our new glorious body." Absolutely, that is my goal to be like Jesus. Paul still wanted to see these good Christian's in the church make their goal to be good citizens in heaven. In the book of Titus, we find the outline of a good heavenly citizen.

Reference: Titus 1: 8; 2: 7

In Titus 2: 7 we might find this is all very difficult to accomplish, we get some reassuring words in Matthew.

Reference: Mathew 5: 12

So this has been a quick revelation to help all of us secure our 'good citizenship,' preparing for our heavenly home in the Kingdom of God and eternal life. Amen and amen.

PASSING THE BUCK

Dear reader, do you know who was the first person to pass the buck in the Bible? Adam was the first. Eve was the second. The serpent had no one to pass the buck to, because he had no excuse, he is always guilty of something.

Reference: Genesis 3: 12-14

I make a habit of finding an excuse for the things I do most of the time. I don't do a lot of bad things, but I do silly or stupid things that I usually have an excuse for. I am not one to say 'right off the bat' that I made a mistake. My little wrongs have never affected anyone the way that Adam's did. His disobedience was so bad that it took over four thousand years, before the debt was paid back. Adam's first sin was the worst sin ever, because man was paying the price of death and without living in paradise for all four thousand years. The gates were closed until Jesus' redemption paid for that sin; all sin was paid for at the cross. God made the most wonderful place for Adam and Eve to live in. They wanted for nothing because they did not know that they lacked anything.

Reference: Genesis 1: 26-28

Think of your own circumstances, wouldn't it be great to have dominion over all of them, to the degree that you would be so blessed and, "Be fruitful, and multiply, replenish the earth and subdue it." That is the way Adam and Eve started off, and they blew it. Instead of facing up to their disobedience, their sin they were just 'passing the buck' one to another. God gave them the chance to repent. This was one of the first encounters with a man. He had just created man and already there were problems. Through the Bible, God shows a great deal of patience with mankind, but here God was so disappointed, that He could not let them slip by. It is one thing to 'pass the buck' while dealing with another person, but it just won't work with God. I have learned to repent daily, because I know I slip up daily and I want to go to bed at night with a content heart and peaceful mind. I have thoughts, words, as well as actions that are sinful without my knowledge, then there are those that I can remember, that I quickly ask forgiveness for. What would I do if God didn't forgive me? When we get into Exodus with Moses, I believe God has a very good idea of how difficult man really is.

Reference: Exodus 4: 30, 31

How long did it take God there upon the mountain patiently explaining every detail to Moses to get him to go back to Egypt? Now he is there things are going quite well. But he has not seen Pharaoh yet.

Reference: Exodus 5: 1, 2

When the brothers went to Pharaoh things didn't go as well as Moses was hoping for. In fact, they went very badly. The poor Israelites were made to work harder and make their own bricks. They had to go and gather their own straw to make their bricks. Making their own bricks and gathering the straw made them work harder and longer. At first, they listened to Moses and gave thanks, worshiping the God of Abraham, Isaac, and Joseph. Moses told them that God will deliver them out of Egypt. But they became angry with Moses for causing them more problems and work.

Reference: Exodus 5: 20-23

Now, 'passing the buck' was in full swing. They were blaming Moses for Pharaoh's harsh punishment, with Moses blaming the Lord for sending him to Egypt, causing all this turmoil. But the Lord is patient with all of them and reassures Moses that things will change.

Reference: Exodus 6: 1, 2

God does not only say things will change, but He reminds Moses of his ancestry and nation.

Reference: Exodus 6: 1-4

God once again reassures Moses that He will deliver Israel out of Egypt.

Reference: Exodus 6: 5-8

Moses was in charge of the situation from that day; although it took some doing Moses followed every word from the Lord and redeemed the children of Israel from their slavery. Praise the Lord. We also read of others in the Bible that always found someone else to take the blame instead of facing their sin. Looking to Paul; he had every reason to blame others for his imprisonment, in a dungeon and in chains, for his suffering and being beaten. He could have blamed and hated everyone, but not Paul as read in Hebrews.

Reference: Hebrews 10: 34-36

Paul always wanted to encourage his disciples and followers. Paul always wants to support the church and the brethren.

Reference: Colossians 1: 23, 24

As Christians we know one day we will suffer and the church will be persecuted and instead of 'passing the buck' and blaming the Lord for all of it, let us rejoice, for all that is happening is a sign that Jesus Christ is coming back soon.

Reference: Hebrews 10: 36, 37

Thank You Lord. Amen and amen.

～

HOLY SPIRIT LET US PRAY

There is a rumour out there dear readers that, "Speaking in tongues is not necessary or beneficial." That is just a rumour, it is not a fact. This rumour started with this verse.

Reference: 1 Corinthians 14: 9

Do we need to always understand the words the Holy Spirit is speaking when He is speaking to God? The answer is, "No," if we trust Holy Spirit to speak to the Heavenly Father for ours or others benefit. Speaking in tongues in church or in the presence of another person can be confusing and it can be a problem to those who hear these strange groaning and ramblings. Paul makes a very good effort to instruct us in the difference of speaking in tongues and praying in tongues. This difference is what the church and church leaders have not shared to Christians. They have put so much weight on other gifts and little interest in tongues.

Reference: 1 Corinthians 12: 4-10

Paul placed 'tongues' as one of the most beneficial gifts from the Holy Spirit in his life. Paul had all the gifts of the Holy Spirit; he was the administrator of many churches. He was a good administrator because he had the wisdom, knowledge, and discernment from the Holy Spirit for the churches he hardly ever got to visit. Paul also had the gifts of healings and miracles; he was a great prophet. So why with all these great gifts did he need 'tongues?' He needed all the gifts because they work together and support each other.

Reference: 1 Corinthians 12: 11

Although Paul was so highly gifted of the Holy Spirit, he was aware of the need of unceasing prayer. Do you know where we read that?

Reference: 1 Thessalonians 5: 17

How is it possible to pray all the time? We can't. We must eat and sleep, work and keep our mind on what we are doing all the time. We can't always be praying. When we start to pray in our normal language and the phone rings or there is a knock on the door, how long does it take us to get back to the same place in our spoken prayer where we were before the interruption? Do we get to finish our prayers everyday or does the world make an effort to keep us otherwise occupied with family or work. In the flesh we are not able to pray without ceasing. The devil on the other hand is able to keep us from prayer any time he wants to, because it is he that can control our flesh. But we can pray in tongues through the Holy Spirit in languages that the devil does not understand. We can turn to Holy Spirit in His language through our tongue and although the phone rings or there is a knock on the door, we are interrupted, but the Holy Spirit is not. Paul made the statement that he spoke in tongues more than anyone.

Reference: 1 Corinthians 14: 18

Paul was referring to his prayers in tongues. Man in the flesh has not the memory or capability to cover all the prayers that are our daily need in our environment. Our thinking is limited; our verbal words of prayer are limited. In the next verse Paul refers to speaking in tongues in church or with others present, not to our personal prayer time.

Reference: 1 Corinthians 14: 27, 28

An example of Holy Spirit's capability of reaching out in prayer through tongues covers things that we do not reach in our daily prayers in our normal language.

Reference: Romans 8: 26, 27

This is the best benefit we have from speaking in tongue. Holy Spirit knows the needs of everyone, everyone I love and like and know. So, when the Holy Spirit brings someone into thoughts for prayer, I say, "Let us pray Holy Spirit." I always have my prayer partner with Him, and I can trust Him better than my own thinking. I can trust Him to say the right thing in my prayers. You may think that is silly, but we many times say the wrong thing in our prayers, so much better for Him to take over my prayer time and get the right thing prayed for. I always feel that when I see someone with visual problems, I can trust Holy Spirit to pray for them the very best prayer to help them.

Reference: John 14: 16

I love the words of Jesus in this verse. I just told you how I trust the Holy Spirit. Jesus says He is our Comforter. Oh, that is great. My Comforter, that abides with me, and in me. The one thing I must admit is not always so easy, that is to be obedient when the Holy Spirit directs me on the path He wants me to stay on. In other words, it is not always easy to obey. And yet obedience is the key to the Comforter.

Reference: John 4: 26, 27

I can't cover it all even though I try to remember in my mind all that is within my heart at the time. I know Holy Spirit is not limited by persons, nations, or religions. He is universal, through my mouth, speaking tongues whatever language He wishes, I am also praying universal.

Reference: John 4: 23, 24

I want to worship the Lord, and I do with the limited vocabulary I have, in my normal language. Is that enough? I used to think it was. Now I know through the physical and spiritual emotions and feelings and tears that can come, my worshipping the Lord in tongues is so much more of thanksgiving and praise to Him. It makes so much difference in worshipping and praying when I can say, "Holy Spirit let us pray." Amen and amen.

~

HIS ARMS ARE OPEN

"I am coming back to the heart of worship, and it is all about You, it is all about You Jesus" It is alright for us that are standing in church to sing, singing to the rafters. It is all about You Jesus, but what about those standing on the outside of our worship time. There are many people that at one time or other in their life had given their hearts to Jesus, but it is like they secretly took back their lives from Jesus. They are not honouring their commitment to the Lord. Our churches are full of Christian that are lords of their own lives. We see many come to the front to be saved, oh what joy. Although, a real wonderful thing to see is, when an elder or helper in the church recommits their life to Jesus with repentance. It is not easy to repent and admit you are backsliding back into the world. We can be so busy serving the Lord in our church, that we forget who we are serving. Our ministries and tasks keep us so busy; we forget our first love Jesus. We forget salvation and cross. It was at the cross we were cleansed and delivered. Let us see what the word has to say.

Reference: Jeremiah 3: 22

When the Holy Spirit called us out of darkness and into the light, we were so in love with Jesus, tears streamed from our eyes as we confess our sins and His forgiveness. We were so full of joy, and full of worship to the Lord. Then we could not get enough, church, prayer groups and Bible studies. Eventually we wore ourselves out, we felt so empty, so inadequate. Now our hearts are broken, and we want Jesus to love us, and we want to love Him as it was in the beginning. Jesus has opened His arms to gather all His suffering children to His breast.

Reference: Mathew 19: 14

Dear reader, do you think that when Jesus said those words, He was speaking to babies? He was speaking to big suffering children in the church. He was saying, "Come and rest, lay your burdens down here at My feet, and let us have some time together." Remember Mary and Martha; let us go to the Word.

Now there you have it. There is a place to rest at His feet and listen to His word. Are you ready to worship? "I'm coming back to the heart of worship, it's all about You Lord, and it's all about You Jesus." We must all go to Him, because His arms are open for us. Amen and amen.

~

HEAVY BURDENS

Dear reader, we all have some sort of burden we are bearing. So long as everything is going fairly well, we feel that our burden is light. But when sin sets in, the result is bad health or suffering finances. Maybe we are burdened by relationships that we hope will go well and they end up going sour. When we have these heavy burdens, we must admit the reason for our burdens is sin, and there is only one way to unload sin.

Reference: Psalm 38:4

That is what sin does to us, it overwhelms us. Sin seems unforgiveable and unbearable, and we have a big problem finding a way to discard it.

Reference: Deuteronomy 1:9

Sin appropriates the body and the mind, it attaches to individuals as they carry it within their very beings, until they find the only way to unload it.

Reference: Galatians 6:2, 3

What is the law of Christ? I believe it is two things, first the witness of salvation and forgiveness. Second is to love your neighbour as yourself. If you are carrying a heavy burden, you would like for someone to come along and redeem you from it. That is what Jesus Christ has done on the cross.

Reference: Titus 2:13, 14

Our verse from Galatians tells us, "To bear one another's burdens," to do that is to reveal our love for them. The law of Christ is always supported with love. When Christ looked upon a sinner, He looked upon them with compassion, and that is the way we must see them also.

Reference: 1 Corinthians 7: 29

We would have to take time from our busy routine to show compassion on a heavy burdened sinner. We would perhaps have to share their burden. Love is truly the only way we can help them. Without the love of Christ, where would we be, and without the love of Christ where will they be?

Reference: James 5: 16

As a Christian one form of love is prayer. Prayer will bring that heavy burdened person to the foot of the cross, and as we lay down our burdens by faith and in your spirit, you will see that person you love walk away burden free and in time that will manifest in their lives.

Reference: Galatians 5: 1

That payer is the sign of your love, and it is that which lightens the burden. The question is, "Do we have time to show love to a sinner today?" Have we time to pray for someone? Another big question is, "Do we have time to bear another's burden today?" If you take time for others, God will take time to bless you both. Amen and amen.

∿

HEAVENLY WORSHIP OR EARTHLY PRIDE

I know you have heard the saying, "Pride comes before a fall." I am not sure where the saying came from, but I believe it should have come from the Bible. How many examples of pride do we find in the Bible? The story I am thinking of now is of a man named Gideon. The Lord called him to lead the army of Israel against the Midianites. We find the story in the book of Judges.

Reference: Judges 6: 11, 12

That is a great beginning for the story. Gideon was a farmer and while he was working was visited by an angel (or by Jesus). He was addressed as a mighty man of valour, and he was told that the Lord is with him.

Reference: Judges 6: 14, 15

You would think that Gideon would run to his house, get his sword and shield and be ready for orders from the Lord. But no, alas Gideon is a wimp. I know the angel called him a man of valour, but so what, Gideon needed excuses.

Reference: Judges 6: 17

So Gideon asked for a sign from the angel, the angel touched his sandwiches lying on a rock, and when He touched them with his staff fire burned them up. So, there was his lunch gone, woof. A very good sign I would say, but not good enough for Gideon.

Reference: Judges 6: 22-24

Gideon worshipped the Lord and built an altar for Him. Gideon was not authorized to build and altar. Well, you think he was ready to go to battle. No, he still had excuses. He was still a wimp and afraid. So, he tested God one more time, and God was patient and let him test Him two more times. Those tests we read in the verses below.

Reference: Judges 6: 36-40

After all those tests finally, Gideon believed. He believed God and began to prepare for battle. Gideon called all his neighbours and all Israel to join him and he would lead them into war against their enemies. When God saw all the Israelites He said to Gideon, "There are too many to send some home." What do you think Gideon thought when God said, "There are too many?" Gideon wanted to win this battle, and he wanted all the help and all the men he could have with him. But God had a plan that Gideon did not know about.

Reference: Judges 7: 2-7

So Gideon heard the orders from God, in verse 2 God said He was dealing with a proud nation. I think if I saw my army 'on their face lapping the water like my dog,' I would feel a bit safer with my army bending down and staying on watch, but God is awesome. The army on their faces lapping the water were not too concerned if the enemy was close by, and these are the ones God is calling to be His army? No, it was the ones that cupped their hands that God chose. We are talking about 300 Israelites against 30,000 enemy soldiers. One hundred soldiers to one Israelite that was God's odds. Also, God had a very special plan that no man would have thought of.

Reference: Judges 7: 16-21

So, what do you think of God's plan, will it work? God's plans always work. God confused the enemy and they turned on each other and killed each other, so that the Israelites won the battle and chased them out of Israel. Then Gideon and his faithful 300 slew all their enemies on all sides of their land. Gideon was a great leader and loved by the people.

Reference: Judges 8: 22, 23

After all the battles and after Israel was liberated from all her enemies the people want to make Gideon their ruler, their king. This farmer was so humble when the angel first spoke to him and now, he had successfully led his nation to victory and was asked to be their king. Gideon replied that neither I nor my sons will be your ruler, only the Lord will rule over us. That was a good reply; you might say it was a humble reply. So why would God not be pleased with Gideon hereafter? Gideon wanted some of the booty and he was entitled to it, don't you think? You can continue with the story of Gideon in Judges.

Gideon asked for all the gold earring and necklaces, so he took them and made himself a fine garment like a king's robe and the rest he put in his vault. Gideon did not want to be king with the responsibility of a king, who must govern his people, but he wanted a king's ransom and a fine house and bank account. In other words, he wanted the booty to sustain him for life. So where was God in all this? Way back when he had built an altar to God, before he was a glorified hero, that altar was still in use for special religious sacrifices according to the laws of Moses. But Gideon never thanked God with a sacrifice or a party, no singing no dancing. All of that was the way Moses and the people thanked God when they had won over their enemies. But Gideon didn't even hold a holiday to give God thanks. Gideon was only aware of his position now and his wealth.

Reference: Judges 8: 28-32

Well Gideon had his day and Israel was at peace for 40 years. Gideon fathered many children and one of his sons he called Abimelech, which means, "My father the king." How could he name his son that? Gideon was not a king except in his own eyes. So sad, because Gideon's pride ruled his life instead of God, he no longer did anything rewarding for his people. He could have been their ruler serving the great Jehovah and the nation of Israel. But he had too much self- pride to share any of his achievements with God. He just fathered many children, was rich and died. Gideon died without a blessing from the Lord. The Lord made no covenant with him or over his household. How Sad.

Reference: Proverbs 16: 18, 19

Gideon's pride destroyed the mighty man of valour that the angel (Jesus) once addressed him as. If Gideon had only given God thanks for the victories or displayed a sign of heavenly worship to the Lord that would have made Gideon a great man also in God's eyes. But because of his earthly pride and lack of heavenly worship, God had no more earthly good for him or his family.

Reference: James 4: 6, 7

God has given us life and abundant life, so remember to always give Him heavenly worship every day and resist your earthly pride. Amen and amen.

~

IS YOUR HOUSE IN ORDER?

Dear reader, I am not trying to offend you. I know you keep your house clean and everything in its place, painted on the outside every five years and the garden is beautiful. That is not what I am referring to. I should put it in another way, "Is your life in order?" We all have a bit of difficulty keeping our lives in order. So how about our lives with God? The question is, "Is your life with God in order?" Because the story is a little long about where I am going.

Reference: 2 Kings 20: 1-6

Hezekiah was not convinced that he was healed, so he asked Isaiah for a sign that he would be healed. Well, the Lord had told him he was going to die, so he was to get his house in order. Hezekiah cried and turned his face to the wall, he reminded the Lord that he had been a faithful servant to the Lord. Hezekiah challenged God saying, "My house is in order because I have walked before Thee in truth and with a perfect heart, and done that which was good in Thy sight." What more order did God want from him? Hezekiah wept to think that God would take his life when all these years had lived for God. God listened to his plea and decided that He wouldn't take his life. Instead in three days He would heal him. This promise came from God, "I will add unto thy days fifteen years."

But Hezekiah felt that he had been through a lot with God so he challenged Him again. God gives him a choice of miracles, an easy one or a hard one? Me I believe I would have backed off and said, "Thank You Lord," but not Hezekiah.

Reference: 2 Kings 20 9-11

Hezekiah answered Isaiah, "It is a light thing for the shadow to go down ten degrees, let the shadow return backward ten degrees." So the Lord brought the shadow ten degrees backward. Hezekiah had faith in the Lord and therefore he challenged the Lord twice. Hezekiah knew that God was just and he had followed the Lord's laws all his life. The question is, "Could you challenge God?" Because your house is in order and you have been faithful, and have not given God any reason to be displeased with you? This question is for us both, to make sure our house and our lives are in order, according to God. Amen and amen.

~

IT IS NOT THE LENGTH OR THE WIDTH, IT IS THE DEPTH AND THE WEIGHT

Dear reader, I was listening to a woman speaking about Christians trying to keep up with other Christians that they had admired. She spoke of a sister in Christ that she so admired, who happened to mention that she prayed four hours every day. So, the woman felt that she must do the same as her Christian sister. The next day she went into her study, got on her knees and started to pray, after twenty minutes she was finished with it. She had worshiped, praised, given thanks, and interceded for all her prayer requests. She looked at the clock, and thought what do I do now? So she began to pray in the Spirit, twenty minutes later, she was asleep on the floor. She woke up later that morning, looked at the clock, and she had been on the floor sleeping for almost four hours. She felt very silly and that was the last time she tried that. Here Paul gives us a good breakdown of what is needed in prayer.

Reference: Romans 12: 8-16

I know how this woman felt there on the floor in her study. I would like to read
more of the Bible: I should be reading three chapters a day by the routine that
is set up for the year. I read three verses to have a chapter and fall asleep. When
I try to read a good Christian book after three to five pages my eyes are closing.
I have a prayer board in my home. I stand in front of it, lay my hands on it and
pray, I give thanks, go over to praise, and then intercede for everything and
everyone. That takes about half an hour.

Reference: 1 Timothy 2: 1-5

I pray for the nations, their leaders, weather conditions and travelling mercies,
so I go to the Holy Spirit, and together we worship the Lord and bring special
prayers. That is all done in about thirty minutes. When I go to bed at night, I
fall asleep in my prayers, and wake up in the same place I was when I fell asleep.
What is going on with me?

Reference: Mathew 6: 7, 8

I feel like I am not holy enough. Others read the Bible everyday as well as book
after book by all these great Christian authors, but I can't keep up with them. So,
I have consulted the Lord, "Why do I always get sleepy when I am reading or
praying?" At first no answer, then He said, "It is not the length and width of your
prayers, your writing or your reading, you're OK, it is the depth and weight of
the time to focus on Me."

Reference: Colossians 1: 9-11

How long I read or write; how long I pray has nothing to do with the depth of
my time. If my time is pouring out my heart, I am blessed, receiving answers,
with deeper understanding of my life and the others around me. With more
understanding from my diligent reading, I am receiving an abundance of
'weight' in peace, joy and perfect contentment in my home and in my life. I have

good health, an abundant life with Christ and I am very blessed.

Reference: Ecclesiastes 2: 25, 26

I hope that you have more confidence in your relationship with the Lord and in your Christian life. Now that we understand God's words our desire is to not think so much about the length and width of our time we spend with the Lord, no we need to go deeper, with our depth and weight that counts more to Him and will give us more of our quality time with Christ Jesus. Amen and amen.

~

IMMUTABLE GOD

Wow dear reader what a mouth full in this title, first we have the definition: 'Immutable, adjective, not subject or susceptible to change.'

I heard that word used on the radio, so I wrote it down and looked it up, to make it a part of my own vocabulary. When I found the meaning I thought this word can only be used when speaking of God. Everything I touch, see or hear changes, but not God. Everything I touch, everything I look at, it goes rotten, falls apart, rusts, gets old and dies, everything but God, He is forever. I don't know about you but giving God this title, is like feeling two strong arms hugging me and making me very safe.

Reference: Mark 12:30

Sadly, some people would not agree with me. They would say that God is always ready to correct us or punish us but not always ready to bless us. In the book of Job we find that he relates to God as immutable or unchanged.

Reference: Job 23: 13, 14

When Job was speaking of God, he was not speaking of a God who only corrects, punishes, although at the time Job was suffering very badly. Oh no, Job was referring to the love of God lasting forever. Job felt safe with God.

Reference: Job 23: 11, 12

When we can repeat these words to God, we are also repeating Mark 12: 30, the first commandment to Him. Staying on His path, is to love Him, following in His footsteps trusting Him, not turning aside, is obeying Him. With all of my mind and with all my strength, I know his words and His commandments, and I do not refuse to follow them. Job goes on to say, "But have enjoyed them more than my daily food." We are flesh and blood, and we need food and drink to live, to sustain us. Job knew that, but he went further because he knew we are more than just flesh and blood.

Reference: Genesis 1: 27, 28

Job knew that as being created in the image of God, he too needed to be sustained by the same nourishment that God was sustained, by the Living Bread and Living Water of the Holy Spirit of God. Job had passed the need for earthly things. Every earthly thing had been killed, destroyed, or affiliated upon him in his life. The misery the devil had placed on him only turned him closer to God. No help did find from his friends, his only help came from his faith in God. His joy was to serve the Lord, an enjoyment better than a daily meal.

Reference: Job 23: 14-17

One more thing about our immutable God is that His plans don't change either. I know you can find places in the Bible where prayer changes what God has said He has planned. But God never reveals all His plans. He only tells us what He wants us to know, so we will change our heart and get closer to Him.

Reference: Psalm 30: 12

Another word for immutable is the word 'forever.' Here in this verse David has taken a vow to God that should be our vow to the Lord also. He has told the Lord; he will thank Him forever. How can that be? Paul says the same thing to us.

Reference: Ephesians 5: 20

When we are born again, we have changed, hopefully for the last time. We are the ones that are to be unchanging, immutable, standing strong in love, faith, obedience and thanksgiving forever. When we stay focussed on our immutable God, we can be more like Him. Amen and amen.

~

GET THE HELL OUT!

Dear reader, have you heard the phrase, using the word hell? Hell is a noun because it is a place. Hell represents evil. So when I say, "Get the Hell out of something!" I am actually saying, "Get the evil out of something."

Reference: Deuteronomy 32: 21, 22

Only God alone can send a sinner to Hell. But, there is hell on earth also. Where there is evil there is hell. In this verse God is angry, because of the idol worship of false gods. God is jealous when He sees Idol worship. His jealousy grows to anger, and someone must pay for this sin. Once again, He is speaking to Moses about the Israelites, about their weakness worshipping false gods. God says that the lowest hell is burning from His anger with the Israelites. They are under the covenant of Abraham, Isaac and Jacob, a blessed people under the protection of their Holy God, and yet they worship other gods also. Taking a chance to anger the Great I Am was only ignorance; it is there in an ignorant man that evil finds a way into the mind and later even the heart. When evil exists in a man's life, he is only looking for Hell in his future.

The Lord put man and woman in Paradise, a garden of beauty and plenty. They were in a blessed place needing nothing more than what they had all around them. So, why did they have a desire outside of their blessings? Was this tree of 'Knowledge' bearing fruit that could be better than the blessings they already had? Could they not graciously obey their Creator? Why did evil have to come to the garden? Where did it come from?

Reference: Isaiah 14: 12-15

My belief is that when God banished Lucifer and all his followers, God allowed them to reside on the earth (ground) before God saw them there. When God looked upon the earth and the condition it was in, dark with no form, a perfect place for Lucifer but not a pleasant place for God, or what He wanted for the earth. So, God brought light (Jesus) and goodness to the earth, Lucifer had to be banished to another dark place, Hell. Jesus spoke of this in the book of John.

Reference: John 12: 31, 32

As we know, that was the mission of Christ on earth, to draw all men to Him and to redeem them of sin through His death on the cross. Therefore, from the very beginning Lucifer or the Devil was present, even in the Garden of Eden. His evil was lurking on the earth. God wanted man to obey Him for their own protection; Paul refers to what happened in Eden.

Reference: Ephesians 2: 2

Paul gives us another name for the Devil; 'Prince of the air.' This even represents the world's weather conditions. So, the Devil has charge of the air, and what happens because of sin that causes havoc on the earth. Why does God allow the Devil to have so much power over the weather conditions? Living in Florida, weather conditions are very much a part of the warnings given in the autumn. When we see the damage from the wind, we believe we have seen hell on earth, and we pray. We remember the Lord stopping the wind and overruling the 'Prince of the air.' Let us take a look in the book of Mark.

Reference: Mark 4: 39

Jesus rebuked the wind, putting a stop to the Devil's power. With the name of Jesus, we can also rebuke bad weather and shout, "Get the hell out." Several times we find in the Gospels that Jesus rebuked evil and the Devil in Hell. He healed the sick, cast out demons, calmed the wind and even rebuked His disciple Peter when he spoke with a proud tongue. Hell had to get out when Jesus was present. Hell represented darkness and death, Jesus represented light and life.

Reference: John 8: 12

There is a protocol for all men to follow if they want to have Jesus get the hell out of their lives. Number one is to be born again.

Reference: John 3: 5-7

To have the Light of Life in your life is to turn over your life to Christ and be born again. The second thing is baptism.

Reference: Colossians 2: 12

Publicly, if possible, be immersed in water so as to bury the dead and proclaim openly your new life with Christ. The third thing is to be fed.

Reference: John 5: 39

The scriptures are our daily bread, our living waters and our refreshments and nourishments that help us grow in our Christian life. James gives us the fourth thing in our protocol.

Reference: James 5: 16

This is the fourth thing in your protocol, prayer. Prayer is addressing the Holy Father though the Holy Spirit in the name of Jesus. There is a fifth thing.

What a great verse and promise. John has given us the key to rebuke evil, fear, poverty, sickness and even death. We have the power and authority in Jesus name to believe and to shout, "Get the hell out." Amen and amen.

~

GREAT IS THY FAITHFULNESS

Dear reader, I love it when we say, "Thy." We are speaking of God's faithfulness and not ours. Where would His faithfulness be without ours? I believe it would be behind the Pearly Gates, it would never be on earth. To experience God's faithfulness in our lives we must have faith in God. I like to watch Christian TV. I like being part of the congregation, listening to the testimonies and the faith that another has in the Lord. Also, I like reading the Bible stories about the faith of the prophets and patriots in the Old Testament. In so many stories we find people that others would not even look at such as street beggars, shopkeepers, and widows. One of my favourite examples of Faith was with a woman like me. She was a Shunammite woman. Let us go to the Word.

Reference: 2 Kings 4: 8-16

First the Holy Spirit must have enlightened her because she says to her husband, "Behold now I perceive that this is a Holy man of God." I believe this woman was an intercessor who spent a lot of time in prayer. Prayer for her country as it was always being threatened by their enemies. I think when she perceived it, she was in prayer. Her husband knew she was a woman of God, so he agreed with her to bless Elisha and give him an accommodation in their home.

Let me ask you, "Does it pay to give to God?" When Elisha asked the woman what he could give her for her kindness, the woman said they need nothing. Here you have a poor farmer with a piece of land and a little house. I am sure very little money. The woman said we need nothing, is that faith or what? I like it where it says, she stood in the doorway when he called her the second time. She didn't go inside; she stayed at the door to receive her blessing. Elisha gave her a blessing, and said, "No way, why are you lying to me?" The woman didn't have faith in what she was told. Her faith in God was strong, and she did deserve a blessing from God, both her and her husband for being kind. She agreed and received the blessing and conceived and brought forth a son. This is not the end of the story, or this family. Their son grew up to be a young man, and while working in the field with his father the boy suffered a stroke and died. The mother has faith and carries the boy to the room and the bed of Elisha. Now she calls her husband and tells him, I have to go to the man of God, so she goes to Elisha and he greets her.

Reference: 2 Kings 4: 25, 26

When he greets her, he asks, "How is everything with you and your husband?" She says all is well. Then she tells him that their son lies dead on his bed in their home. She still has faith. Elisha goes back with her. Goes in the room, revives the boy, and delivers him to his parents. Later in the chapter, Elisha sends word to the woman of faith, that there is to be a famine, they must go to another country until the famine passes. They are away 7 years, when everything is gone. Their house and land is gone. So, the woman of faith goes to speak to the king.

Reference: 2 Kings 8: 4-6

The king had just heard everything that has happened to this woman and her family from the miracle of Elisha reviving their son. Therefore, they knew this woman of faith was telling the truth and he appointed an officer to restore all that was theirs as well as all the fruits of their field since the day they had left, 7 years earlier. What a wonderful story. Because of this woman's faithfulness and her husband's generosity, they were highly blessed. I hope this story increases your faith and your faithfulness in God. We can sing that hymn, "Great is Thy faithfulness, Great is Thy faithfulness, morning by morning new mercies I see, all I have needed Your hand has provided, Great is Thy faithfulness, Lord unto me." Amen and amen.

GOD CAN

Who says God can't? If the Bible says that God made the earth in six days, and He made man in His own image. Who are we to say God didn't just like that. Wow, it is because we know that God said, "One day to Him is like a thousand years to us." So, we have presumed as some scientists that are also Christian say that the earth is now several million years old, and they insist that God took, by our standards six thousand years for things to develop into the creation of the earth and mankind. The Bible says He took six days.

Reference: Genesis 1: 31

Well, the way I see it is, if we want to change our twenty-four-hour day into a thousand years to please the scientists, we are still within Bible explanations. But, do we also change Genesis chapter one? If we do, then we are doing what we have been told not to do. It is all very confusing, and it should not be as long as we have God's Word in the Bible.

We true believers also must exclude Darwin's and the 'Big Bang' theory. So where does that leave us? Perhaps we are looking for a spiritual explanation, one that we Christians would be happy with. Whatever we are doing we are in trouble; our only safe direction is believing the Bible just as it is written. Just think, would we be saying that God was not telling the whole truth about creation, accusing Him of leaving out some important details about the earth's creation as well as man's creation. I don't think so. God almighty, all omnipotent and all omnipresence, is the God I worship and love. In other words, "God can." Questioning God's capability to create the earth and create mankind in six days that would be to question, "Can God?"

And why have I written on the subject of creation? I have written all this down on paper. It is easier to explain to others when they come with these questions. This is not just a revelation, "Oh no!" This is definitely a declaration of the almighty God. The God who opened the Red Sea, that took some doing.

Reference: Exodus 14: 21, 22

The almighty God that stopped the movement of the earth, so the sun stood still until the Israelites won their battle that took some doing.

Reference: Joshua 10: 13, 14

The almighty God joined three planets together to create the 'Bethlehem Star,'* another miracle. I believe that He did all these marvellous things with the earth and the universe, so why is it so hard to believe that God created them in six days. Whoever says God can't has not met Jesus, they don't know him, have Him in their heart or their life. They don't have faith in Him, they don't walk with Christ. When we have faith in Jesus, we know within our hearts that 'God can.' All Glory be to God. Amen and amen.

**One possibility is a set of conjunctions of the planets Jupiter, Venus, and the bright star Regulus. In this case, the mythologies associated with the objects become important. Jupiter in Hebrew is known as 'Sedeq', which is often translated as meaning righteousness. Jupiter is also often viewed as being the 'king' of the planets. Regulus itself is Latin for 'prince' or 'little king', and Venus is often viewed as a symbol of love, fertility and birth. As such, the combination of these objects close in the sky could have led to the interpretation of the birth of the 'King of Kings'.*

~

GRACE

I know a girl named Grace. I also know a dancer and she is graceful. I like people that are gracious. I have heard a testimony of a judge that gave a young man, who was a thief, a full pardon, in other words, the judge showed the young man grace. So, grace can be applied to many things.

Reference: Exodus 34: 6

The grace of God is not equal to the grace from the judge or the gracefulness of a dancer's movements or even the beauty of a pretty girl. No, the grace of God surpasses all these things. God is love and He is also grace. Dear reader, God is not like us that we must think to act in such a way. We need to think before we show love or grace. God is mercy and goodness, also God is truth. For us to act on these things we must plan and accept our good thoughts, then in accordance with how we manifest those thoughts, we come close to showing more of God to others. Being merciful and gracious is easier for God than for us. Our need for God's grace is a constant need; we cannot express our Christian lives without God's grace.

Reference: Acts 15: 11

Our salvation through Christ Jesus is so dependent on God's grace. One day we are going to have to face the high court of Heaven and Earth. Our expectancy of God's grace is the only entrance available for us. The redemption of Jesus Christ can only be received here on Earth.

Reference: Romans 5: 19-21

Even the grace of God was extended to His precious Son as He was there hanging on the cross covered with all the sins of the world. Jesus knew the plan, therefore He asked His Heavenly Father; if it could be possible to skip Calvary and redeem the world another way. We sometimes forget that Jesus was a human man, and it was through excruciating pain what He did on the cross. He was able to face the cross in the same way we find the strength to face our trials and that is through the grace of God.

Reference: Romans 11: 5, 6

There are many false saviours in this world. They ask us to receive our salvation through our good works or our donations to good causes. But alas Paul tells us that this is not the way, because they are offering grace through your works not through God's grace which is given to us through our faith.

Reference: Ephesians 2: 7, 8

Let us look closer to that gift.

      G - God's
      R - Riches
      A - At
      C - Christ's
      E - Expense

Reference: 2 Corinthians 12: 9

When we find ourselves in a place where we need to call out to the Lord to remove problems. Paul said his problem was, "A thorn in the flesh." That was to say, he was having problems with possibly another person or situations. Perhaps your problem is illness or a relationship or maybe it is your finances. Whatever the problem, there is only one answer: God's grace is sufficient for you. My last verse is the benediction that Paul encourages the churches to share with one another, brotherly love as well as the grace of God.

Reference: 2 Corinthians 13: 14

Amen and amen.

~

'I AM' WITH YOU ALWAYS

Dear reader, I am sharing this with you now in February 2002, but it happened to me at Christmas time. This was a revelation and manifestation in one day. I was so blessed. This slipped my mind with all the Christmas holidays and return to my new home. I was reminded when I was attending a testimony service at my Norwegian Church, while I was listening to what others were sharing I was reminded of my blessing at Christmas. So, I also stood up and shared my miracle, and gave all the glory to the Lord.

Reference: Psalm 24: 9, 10

To cover the situation quickly, I had to move and there was very little space for all the things that I had from my family home. So I would take these things with me to Norway at Christmas. I was happy to give them away, now I knew one day they would belong to the family, why not now?

Reference: Mark 10: 21

So I packed a large suitcase and only a small amount of clothes. I did not know because my ticket was purchased in Norway that I was only allowed 20 kilos in luggage. My friend that drove me to the airport warned me that I might have to pay a large sum for overweight charges. I said to myself, "Help me Lord." I had very little pocket money with me and if I had to pay these charges I would have less for my travel expenses.

Reference: Psalm 40: 17

As I was standing in line, waiting for check-in, I was still praying for deliverance from these charges. I was praying with a confident persistence, I knew that these things belonged in Norway; it was time to pass them on to my family.

Reference: Proverbs 13: 22

As I was still standing there with my (perhaps over weight case) an unknown man came up to me and asked me, "Are you going home for Christmas?" I am sure that I had never met him before.

Reference: Isaiah 48: 6

I asked him to lift my case and tell me how much he thought it weighed, he smiled and said approximately 20 kilos. I shared my dilemma with him, and again he smiled and said, "No problem, I only have this small hand luggage we can sit together, and I will share my 20 kilos with you."

We checked in together on the plane. That trip was one of the loveliest flights I have ever taken from Spain to Norway. He had time to talk and he had some problems with his family. So, before we landed, we prayed together and shared e-mail addresses. This gentleman was an angel sent from God to answer my prayer and need.

Reference: James 5: 13, 14

Prayer works, time to praise Him and give him thanks. Our Lord said He would be with us always, I talk with Him daily, I tell Him everything, and then I get myself a problem and start thinking, "How am I going to solve this problem?" How stupid of me to think or spend a minute trying to solve a problem without first going to Christ."

Reference: Mathew 28: 20

"Thank You Lord." Amen and amen.

~

HOPE IS GONE, GRAB YOUR HARP

Dear reader, when we think of a harp in the Bible, we usually think of an angel or perhaps you think of a young shepherd boy named David playing a harp.

Reference: 1 Samuel 16: 23

David used his harp just as often as he used his weapon. He did have just the responsibility to protect his flock; he also had to quieten them with soothing music. Perhaps an episode with a wolf or a bear had frightened them and there was David to reassure them that now they were safe in his care by playing his harp. In the verse above David was in the court of King Saul. The king had a troubled mind and was very unhappy. He brings the young shepherd boy that had just slain a giant, to his court and asks him to play his harp and sing for him. Then out of nowhere the king tries to slay David, by throwing a spear at him. From that moment on for many years David and the king are enemies and David must run for his life. In the book of 1 Samuel is the whole story of David and King Saul.

Reference: Psalm 43: 4

In the book of Psalms David mentions his harp fifteen times, where he only mentions his sword thirteen times. David's nature was of a man of peace and praise, not war. He became king, as God said he would, and he didn't have to kill for the throne. David knew that when all hope was gone he could turn his thoughts to praise and to God. He knew that peace came with praise, and that power came with praise. David lived many years before Jesus, but the beatitude in Mathew was directed to him.

Reference: Mathew 5: 9

Peacemakers are also praise makers. You may not have a harp, but you have a voice. You have a voice so you can sing, worship and praise God. You may ask how can I do that when I am worried, fearful and troubled? My answer is, if you are all those things, then you are in the right place to begin. Grab your harp, it is right there, when all hope is gone you begin to sing hymns, you begin worship and praise God, and you begin to thank Him for life and your salvation through the cross and Christ. What better example do we have than Paul and Silas in prison. Perhaps you have been in prison or have visited someone in prison, believe me you have never been to a prison like the one those men were in.

Reference: Acts 16: 19-21

The church had sent these men out to minister; they were the first missionaries from the church. How hopeful they were when they first started out on their new adventure. How hopeless they found themselves the next day. All they did was to save a slave girl from eternal damnation; they had cast out the evil spirit in her, in the Name of Jesus. She had been a fortune teller and now her owners had no business without her.

Reference: Acts 16: 22-24

The inner cell was damp and cold. There was Paul and Silas in stocks on the wet floor freezing and in the dark after they had been beaten. How hopeless does it get? But these were not men who complained to God, these were peacemakers, praise makers they decided instead of whimpering they would worship.

Reference: Acts 16: 25, 26

How did they know that by praising God would cause the biggest revival in town? They didn't! They were in the inner cell encouraging themselves whilst sending hope to all those in the outer cells. The Romans on one hand were very happy to put Jews in prison; they did not like the Jews and were always pleased when one was sentenced to prison. Jews on the other hand knew how to sing unto the Lord, but there in prison they believed God, Jehovah, to be so far off. They had no idea of Jesus or His salvation.

Reference: Acts 16: 26, 27

The praise and hymns had reached their Heavenly Father. No damp, cold cells were hidden so God could not reach them. No prison bars could keep the Lord from His faithful servants. It took an earthquake to release God's blessings on all the prisoners. Not one tried to escape because they were free. Free of their chains and free of their sins.

Reference: Acts 16: 27, 28

The jailor woke up, and when he saw the prison doors open, he drew his sword and was about to kill himself because he thought the prisoners had escaped. In verse 28, Paul shouted, "Don't harm yourself, we are all here." Have you ever been in a revival meeting where the presence of God was so strong that you felt your chains fall to the floor? That is what the jailor found that night in the prison cell, all the chains were on the floor and the prisoners were all singing and praising God. What a sight. The jailor could not believe his eyes, but he knew he wanted whatever Paul and Silas had.

Reference: Acts 16: 29-32

That night was the beginning of prison ministry. When or if you visit a prison, practice a song of praise. Paul and Silas were singing hymns perhaps from Psalms.

Reference: Psalm 42: 11; Psalm 71: 14

There may be a time because of illness or your finances, perhaps it is a relationship or like Paul and Silas you are unjustly accused. Whatever the situation is for you, praise is the answer. David knew praise and worship was in his life and in time it made him a king. Paul and Silas knew also the power of praise and at the darkest hour of midnight their revival had just began. I hope that you too will practice praise and play your harp.

Reference: Psalm 98: 4, 5

"Sing unto the Lord with the harp." Amen and amen.

GOD'S WILL

Dear reader so many times we use the phrase, "If it is God's will." We use this phrase as if we are not sure of what God's will is. The will of God is written clearly in the Bible. Did you know that a person that cannot hear or see could understand the will of God? Even the deaf and blind can understand the will of God. David wanted to know the will of God better, so he prayed this prayer. This is a good daily prayer.

Reference: Psalm 51: 10-13

David wanted a new heart and a new spirit so he could teach the will of God to others. In Hollywood when I was growing up, they made a movie called Frankenstein. This film was about a monster. The monster was mostly evil, but to the end of the movie some good appeared in his character. This reminds me of the heart of man both good and evil. Hollywood was making big bucks making these evil films. Today it is the same; Hollywood exploits the evil side of man, because the evil side likes being entertained by its own kind. When I lived in Florida, there was a church on every corner in the area I lived. Those churches did not put a stop to evil that the flowed through Polk County like a river. This large, evil river flowed right through the Bible Belt, the southern states in America. Drugs, alcohol, divorce, child and wife abuse, rape murder, homosexuality and abortion are what filled the evil river there. Christians are standing on the opposite banks, calling out to each other, "Keep praying that the river will dry up."

Reference: 1 Peter 3: 17

God had informed the Israelites and the nation of Israel in all the books of the Old Testament through the Patriarchs and Prophets, what He wanted of them. Telling the people for many hundreds of years, just what His will was and is, but in all that time people could not understand what they were being told. In the New Testament the will of God was told to the world through Jesus. I just finished my will and testament. This paper says what must be done at my request after I no longer am able to do them myself. I had to have a notary, two witnesses to sign and stamp it before it is legal. Then the lawyer must probate it also. The will and testament of God is in the Old Testament. Here are some verses from it.

Reference: Deuteronomy 28: 3-6

As there can be clauses in a person's will, so there clauses in God's Will.

Reference: Deuteronomy 28: 15

To be blessed from the Will of God, one must have obeyed Him, if not the blessing becomes cursing.

Reference: Deuteronomy 28: 16-19

God has made it very clear what His will is. The Patriarchs and prophets recorded everything God said; they were witness and notaries for the Will of God. The problem was there was no lawyer to probate His Will in the Old Testament. In the New Testament we find a lawyer, an advocate. One whom God has appointed to probate His will, not only for the Jews but also for Gentles. We now have Jesus the Son of God here on earth for that very reason.

Reference: 1 John 2: 1, 2

If someone wanted to change my will they would have to hire a lawyer, go to court and in front of the judge, they must present evidence so they have the right to change what I have requested. No lawyer, no court, no judge, and no evidence can change the Will of God. David tells us that our destiny was planned before creation of the earth. In other words the Will of God was written before then.

Reference: Psalm 139: 14-18

The Patriarchs and prophets were not able to probate the Will of God because they were only notaries and did not have the last word on God's behalf. The lawyer that is appointed by the one that is leaving the Will is the only one that can speak for them on their behalf.

Reference: Mathew 5: 17, 18

Through the words of Jesus and the teaching of Paul we can understand the Will of God. God's advocate was and is Jesus. He is the only one that can speak on behalf of God's Will. A lawyer cannot probate a will before contacting, communicating, and informing the beneficiary.

Reference: John 5: 30

God's Will was to send Jesus to contact, communicate and inform the beneficiaries of the Will of God. If you ask, "Who are they?" They are the ones saved, sanctified and waiting for their eternal life in Heaven. Only with these qualifications can one be considered to be a beneficiary of God's Will. Jesus at the Cross was probating the final request of the Will of God. It was there at the Cross He said, "It is finished."

Reference: John 19: 30

The total package that God had and has for His beneficiaries was presented on that Easter morning when Mary Magdalene cried out, "He has risen."

Reference: John 20: 1

The ultimate understanding of God's Will is recorded in this verse.

Reference: Isaiah 53: 5

There is no evil, no tempter, no devil, and no sin that survived the cross at Calvary. Every sin that is in that evil river that flows through the' Bible Belt' has been redeemed. God's Will will never change, although His answers may be unlike His will. God is also a Father; He is the maker of all things.

God may answer, "Yes, no or wait," He does not always answer, "Yes." Our destiny is not for us to know; only God knows that. Only God knows when we ask the Holy Spirit for something if it is in our destiny to receive it. We don't have to add to our prayers, "If it is God's will." When we pray to God, even by the Holy Spirit in tongues, we should be aware and understand the will of God.

Reference: Romans 12: 2

God wants to have a good relationship with us; He wants to bless us beyond our requests. Amen and amen.

~

GOD MOVES

Dear reader, I read a sentence the other day that the Holy Spirit placed in my spirit to write about. I don't remember where I read this, 'I love the way God moves into impossible situations,' but I can't forget it. I live in Spain and here they have many religious parades throughout the year and in all these parades they carry large figures of saints and virgins walking through the streets. The public, who are standing in the streets, run up to the figures and throw flowers onto the platforms and kiss them. It is a beautiful thing to see with all the lights and music, but it is so sad to see them standing there in the streets for hours. What is the principle behind it? The first time my family saw the parade on Easter week we were so impressed with the beauty and spectacular procession, just like all the tourists there. But later in my quiet time, I started thinking of what we had seen and how the public was showing a kind of worship to these figures. I felt uneasy in my spirit and prayed about it asking the Lord for some answers.

Reference: Psalm 115: 4-8

When God answers our questions He gets right to the point. He was telling me that here in this new country, where we now are living, they are practicing idol worship.

Reference: Deuteronomy 4: 28, 29

Wow, I was not happy thinking that there were idol worshippers as my new neighbours. These false gods that were being paraded on the streets, had no soul, no spirit, no heart and no mind, all they had was a body of wood, metal, and cloth. The expressions on their faces would never change. The prayers and all the crying around them are never heard or answered. These false gods only move by the hands and feet of men that carry them on their shoulders. By the way these figures are up to 10ft high, locked away in their adorned storage houses close to the church.

Reference: Deuteronomy 4: 29

This verse follows the verse where Moses warns the Israelites of their stupidity to serve these false gods. Moses puts a big 'But' in there. The idols in Spain are powerless, they cannot move themselves. If they cannot help themselves why would this nation expect them to help it? God moves by Himself, and He moves everything around us by His power. Everything around us means sky, weather, and all forms of life.

Reference: Psalm 62: 11

I am only a small seed bearer, but I know that Spain is in need of seed bearers with the Gospel. This country needs God to move it completely around and back to Christ, not just a baby in a manger. God moves in impossible situations and here is one. The way to get God moving is prayer. God is a gentleman; He would never impose where He has not been asked. Intercessory prayer for Spain is just the invitation God is waiting for.

Reference: Psalm 66: 3

We must pray and extend an invitation to the Lord to reveal His power against these false gods and their makers. Our God Jehovah moves with power and grace. As we invite Him into this impossible situation, He sets us afire to get moving also.

Reference: Psalm 106: 8

We are servants of Christ if we are saved, sanctified, and baptised by Him in His Name. When we become His, we are also mighty with His power. To achieve this is a daily process with prayer and the Word.

Reference: Eccl. 5: 19

As God moves in our lives, so does His power, as a gift for children. It is in God's Word we find our greatest gifts and rewards.

Reference: 2 Thessalonians 1: 11

From the time I came to Spain 40 years ago, I have seen God move in so many people's lives including my family and the church. With things as humans we would say, "No these things are possible." But now we testify that the Lord did the impossible. God is moving all the time, take my word for it. Look around you and watch what is going on, so that you can see God making it happen.

Reference: Luke 1: 37

I started this revelation with a sentence, 'I love the way God moves in an impossible situation.' When we are facing the impossible, we can be sure that God hears our prayers and will answer them. He is not manmade and powerless like the idols in Spain; He is the maker of man and the almighty creator of the universe. Amen and amen.

GOD BLESS YOU

I happen to know a person that sends a 'God Bless U' on all my mail. I use that phrase whenever I am speaking to anyone, although it doesn't always happen. Perhaps you, dear reader, think I don't have faith in God to bless these people. You're wrong. I have faith in God's blessing. There is another reason it doesn't happen. Let's go to the Word.

Reference: Genesis 1: 22, 23

We read God did not bless the earth that He created until He had been working on it for five days. Then He made man and blessed him.

Reference: Genesis 1: 27; 2: 1

Everything He made was good and God was content with His handiwork, so He blessed and sanctified it, then He sat back to rest and enjoy it. We know what happened next. Adam and Eve sinned, and God had to punish them. So what about God's blessing? God's blessing continued. God blessed a lot of names in the Old Testament. These you read about; Noah, Abraham, Isaac, Jacob, and we know of Joseph and Moses. We must never forget the blessed David. I am sure you have many names you could add to the list. Why were they blessed? They weren't blessed because they were perfect; they were blessed because they were obedient to God and honoured Him. They had it in their hearts to do good. Also, they prayed for their families and their nation. God Himself makes it very clear whom He will bless like those that keep His commandments. One of my favourite chapters is in Deuteronomy.

Reference: Deuteronomy 28

God points out His blessings and to whom He will bestow them on. He also points out those to whom He will not bless and remove His blessing from. It is very worthwhile reading for those who are asking for favour from God. The Bible has a continuation of books that repeat God's blessing.

Reference: Mathew 5: 3-11

I this chapter we find that Jesus extends very special blessings in the 'Sermon on the Mount;' and Jesus our Lord and Saviour, after He had been resurrected, gave a blessing that is for all of us.

Reference: John 20: 28, 29

Yes, we believe in Jesus and have received Him as Tomas did that day.

Reference: Revelation 22: 14

In this verse we have a greater blessing in store for us. We that are saved through the Blood of the Lamb, the Son of God, Jesus Christ, have the blessing of eternal life with God in His Heavenly home. We may 'enter through the gates of the city.' Wow! A big Wow! So, what about this that I am always saying, "God Bless You," to, what about them? Sadly though my thoughts are; if my prayer time is not also devoted to them, their need of being saved and repenting of their sins, my words are empty and have no meaning. This is something I need to think long and hard about and perhaps you need to do the same. Amen and amen.

~

GOD AND YOUR FINANCES

Dear readers, are you willing to let God get involved in your finances? Perhaps you are thinking that you must give away all your wealth to please God. Then you would be poor and humble. Wrong, in God's Word He makes it very clear that when you give you get back.

Reference: Luke 6: 38

If you are having problems with the economy as many are right now we hear that our world is in trouble financially. Do you really believe that the rule of giving can work for us? Maybe we need some proof that it works. In the Bible the finest proof is found with Abraham. James tells us that Abraham was a friend with God. How wonderful to be known as a friend to God.

Reference: James 2: 23

God taught Abraham everything about the law of giving and believing. Abraham had to follow four steps to become the wealthiest man in all Israel.

Reference: Genesis 12: 1

The first step Abram (God later changed his name to Abraham) had to do was to listen to the voice of God. To do this Abram had to be searching with his heart for the Lord. He was not raised to serve the Lord. His family worshipped and served other gods. As a young man he must have lost faith in these false gods and a desire grew within his heart to worship and serve the Lord, Jehovah, therefore he was listening for the Lord's voice. God knew Abram's heart and He wanted to use him to father His nation. God did not only tell Abram to leave his birthplace and go out into the world on his own. Oh no, God assured Abram that as he obeyed, he would be abundantly blessed.

Reference: Genesis 12: 4

So, step one that we must take is as Abram took, to listen and obey.

Reference: Genesis 12: 7

Well, Abram arrived in this far country safely but was wealthier than he was when he left his home. He had travelled a very long way with his wife and nephew, they had no home, no friends, and they had only what they left home with. Abram did not think himself in trouble. He knew with the little he had arrived with, it was a blessing. He wanted only to honour God; his first priority was to honour Him. He built an altar to the Lord for all to see, instead of a home to his family. Abram had not seen any more blessings, but he wanted to give thanks, before seeing them. So, he honoured the Lord when he first arrived in the new country. The second step is to honour God.

Reference: Genesis 13: 5-8

The third step that we definitely must learn to take is generosity and to avoid any regret or strife. When things are not going the way we wished they would, we need to find someone less fortunate than we are and bake them a cake. Does that sound crazy? Well step four is dependent on our heartfelt compassion and love for the others.

Reference: Genesis 18: 32, 33

What have we here? Abram has been pleading with the Lord to show mercy on his nephew and his family. Abram did not say to himself, "Well that ungrateful lad, after all I did for him, he chose the best land available and went off to live his merry life in Sodom, serves him right if the city is destroyed." No! He pleaded with God five times for Lot and his family. His compassion overtook his nature of revenge. Although he had been treated badly, he loved Lot and did not want to see him come to harm. Showing compassion to others is step four to please God. As we take each step we also please ourselves and we come into a state of joy and happiness. We are not to be boastful for our obedience but be thankful that we accomplished all four steps. The problem is that the Lord does not want us to take the four steps only when we are in need or have a problem. No, God wants us to adopt this behaviour as our lifestyle.

Reference: Genesis 13: 2

Because Abraham's lifestyle was solely involved in following these four steps, he was the wealthiest and blessed man in all the land. When we find ourselves in a financial bind and in need of these blessings, what do we do and what do we say? Or do we do anything? Sadly, our biggest problem lies in what we do say. Because our words can hinder what God has out there for us.

What you have to say about your situation is what controls the outcome of your problems. It is not easy to be positive when everything looks so negative. That is what makes God's supernatural law so different from man's normal law. All the power of both laws lies within your very words, whether they are positive or negative, so how does this affect your giving? In every way it affects your living. Who are you living for, yourself or your creator? Some of us are living only for ourselves and all that we can gain on our own terms with God. I am sure most of you have found out that it doesn't work that way. The only terms we can make with God are written in His Word for us.

Let us look at some financial problems that could be our problems today. Past due bills, mortgages, in need of work, to sell or buy property, all these problems can be the cause of sleepless nights. To overtake them all we must take control by speaking to them. Maybe you are smiling or even laughing at what I just said. Well, you tell me how God created the earth. He did it by taking control of this planet and by speaking to it. One by one He called for the elements to appear on the earth, and they obeyed His Word. This same power God had in His Word you have in your word through Christ. Speak in the Name of Jesus with authority He has given you.

Reference: Mathew 18: 18-20

Jesus says that when we speak up and claim the authority He has given us, we can stop things from happening or we can get things to happen. In other words, we have the power over circumstances in the Name of Jesus. Also, He says if there are two of us in agreement, it will happen. The next verse is one of my favourites. It is so comforting to know, when I speak up Jesus Himself agrees and His presence is with me. That is when I feel the close presence of the Holy Spirit. Also, I am convinced that what I am asking for is correct or not but stay in the will of God. How happy God confirms our request.

Reference: Psalm 37: 4, 5

I am sure if you have debts, you have prayed about them. But have you spoken to them and given a tithe on their behalf. Oh, you are laughing again, but in God's Word He makes it clear that if you give a tithe He will open the windows of Heaven for you.

Reference: Malachi 3: 10, 11

In this verse God says, "Prove me," He is given us the right to prove His word and hold Him to His promises. God doesn't make promises that He doesn't keep. On the other hand, man makes promises to God that he doesn't keep. Remember I said we must direct our lives to live with our convictions and our commitments to God. We must program and train our thinking to only speak words of power and victory over our problems before we see the final results. We must learn to speak in faith, repeating many times a day the power we have over our problems in the Name of Jesus. These Bible verses are not just for our evening and morning prayers, they are for every hour of the day. When a negative phrase pops out of our mouth we must repent and reverse it. As long as it takes us to build our faith through our words and our giving, to apply them totally into our daily lives, is just as long as it will take our problems to be resolved.

Reference: Philippines 2: 10

God and your finances must always be in order. In the verse above we are told that all things, not some things, but all things on earth will and must bow to the Name of Jesus. So, take control of your finances, speak out, use the precious Name of Jesus and take over. Amen and amen.

~

HEADS AND TAILS

Dear reader, what is so important about this phrase, 'Heads and Tails?' I think it is the position they are on the body. The head has the eyes to see everything around so it can protect the rest of the body from any danger. The eyes can see the good things and the colourful things that the body enjoys and likes to participate with. It is a good thing our eyes are on our head, we need our sight!

Reference: Mathew 6: 22, 23

The ears are also on the head of the body; they are there to listen to what we want to hear from others and what we want to remain in our thoughts. It is what remains in our thoughts that will occupy our thinking. With our ears we can hear pleasant things that we want to save, but at times we hear things that are not pleasant, and it is those things we try to discard from our thoughts. So, another good thing is that God placed our ears on our head because we need to listen.

Reference: Revelation 2: 29

The mouth, I believe, is the most prominent tool on the head and in many cases is badly used and abused. Its true function was to communicate kindly to others, to communicate love, to give thanks and to praise God. We also find that the mouth is good for giving instructions and information. That is why our mouth is also on our head we need to communicate.

Reference: Romans10: 8-11

Another part of the head is the mind, and it is the mind that really makes the greatest difference between the head and the tail. All the parts of the body do their duties by commands of the mind. That is why the mind is in the head, we need the mind for leadership.

Reference: Philippians 2: 5

So, to be a good head is to be a good leader, with responsibility of the other members of the body, to do the best of their abilities.

Reference: 1 Corinthians 12: 18

In this verse we find the joy to know that God is pleased with how our body is and that is a gift for any woman. But here Paul was also referring to the members of the church, which is the body of Christ.

Reference: 1 Corinthians 12: 27

The head of the church is Christ, and we need Him as our leader. We have many leaders in this world. We have leaders in our government, in our communities, in our workplaces and in our schools and homes.

(Footnote: If we want a good leader, we must have a good head.)

Reference: 1 Timothy 2: 1-3

We must pray for our leaders and those in authority, we also pray that we have the guidance we need to elect good leaders. If we don't have good, God-fearing leaders making our laws and governing our daily lives, we will find ourselves in the position of the tail. The tail has no sight, no hearing, no communication, and no thoughts. All it does is hang on and follow the leader. It takes no responsibility of where it is going, it just hangs on and hopes all will be well where it ends up. Now these are things to think about. If you are the head, you will use your eyes, Psalm 25: 15. Also you will use your ears, Acts 28: 27, "And they hear with their ears and understand with their heart." You will always need your mouth, Psalm 19: 14, and at last we use our mind to think before we act, Isaiah 26: 3. If you are the tail then you just sit back, hang on, and hope for the best. Question: which position are you? Perhaps you need to pray for a better position? Amen and amen.

~

HUMAN SACRIFICE

Dear reader, I am not one to see squeamish movies, so I really don't much like to think of how sacrifices were done, and I certainly would not want to see one. We are reading the book of Leviticus, 'the book of law,' in our Wednesday night Bible Study. We are up to chapter eight and so far, every chapter has been squeamish. God is so precise about every sacrifice and how to do them properly. Each sacrifice is done for a very significant purpose. The big one is the 'sin offering,' which is only correct. There are offerings for precise sins also, stealing, lying cheating, adultery and there is a peace offering and an offering for your trespasses. God dedicates how each poor animal must be sacrificed. I will go through it very quickly, and then give you some references. First God tells Moses how to kill the bullock and save the blood. He says the offal and innards are to be separate from the heart, liver, and kidneys. Everything that is required to be burned must be burnt on the fire. After the offering is over one choice piece of meat is to be given to the priests for their dinner, they work all day to make these sacrifices. All of this takes place in the Tabernacle that God had Moses build for the people and the priests. Now it is time to go to the references.

Reference: Leviticus 1: 1-13

The most important thing to remember is that God is giving Moses instructions of how He wants to be approached and worshipped in the Tabernacle. In verse 1 is a little word that is wonderful when you think of what it means. The word 'from,' wow! God spoke from the Tabernacle. Is there anything in this world that could be better than to have God speaking from some place in your home or church? As you read the verses you can see how precise God is in every detail in the preparations. All these details are what I call squeamish, cutting up the offered animal and parting it for the altar fire in the tabernacle and the rubbish fire outside the camp. Also preparing the portions the priests were to eat. Personally, I would not have an appetite after the offering. In the first verse we find that God speaks. He says, "Take a male without blemish." He also says from the cattle herd, or sheep from the flock. I like when He includes those with no cattle or animals, they can sacrifice the proscribed birds.

Reference: Leviticus 1: 14, 15

The Lord knew not everyone could afford to sacrifice an animal, so our merciful Lord said He would be pleased with the bird sacrifices also. Perhaps you recall a poor family that had only birds to sacrifice at the Temple.

Reference: Luke 2: 22-24

There were also those who had nothing but grain or meal to offer and God was pleased with that also. God knew that they were offering the best they had and that pleased God.

Reference: Leviticus 2: 1-3

The Lord included everyone for the offerings.

Reference: Leviticus 2: 8

All these laws of sacrifices and offerings were first spoken to Moses. When Jesus was growing up He learnt what His Heavenly Father wanted in those offerings.

Reference: Mark 12: 41-44

Jesus made it quite clear how precious sacrifices and offerings can be when He told of the widow and her gift. God looks on the heart and He knows whether our gifts are from overflow or truly a sacrifice. Our tithe is 10% of our property and our overflow. Our offerings are over and above our tithes. Giving in this manner gives us favour with God and our prosperity. Getting back to the Tabernacle there is one more thing Moses is told to do.

Reference: Leviticus 4: 3

I want to look at this verse and take it apart. Here it says if the priest has also sinned they must do their recompense. Even in that time priests were not above the law of God, in fact their designated duty was to keep His law. Therefore, not only must they repent, but they must do it in front of the whole congregation. In other words, no one is without sin, and no one is above repentance.

Reference: Leviticus 4: 4

As the priest is about to slay the animal, he consecrates it to be worthy as an offering to the Lord. As we know there was and is and always shall be only one offering worthy of the Lord and that offering is 'the Lamb of God.'

Reference: Leviticus 4: 5

The blood was the life of animal. The blood was the only part of the offering that was brought to the church. The other parts of the animal were gifts to God: the blood was a gift to the church. Only the blood could cleanse the congregation of their sins.

Reference: Leviticus 4: 35

Once the offer is done there is an atonement established with God. Atonement signifies the 'wholeness of one.' If two things are brought so close together that they become only one that is what atonement is, for us it is 'being within the wholeness of God.' Now we have spoken of these animal sacrifices, what about a human sacrifice? A man in his thirties sacrificed as a sin offering for mankind. This sounds a bit barbaric, but it was done because God wanted it so. God sent His only begotten Son, Jesus, to this Earth, to be sacrificed on an altar, 'where the timbers crossed.' His only Son was whipped and beaten, preparations for the sacrifice. As the 'Lamb of God,' He uttered not a word until He was on the altar, on the cross. The Tabernacle was called Calvary. You may think I am telling a tale, but all this is true and written in the Bible. I want to start with this verse.

Reference: Luke 22: 15

Note: the Passover was when all the Egyptian's first born died and God let the angel of death pass over the Israelites homes, that had the lamb's blood on their doorposts (Exodus 12: 11 and Leviticus 23: 5). It was at this last meal that Jesus was preparing His disciples and Himself for a 'human sacrifice.'

Reference: Luke 22: 15-20

After sharing their meal together, Jesus went to the Garden of Gethsemane, I am going to just give you references now that all Christians know in their hearts.

References: Luke 22: 40-44, 47, 48

Now we go to read what Paul had to say about this 'human sacrifice.'

Reference: Romans 3: 23

The little word 'all' means we are included; just as God called for the sin offerings in Leviticus chapter four. He called for a sin offering on Calvary. The difference was that there in the Tabernacle Moses preformed that sacrifice every year because there was no ultimate offering for sin.

Reference: Romans 8:3

For even those who came faithfully to the altar every year with their sin offering: they left the Temple and went back to their sins. More references.

Reference: Hebrews 9: 12; 13:11-16

God was and is pleased and thankful with the sacrifice of His Son, Jesus, on Calvary's Cross. Now Paul gives us the GOOD NEWS. Romans 6: 8-12: It is a good thing we can recall all Jesus did for us on the Cross. He paid for our sins once and for all time. No more sacrifices have to be brought to a Temple or an altar, we are not worthy of His 'human sacrifice' at Calvary. Yet if we believe in Him, we are sinners, saved and washed clean by the blood of the Lamb of God. We have only to thank Him and follow Him, our King of Kings. In the same way

He gave His life for us, we must give our life to Him. This last verse is the best. My boys and I always repeated this at bedtime.

Reference: Galatians 2: 20

Amen and amen.

~

GLORY FROM THE TONGUE

Dear reader, I know that we as Christians would like to bring glory to Christ when we speak. But we don't always do that, in fact we seldom do that because our tongue is so wild and untamed at times. I don't mean we curse or take the name of Jesus in vain. No, I mean we do not always think before we speak, or we let our emotions rule our tongue.

Reference: Psalm 5: 8-10

This verse is a prayer, it should be our daily prayer as we are waking up in the morning and getting ready to start our day. David said he knew his enemies were out there. David had discernment of who was for him and who was against him. We also need that discernment. In verse 9 David knew the enemy did not love or serve the Lord, and they were dishonest. Second, he knew they were deceitful and evil. Third, he knew they were dangerous. Fourth, he knew they were mischievous and liars. With all these bad characteristics, I would say they served the Devil and Beelzebub, who is also our enemy. In verse 10 I am reminded of a comment that I often make when I hear a Christian repeating bad news, problems with finances, sickness, or troubled relationships. My comment is, "Bite your tongue; you're giving the Devil his due." In other words, in verse 10, we want to turn it around, when we get bad news we replace it with the Good News, we can claim through the Blood of Christ, our prosperity, our health and loving relationships. God will bring destruction to the bad news, rumours, and gossipers. We can and should speak the Good News.

Reference: Psalm 35: 28

David was a blessed man, and he loved the Lord, although he sinned many times, and he had to repent many times before the Lord. The Lord continued to bless him because He knew David's heart. I especially like these verses so why not take a peek at Psalm 51, the last part of verse 14 and verse 15: "O God, thou God of my salvation, and my tongue shall sing aloud of thy righteousness. O Lord, open thou my lips; and my mouth shall show forth thy praise."

Reference: Psalm 51: 12

David lived many years before Jesus, he knew of Him, and he wrote in his own words in the Psalm 22 as he envisioned the Messiah on the cross and His crucifixion at Calvary. David was blessed with the prophetic for the Messiah, and Pentecost, the day that the Holy Spirit made his visitation to the upper room in Jerusalem.

Reference: Acts 2: 25

In the upper room the hundred and twenty were there waiting on the Comforter that Jesus had said would come. It was then the Holy Spirit visited them in that room by the shaking and with tongues of fire and speech in unknown languages, to those who were present there. The shaking and shouting in many languages were the confirmation of the prophets in the Old Testament. One of them was from David (Psalm 16: 8). And Peter spoke the words of David, except for one change.

Reference: Psalm 35: 26

The change regards the tongue. The day of Pentecost was the day that the disciples were given a new language straight from Heaven. There were visitors from many different parts of the Rome Empire, all speaking in their own language, when they also heard Peter witnessing about Christ and His resurrection. He was so blessed to be witnessing to all these nations visiting Jerusalem that day. Although Peter was not in charge of his tongue, it was the Holy Spirit that was in charge of it and who was the witness. Surely when Peter said, "My tongue is glad," he was speaking the truth. David was a prophet; he knew the Messiah and the Holy Spirit that God had promised to His people. He did not know in what form God would send His Spirit. David knew in the time of the Messiah; God would be glorified. Peter knew that only through the tongue God could be glorified.

Reference: Psalm 119: 172

We can glorify God with our tongue or dishonour God with our tongue. Yes, with the tongue, we have the power to do either one.

Reference: Proverbs 18: 21

We are all very weak in this area of our Christian walk. We do not always think before we speak. One verse that I have always liked is also a daily prayer and a reminder to, "Bite your tongue and 'Do Not' give the Devil his due."

Reference: Philippians 2: 5

We all have to think and remember how to bring glory to God through our tongue.

Reference: Psalm 96: 8

Amen and amen.

~

HEAVENLY WORDS

Shalom dear reader, have you ever thought of giving us Heavenly Words? I mean we can use words that are so pleasing for God to hear us say. I have four words that I believe are words that came down from Heaven so we can share more of Heaven in our lives. The first word is "Abba."

Abba. The dictionary explains it as, "This Syrian or Chaldean word is found three times in the New Testament (Mark 14: 36, Romans 8: 15, Galatians 4: 6) and in each case is followed by its Greek equivalent, which is translated, "Father." It is a term expressing warm affection and filial confidence. It has no perfect equivalent in our language." *(Easton's Bible Dictionary.) (But we, English speakers, would say, "Daddy.")*

Reference: Mark 14: 36

Jesus told of God, His Father, throughout the three years of His ministry. He was teaching, healing, and ministering. He spoke of His Father at the time He was performing miracles. Now He calls His Father 'Abba,' when He was in the garden waiting to be taken and preparing for His death. The angels are ministering to Him, wiping the drops of sweat and blood from His brow as He prayed. The name' Abba' was the name He used in Heaven when He was speaking to His Father. This name represented the endearment and love He felt for His Father. The Heavenly Father must have been so sad to hear His Son's prayers; all He could do was send Him angels to comfort Him there in the garden. Abba, Father had given the cup to His Son Jesus in Heaven and now He must drink from it here on Earth.

References: Romans 8: 15; Galatians 4: 6

The closer we get to the presence of God, the more natural it is for us to call Him Abba. The heavenly word should also be in our daily prayer language and thoughts. The second word is, "Agape."

Agape: Developed in Christian theology as the love of God or Christ for humankind. In the New Testament it refers to the covenant love of God for humans, as well as reciprocal love for God. Christ going to the cross and dying there was the greatest example of agape love. Before the cross, John gives us the explanation.

Reference: John 3: 16

There is the first example of 'agape' love. God gave His Son to die in our place because of our sins and Christ did it on the cross because He followed the example of 'agape' love from His Father, 'Abba.'

Reference: John 13: 1

Jesus invited His 12 disciples to the Passover feast, but only 11 finished their dinner. Jesus washed the feet of all 12, before sitting at the table. Jesus loved them all, even Judas, because of His 'agape' love, no-one was left out.

Reference: 1 John 4: 8-12

Christ was the man in the flesh that showed the great example of 'agape' love to His followers and to us to bestow that love to the world. To manifest 'agape' love is almost impossible for mankind. But to make it our goal is what the Lord expects from us. The third word is used daily, "Hallelujah."

Hallelujah. Or 'Praise ye the Lord' stands at the beginning of 10 Psalms. (Some of which are: Psalm 106, 111,113, 135, 146, 150.) These are contained in the book of Psalms called the 'Hallelujah' Psalms. From its frequent use it grew into a form of praise. The Greek form of the word, 'Alleluia,' is found in Revelation 19: 1,3,4,6. *(Easton's Bible Dictionary.)*

I am afraid this word for worship and praise to our Almighty Lord is so misused in the world. David wrote Psalms to express his worship and praise to God. He used this Heavenly Word to exalt the Lord to His highest glory. I will comment on some of the verses.

Reference: Psalm 147: 1

There are a lot of good churches today and the witness is strong, but the praise and worship are not as strong as they should be. David tells us that praise is the right thing to do before the Lord. Therefore, I think he was saying, "Hallelujah, praise the Lord," not just using the word on its own. 'Hallelujah, praise the Lord' should be the first thing we say when we come into the Lord's House. I love to say, "Hallelujah praise the Lord," because I know it is a whack against the Devil. We can look at John's book of Revelation.

Reference: Revelation 19: 4, 5

The word 'Hallelujah' is definitely a Heavenly word. We are so favoured of the Lord that we can use it to express our praise for Him. The Lord in Heaven has shared these very Holy words with us so we can return them to Him and please Him that way. The fourth word is, "Shalom."

Shalom: The use of 'Shalom' in the scriptures always points towards that transcendent action of wholeness. 'Shalom' is seen in reference to the well-being of others (Genesis 43: 27, Exodus 4: 18), to treaties (1 Kings 5: 12) and in prayer for the wellbeing of cities and nations (Psalm 122: 6, Jeremiah 29: 7). Coincidentally, the root 'Shalom' means peaceful. *(Easton's Bible Dictionary.)*

I have used the word 'Shalom' almost thirty years as my greeting with everything I write from prayer requests or Facebook and e-mails. I believe that 'Shalom' is the best greeting to begin any written communication. What can be better than to place God's peace (Shalom) on another person when writing to them? As you know in Israel it is the Jewish greeting spoken when visiting another person or meeting one another. This word is surely from Heaven, Jesus always said, "Peace be unto you," when meeting His disciples.

Reference: Galatians 6: 6

These five Heavenly Words can build us up. They can increase your relationship with Jesus, speaking more like Him. Using these Heavenly Words correctly will always please the Lord. They are words that will enrich your spirit; just those four little words. Amen and amen.

~

GOD'S TREASURES OUR TRASH

In most cases dear reader we consider trash useless, but sometimes what we consider useless God considers useful. First, I would like to know what keeps you feeling good about yourself and what do you need to always feel good about ourselves. I think the things we need and never really want to live without is love and security. From birth, we have the love and protection from those who are caring for us. I know that in some cases children have very little and in other cases they have too much. Only God, our Heavenly Father, knows what is just right for us. Like a mother bird caring for her young. He knows just how much love and protection we need until we will be able to fly and fend for ourselves, away from the protection of our parents or guardians. When I say, "God knows our needs;" that is not just my words, it is His words. The spoken word to a child is what they remember better than material things. When God speaks to us through His word, the Bible, we can be sure of every word. We can put our confidence in Him. We can dwell in the word of the Lord. In the same way we feel safe and cared for in our homes, we can feel safe and cared for in the Word of God.

Reference: 1 john 4: 16, 19

This is a dwelling place I spoke of, and a safe place in the Word of God. We are cared for and loved by our Heavenly Father, God.

Reference: Deuteronomy 33: 12

All the love and security we need we have in God, and we find it in His precious Word. So, what is it that keeps from experiencing the safe dwelling place? Is it our confidence? It is our confidence that we so easily trash and try to go on without it to proceed in our normal lives. It is our confidence that God treasures and wants to have us expand in our lives. He wants that very thing that we so ignorantly throw away to be our rich reward that He has promised us. Our confidence is our weapon against fear. As we dwell in God's Word our confidence grows and so do we. In this verse everything I have said is repeated.

Reference: Hebrews 10: 35-37

First, we have to know where our confidence comes from.

Reference: 2 Corinthians 3: 4, 5

When you turn your life over to Christ, He, in return, rewards you with confidence. That was then, what about now? Has time worn down your confidence in God? Actually, the more time you make for God in your daily life and in the Bible, your confidence should grow and be a useful tool for Christ and the church as well as yourselves and others. Oh, what has gone wrong? The answer to that is too much 'fear.' Fear is the foe of confidence. Our daily lives present so many fearful areas that we become weaker and less confident, our faith gets a beating, and our confidence gets trashed.

Reference: Hebrews 4: 16

We have only to wait on the Lord to get our confidence back. I do not mean we sit in a chair with our arms crossed and wait on Him. Oh no, we wait on Him in His Word. We find restoration in His Word. Our strength and faith is revived and our confidence restored through His word.

Reference: Psalm 27: 14

In this verse it says God will strengthen your heart. Did you know that when your heart is right so is your confidence? Jesus said that when we love God and we love ourselves then our heart will be right.

Reference: Matthew 22: 37

There is no way we can have confidence without love.

Reference: Hebrews 10: 32, 33

In this verse we are being asked if we remember after giving our lives to Christ and being filled in the Holy Spirit that we had our confidence and we stood our ground against anything that wanted to hurt us. We had victories and we want more of them.

Reference: Hebrews 3: 14

The word 'partakers' actually indicates that Christ's completeness is made up with us. It might be hard for you to do that, but Christ works are only manifested through Christ's followers that the Holy Spirit lives within. The Holy Spirit, with the grace of God, and His Holy power only is manifested through those that have that steadfast confidence. We cannot continue trashing our confidence. We must reclaim it and recognise how God treasures it.

Reference: 1 John 2: 28

We know that Jesus is returning soon, and we need to take care of our confidence because it is a treasure. Amen and amen.

INTERCESSORY PRAYER

Dear reader, I am very thankful that my Heavenly Father reprimands His children. If He had not reprimanded me many times, I could have been back where I was, but praise the Lord; He has not let me go back there. He keeps His eye on me and He knows I need a lot of instruction. That term, "Intercessory prayer," and all the talk about intercessors in church, really didn't move me much; I thought they were building themselves up, 'holier than thou' people. Well, the Lord put up with my ignorance long enough and I heard a good preaching that opened my ears and my eyes to what it was all about.

Reference: Genesis 1: 26

All of us know this verse, but have we ever really taken it as an appointment for learning? Learning more of God's relationship with man? God gave man dominion over what He had just made; the earth and everything in it. Why did He do that? We make such a mess of our own lives, how could God expect us to do anything good, with man or beast? I believed God was lazy, so, why give us dominion over all His beautiful creation? Well now I believe I have the answer, and what a change it has made in my life. God is not lazy, but He knows we cannot handle it without Him, so He wants us to be close to Him. God wants to be glorified on earth and He could not do it Himself, He needed man to do it. Jesus the Son of God was and is our perfect example. True, God gave man more that he could handle, so man would call on Him to intercede in the affairs on earth. God always knows what is going on with us and He has the devil in check also, but He wants to hear from us and stay close to us.

References: 1 Timothy 2: 1-3; 2 Thessalonians 5; 17-19

Now we have it all together in these verses, God has given us dominion so; we will be dependent on Him to care for His creation. God wants us to intercede, so that He can have the glory of the victory. God has given us the Holy Spirit to be our intercessor, so that we can be partakers of intercessory prayer to God. Amen and amen.

INTIMATE RELATIONSHIP

Dear reader, I know that we all have different kinds of relationships in our lifetime. From birth we start a relationship with our parents. From the beginning we think about what we need and want, we only have to go to our parents, and we will get it. That was when we were very little, growing up we found out that this is not always the way. Some of our dear parents, as much as they would like to, just could not give us all we wanted or needed. But, there are those that could give us all we wanted or needed.

Reference: Ephesians 6: 4

Our parents wanted to raise us properly and responsibly, so they made a point to give us what we needed, but not always what we wanted. One thing we needed was to learn to love the Lord.

Reference: Colossians 3: 20

Then we have a new relationship in school, where we learn the meaning of a 'good friend.' We all had one through our school years.

Reference: 1 John 4: 7

During those precious years of growing up and going to school, we spent most of our free time with our best friend maybe we were 'a duet' or perhaps the 'Three Musketeers,' whichever it was: two of us or three of us, we were in a relationship.

Reference: 1 Corinthians 13: 10-12

Then what? Some of us just went on to find work or continue our education in pursuit of a career to start making our new way in life.

Reference: Ecclesiastes 2: 10

But for us that got married, we had entered an 'intimate relationship.'

Reference: Mathew 19: 5

We are sharing our life with another person, we are sharing our bed with a new person, our home, our wages, these things are no longer just for us, and everything must be shared. Our dreams, our wishes, our thoughts, we are sharing them all with the person we love and that is why we have married them.

Reference: Proverbs 31: 28

In time we became parents and more relationships developed. It was at this time after my husband and I had become parents. First, we married, a new relationship, became parents, a new relationship, then we met Jesus, a new and wonderful relationship. We got saved and baptised. I remember so well that Christmas Day in Norway my hubby and my sons were in the living room around the tree, I had not heard a word from my family in the states. I was in the bedroom, listening to their laughter, but at the same time I was feeling a little sorry and guilty. I was feeling guilty, because although I was so fortunate with a loving husband and my beautiful sons, I was feeling sorry for myself, no card from my mother. I was in quite tears feeling very low, when Jesus came and warmed me with His presence, and His words, "Daughter don't you know that my love for you is greater than your mother's love, my love for you is greater than your love for your children."

Reference: 1 John 4: 19, 20

Here was Jesus warming me with a hug, comforting me with His words and He was feeling my pain. Jesus had heard my crying and knew everything in my heart. He knew my thoughts, my dreams, my wishes He was with me, and He knew everything about me.

Reference: Psalm 139: 1-6

Here in these verses from David we are told of the "intimate relationship he had
with the Lord. That is the same relationship I became aware of on that Christmas
Day. I am having an 'intimate relationship' like none other in the world. When
I call His name, He is with me. When I wake up in the morning I say, "Good
morning, Jesus, I love You," and He answers, "I love too." At night when I go to
sleep, He accompanies me in my prayers and lulls me off to sleep sharing His
thoughts with me.

Reference: Psalm 92: 1, 2

During the day He is always with me, He shows me the best course to take
to get through the things that must be done that day. He shows me how and
where to shop. He blesses me all the time with my purchases, whether it is food,
clothing or something for my house, the garden, or my pets. He blesses all of us
throughout the day, every day.

Reference: Deuteronomy 28: 8

My Jesus is my Lord. He owns me and everything and everything I have and
everything around me.

Reference: Romans 10: 9

I belong to Christ, therefore He is responsible for me, He is responsible for my
health, my family, my relationships, my home ,my pets and most importantly my
money. What to keep and what to give away, what to spend, what to save. He is
responsible for it all, my peace, my joy and my happiness. I have given Jesus my
life; He is responsible for that also.

Reference: Romans 11: 32

When I am naughty or disobedient, He is responsible for me, He must help me
to make amends and repent, turn it around so I am back on the narrow path
walking with my King, my best friend.

Reference: Exodus 15: 26

When I am not well, He is responsible; He must heal me, restore me and make my body work properly. He made me, He owns me, He is my Lord and responsible for everything He owns and everything He has made.

Reference: Hebrews 13: 5

When my finances are in trouble, He is responsible, He must show me where and how to plant a seed to refurbish my harvest. He is responsible for my seeds and my harvest and how much I am to keep for myself.

Reference: Romans 2: 17

I have an 'intimate relationship' with my Lord, I trust Him with my life, I have no secrets from Him, no relationship I have is as precious as Jesus.

Reference: John 15: 16, 17

If you call on His Name, Jesus, and believe you can, start a wonderful 'intimate relationship.' He will never let you down. Amen and amen.

~

IT IS ALL ABOUT LOVE

Dear reader, the first love of a new-born child is their parents.

Reference: John 3: 5-7

When we are born-again of the Spirit our first love is Christ Jesus; He is number one in our life.

Reference: Mark 12: 29, 30

So who do you think is number two? Some of you will say that we have to love others and be concerned with their needs as for number two. That is very true, but it is how we know our needs, that we are aware of their needs. So, when Jesus was asked the greatest commandment, He summed them up into two commandments, both founded on a foundation of love.

Reference: Mark 12: 31

When we love Christ as number one, we learn from that to love ourselves as number two. The most important is the way in which we can embrace others and with the love we have for Christ and the love we have for ourselves will cover the love we have for others.

Reference: 1 John 4: 7, 8; 5: 14, 15

To begin the process of love, which is Christ first, myself plus you second, is called the 'agape love.' Agape love is taught properly through the Holy Spirit, and it is the same love which, in time, will be manifest in our life.

Reference: Mathew 14: 15

It will be through the love of the Holy Spirit that will be the only thing we reveal to the world our 'light' which shines with our love.

Reference: Mathew 5: 13

It is our love through the Spirit of God that Jesus was speaking of. That is the 'salt of the earth that cannot lose its saltiness.' It is impossible for the love of God to lose His love because He is love. When we substitute His love with the love and lust of the flesh is when our 'salt' loses its saltiness and cannot regain its savour; it is good for nothing. So, let us hold fast to the love of Christ to be 'salty' and recognise through our lives and our effect on others lives.

Reference: 1 Corinthians 2: 14

Contrary to many opinions, emotions of true love are not part of human nature. True love is spiritually induced. As we love Christ and obey His few simple laws of love, the Holy Spirit will instil in us the desires of love. Why let us be tormented and abused for the sake of human love, when it is much easier to turn to Christ and receive His love and give His love. If you find trouble comprehending love, look at how much love Christ bestowed on man while He was on earth. None of us are worthy of so much love. That same love is still available to us today.

Reference: Ephesians 5: 1, 2

This same love can be our love for Christ, for ourselves and for others, all through us, in us, and around us.

Reference: 1 Corinthians 13: 4-13

When a child is born by his earthly mother, it relies on her for everything from its birth. So, we are new-born through Christ and we rely on Him for everything from our new birth, "It is all about love." Amen and amen.

~

GOD'S CALLING, OUR COMFORT

Dear reader, do you think your comfort is important to God? When God calls you to serve Him, it is His will and for His purpose.

Reference: 1 Samuel 3: 9-10

Samuel was called as a young boy to serve God and he became one of the greatest prophets and leaders of Israel.

God had him travelling on a circuit of Bethel to Gilgal and Mizpeh, judging in these places and from his home in Ramah. He judged Israel throughout this

ministry he was called to. He didn't have a lot of time to spend with his wife
and children while he was on the circuit. When he was old he returned home to
Ramah, and made his sons Joel and Abiah judges, but they did not follow their
father's commitment to God. Samuel didn't have an easy life serving God and his
friendship with leaders and kings did not make him wealthy.

Reference: Psalm 63: 6

I find it very hard to visit other people and sleep in another bed. I went
on a 5-day cruise in the Mediterranean, I liked the cruise and the special
environment I was in, but I couldn't get comfortable in my bed.

Reference: Psalm 4: 8

Then my bathroom, I like my own bathroom not having to share with anyone.

Reference: Luke 12: 24

And how about my wardrobe and drawers, I like all my things in order and easy
to lay my hands on.

Reference: Luke 12: 27, 28

My cosy chair in the living room is where I spend a lot of my time. I don't like to
give it up.

Reference: Revelation 3: 21

And our car, our van, for the last ten years I didn't drive, but my husband
did, and I liked my front seat, where I could stretch my legs and feel very
comfortable while travelling.

Reference: Joshua 1: 9

Everything I have mentioned makes up my 'comfort zone,' they probably are a part of your 'comfort zone' as well. You can see that God has our 'comfort zone' covered in His Word, and in His will. Praise the Lord. Jesus called each of His disciples to leave their homes and their families to be 'fishers of men.' And, it was for that reason that they spread the Gospel and that all but one died a martyrs' death. I would think that the ministry of Paul was the greatest calling of the Lord after His resurrection.

Reference: Acts 9: 4-6

The Bible records the lives of many that were considered the first missionaries. When we study the lives of these men, we find that they made many journeys out to far away countries professing the salvation Gospel of Jesus Christ and the Cross. So, what about their comforts? Did they have any? They had no homes. They had very little money, so their food was usually a gift from other believers. Not only that, but they were persecuted, beaten, and thrown in jail many times. What comfort did they have?

Reference: John 14: 25, 26

They had little comfort in the flesh. Although they, perhaps more than we, always knew they had a comforter with them. They had the same Holy Spirit we also have with us. But the acknowledgement of Him is very little manifested in our lives, as it was so greatly manifested in their lives. And why is that? Because we are so comfortable in our 'comfort zone,' we are guilty of putting our comforts before our calling. This doesn't make us bad Christians, but it does make us lazy ones.

Reference: Acts 3: 2-6

Peter and John had other plans than to spend time with this man. They wanted to go and have their evening prayers and then home for a nice meal and perhaps an evening with friends. So why bother with this beggar? I will tell you why, because they put their calling before their comfort and the result for them was very rewarding.

Their evening prayer time turned into an all-night praise time. What can we do for the Lord that pleases Him as well as is comfortable for us? We can build a better relationship with the 'Comforter,' the Holy Spirit. We can be more aware of what He expects of us. Also, we can learn to follow Him instead of going ahead of Him. We all do not have to be martyrs for Christ, but we should be His servants. Christ comforts us with these verses also.

Reference: John 15: 15-17

We are all chosen, and we are all called. So how do we begin today to answer God's calling and at the same time find our comfort in Christ. Amen and amen.

~

GOD'S FAITHFULNESS AND MAN'S FAILURES

Reference: Nehemiah 9: 1-3

Dear reader, ninety verses in the Old Testament relate to the Children of Israel asking God to forgive them their sins. They always believed that they would receive forgiveness from God. Many times, God would have to do something drastic to shake them up and wake them up to the reality of how bad they really were. They had different offerings that pertained to different sins. All through Moses writings, Genesis to Deuteronomy, we read of these offerings and their purpose. Man is a failure when it comes to following all the laws of Moses. There is no way men could live up to these rules in their lifetime. God's mercy continues in our lifetime today. Before Noah it was not strange for a man to live 900 years, but not so after the flood. Now a hundred years is a long time for us. Before the flood God gave man 120 years in which to repent, while having Noah build the Ark.

In other words, Noah had 120 years to witness and tell the people they must repent and bring God back into their lives, but they didn't listen and they all perished. These verses in Nehemiah chapter nine are so full of God's mercy and faithfulness. They had a very good revival meeting that day. First the preachers gather all the people in one place. Then they started a praise and worship service.

Reference: Nehemiah 9: 5

Ezra followed the praise and worship with prayer. What a prayer. If only we could pray like this today. Ezra was a prophet and leader of the church. When he prayed, he glorified God.

Reference: Nehemiah 9: 6

After the opening of his prayer, he begins to acknowledge God's faithfulness and mercy on His children. Ezra has a long list of things that he wants the congregation to remember about how God loves them and has always cared for them. Thanking God for their forefathers: Abraham, Isaac, and Jacob, then for rescuing all of them from Egypt and the Red Sea.

Reference: Nehemiah 9: 9

Ezra continued thanking God for leading them with a cloud by day and a pillar of fire by night.

Reference: Nehemiah 9: 12

The meeting goes on and all the people are very attentive. Ezra also thanked God for Moses and the commandments. He wanted the people to always be aware of who they were and where they came from. He wanted them to know their God, Jehovah, and all that He had done for them. These people had never seen Moses. The people were in good spirits during this prayer, because they were remembering how God had blessed them and their nation. They had forgotten why they were called to this meeting. Now Ezra reminds them of their sins and the sins of their ancestors. All the good news is over now. He is reminding them of why they must repent for all their sins and wrong doings.

Reference: Nehemiah 9: 16, 17

There's nothing much for them to be so proud of when they hear of how their forefathers failed to live up to the laws of Moses. Now they are feeling very guilty of doing the same. Ezra is recalling the sins of the golden calf, the anger, the ungratefulness and arguing that all took place while the children were in the desert. Ezra praises God for His long suffering heart. How would you feel being at a meeting like this where all your foolishness and failures are reiterated?

How many times in this chapter do we read of God's faithfulness for these sinners? How many times in your or my life has God's mercy been so overwhelming, considering how wrong we have been? Ezra goes on for many hours. Thirty- seven verses that records God's faithfulness and man failures. Six 'buts,' each one indicating one more way in which the people had disobeyed God. The truth had to be told, the commandments and statutes were too difficult to follow, there were so many, the people couldn't remember them all or couldn't follow them. God had to do something to renew a good relationship with mankind. Man had stopped loving God, they only feared Him. This was not God's desire when He created man. He wanted to b e a Father and to have mankind as His children. Let us find what God planned to do.

Reference: John 3: 16-19

God's plan was to come to earth in the body of a man in the flesh.

Reference: John 1:1; 14

God sent His Son Jesus into the world to be the ultimate sin offering for all mankind forever. That means that as you and I accept Jesus as our Saviour the door is opened that kept us from having a heavenly relationship with our Heavenly Father, God. That opportunity came when Jesus died on the Cross and rose again on Easter morning.

Reference: Romans 5: 9-11

God's faithfulness has extended to this year and will continue forever. Man's failures will also continue forever, but now we have a Saviour Jesus. It is to Jesus that we now say, "Thank You," for our everlasting salvation and our oneness with our Heavenly Father. As long as we repent daily and as long as we give thanksgiving and praise daily, we will live forever with God's faithfulness which will cover our failures. Amen and amen.

~

GO INTO THE CLOSET AND SHUT THE DOOR!

Reference: Mathew 6: 6

What does that mean? Does it mean that we should go into a closet and hide ourselves away when we are praying or giving thanks? Does it mean that we should only read the Bible when we are alone or in privacy? I think it means when we are repenting or interceding in prayer, when we are seeking wisdom or understanding. Is it a good idea to do it privately with Lord 'in the closet?' That way we are two and united in our prayers with the Heavenly Father.

When I am alone, I hear the Lord's voice much clearer than when others are around; I must admit sometimes His voice is very distinctive when He wants me to share with others. Jesus knew that our intimacy with Him 'in the closet' is very important in our Christian lives. Jesus knew that behind closed doors, we can be more comfortable with Him as we repent and ask for forgiveness. In this verse He gives us this 'instruction to prayer' in His Word. Our journey with the Lord is to be a 'good Christian,' but this can be very difficult in the world we live in. Thank you Jesus for considering our every need by letting us get closer to You. Thank you God for being Heavenly Father and for Jesus for being our Saviour and thank You Holy Spirit for being our closest friend in or out of the closet. Amen and amen.

~

GLORY CAME DOWN

Wow, dear reader, when and how does this happen?

Reference: Exodus 16: 7, 8

We always find something to complain about, so in that way we are no different than the Israelites and their murmurings. We need a Moses who humbly stated, "I can do nothing about it." He recognised in an instant his limitation to solve the problem. They were in the desert with little to eat. Moses said, "Don't bring your requests to me, bring them to God." Moses was a great teacher. The Israelites were ignorant to the ways of the Lord. They had been in bondage for so many years; they were used to relying on only their own abilities all that time. Now Moses is teaching them to rely on the Lord.

Reference: Exodus 16: 9, 10

I like this verse because the Israelites had come to Moses for answers, and Moses goes to his dear brother Aaron who God has appointed as High Priest. These two have heard the complaining and now they say to the congregation, the Lord has heard you and is waiting for you. How many times have we been in that place where we feel doubtful that God has heard us? We have all been there because that is the flesh. Here Moses ensures the people that God has heard them, but before He answers their request, they must make the first move. "Come near before the Lord," what a lesson to learn.

In verse 10 we read, "At the same time they came near to God, His Glory was present with them."

Reference: Exodus 24: 16

Not only did the Glory of the Lord visit them, but it stayed with them throughout their journey to the Promise Land. There are ten times, from Exodus to Numbers 14, where Moses writes of how the Glory of God appeared, filled and abided in the Tabernacle. I know what you are thinking, "That was then what about now?" I do have the answer for you. Jesus is the now factor.

Reference: Mathew 14: 15

Here we are right back in the same situation where we were with Moses, the people are hungry. But there is a big difference here. The people had followed Jesus into the dessert. They had already 'Come near to the Lord.' They are there already to be fed by His teachings and His love. In the desert Moses was the leader and teacher of two million Israelites. Here on this mountain far from the town Jesus is the leader and teacher for five thousand Jews and Gentiles. Moses prayed to Jehovah; Jesus prayed to His Father.

Reference: Mathew 14: 16, 17

Here again, as with Moses, Jesus is teaching the people to have faith. Here comes the lesson, boy! Is it a whopper? Moses said, "Come to the Lord," and what happened?

Reference: Exodus 16: 13-15

God fed the people with a provision that came directly from Heaven. Out there in the desert, there was nothing for quails to eat, therefore quails would not have been there to be caught, and they came from Heaven. Manna never existed before God provided it from Heaven into the desert. God was not in need of angels or men to give or pass out His provision, it was all done by God, and it all came from Heaven.

Jesus said bring them to me. Once again to receive what they needed, they must make a move in the right direction to the Lord. Moses instructed Aaron what to say, Jesus instructed His disciples what to do. Before Moses could calm the people, He needed the help of his brother Aaron the priest to have them all in the congregation. Jesus had the same need to 'sit them down.' Anytime we come with a request we must be calm before the Lord, so we hear from Him. The provision for the congregation in the desert came down from Heaven. Moses had to look up to see it coming. Jesus did the same. Do you remember Jacob's dream?

Reference: Genesis 28: 11-13

Jesus knew where to look for the Glory of the Lord; He looked up to Heaven. He knew not to look at what He had in His hand but look up to what He was about to have. Looking at five loaves and two fish would only deter Him from the real source of supply. Jesus had come from Heaven; He knew what was up there, the disciples didn't. They would naturally look to the provisions at hand; they had never seen the provisions in Heaven. This lesson took them sometime to learn, sadly some never learned. We too, like the disciples, have the grandest opportunity to take advantage of this lesson. When we have received Christ as our Saviour and Lord, we can look to Him in Heaven and His Glory will come down to us here on earth.

Notice: "I didn't say could come down, I said will come down"

Reference: John 1: 14

Glory came down, and we have a lovely song when we worship the Lord. Let us sing, "Heaven came down and Glory filled my soul." Amen and amen.

〜

GOD CLOSED THE DOOR

Noah did not have the responsibility of who was to be saved in the Ark, whether they were people or God's creatures. God told Noah to take his wife, his three sons and three daughter- in- laws in the Ark.

Reference: Genesis 7: 1

God was already in the Ark that is why He told Noah to come in. Noah had been building the Ark according to God's design for one hundred and twenty years. In all that time Noah's cousins, uncles, aunts and all the family members had the chance to change their ways and offer to help Noah with the building of the Ark. Noah must have tried everything to get his whole family to believe that the Ark was the only way of their salvation.

Reference: Genesis 7: 15

God closed the door. Noah had gathered all of God's creatures on the earth that God wanted saved. Two by two, they went to Noah and into the Ark. Noah and his wife and three sons and their wives all had been obedient and done everything that God had instructed them to do. By faith Noah, being warned by God of things not seen as yet but believed, and prepared the Ark to be the saving house; by that condemned the world and became heir of the righteousness which is by faith.

Reference: Hebrews 11: 7

God was going to reward them for their hard work, for their faith in Him: they were made fun of for their foolishness, building a boat in the desert. God closed the door. Noah's job was finished, he had for 120 years tried to convert others to believe in God and be saved, but he had no converts. Everyone he wanted to see saved was but for those who had not believed was not on the Ark, Noah must have felt like a failure, no one converted in 120 years. God didn't see Noah as a failure, He saw him as an obedient servant, God loved Noah, and He had a great plan for Noah's future.

Reference: Genesis 9: 1-13

God blessed Noah and his family on the Ark, He said,, "Be fruitful and multiply, and replenish the earth." God promised Noah with a sign of a rainbow.

Reference: Genesis 9: 13

God promised He would never again destroy the earth or mankind with water. God established a covenant with Noah. Noah was made the father of all mankind, read Genesis 9: 11. Amen and amen.

~

IN GOD'S WAY

Dear reader, this title can be taken two ways. The way I felt it was to be presented was to follow in the way of God. The other way it was shown to me by the Holy Spirit was getting in God's way. The verse that comes to mind is when the Lord was in the garden of Gethsemane.

Reference: Mathew 26: 39

He says so clearly that He wants to do God's will. Isn't that the same as saying the first thing in the morning prayers before we start our day? Our intentions are to do God's will all through the day. But what happens? Let's go back to the verse, "Nevertheless not as I will." There you have our problem and the second part of the title 'In God's Way.' We want it our way and we want God to make it happen, like we want it. We get in God's way. Paul tells it like this.

References: Romans 7: 14; 8: 1

So, what is really getting in God's way in our lives is sin that we allow to govern us. That sin is labelled 'self-will.' Is this how we deceive ourselves and at the same time try to deceive God? Let it be this way or that way Lord according to Your will. It is not God's will or His way we want it, it is this way or that way we have presented to Him in our prayers. David tells us.

Reference: Psalm 19: 14

We don't have to swear or use other words or sentences that come out of our mouth, like negative complaints and criticism, giving the Devil his due, instead why not rebuke him through the name of Christ. What about our thoughts? I can't believe some of the things that enter my head. Silly, senseless, and sometimes cynical thoughts keep Christ out. What do I meditate on? Sadly, I am afraid the flesh gets most of my meditation time, worrying about this and that and how, when and why is always in my thoughts instead of meditating on and with my Lord and His everlasting love, care, protection and supply, He has for me throughout my life. One of my favourite verses is.

Reference: Philippians 2: 5

As we strive to have Christ's mind in us through the Holy Spirit, we find that our communication with the Holy Spirit improves daily. We learn at times the hard way to get out of God's way. "Lord, You go first, I am right behind You hanging on all the way." After we are walking a narrow path there is only room for one to lead. As a vessel of the Holy Spirit, we step by step advance closer to having that same mind that is in Christ Jesus. At times we have to take a look and retreat from the position we are in and return to the narrow path. When we look where we are we understand that we are in God's way, and we need to move to the His side. Amen and amen.

∾

ON TOP OF IT

Dear reader, do you feel sometimes you are down and feel as if all the problems are on top of you keeping you down?

Reference: Mathew 14: 22-35

I like it when we are alone with our Heavenly Father, we can see things more clearly. He reveals in pictures and words the answers to our prayers and problems. As Jesus was praying, He saw His children in distress out at sea. He had said to them, "You go and meet me on the other side." The disciple did that, they got into the boat and sailed to the other side of the sea. Isn't it funny why they did not ask Jesus, "How are you going to get there?" When the Spirit is directing you, you don't question Him, you just obey. The problems started in verse 24; these fishermen knew the sea well, they would not have taken off in their boat if the signs had shown that a storm was coming. There was no bad weather sign, it was a clear evening, and they could sail calmly to the other side. But as they were far from shore in the middle of the sea the storm came unexpectedly. They toiled most of the night bailing out the water and fighting the waves. In verse 25 the unbelievable is believable; Jesus was walking on the waves in the storm. What the disciples feared most was the wind, and the storm and Jesus was on top of all their fears in complete control.

In verses 26 and 27 Jesus was going off to pray when He sent them to the sea. Everything Jesus did for His disciples were to teach them, encourage them and strengthen them for the future storms in their new ministries. This was also the reason he sent them away on their own, as seen in the middle of the raging storm. They thought they were seeing a ghost on the waves. The disciples had not yet come to the realisation that it could have been an angel, they did not understand the spiritual realm in which Jesus was about to teach them. Jesus knows that although they were rugged fishermen, they were still as fearful as a small child, before He could teach them, He had to comfort them.

Then in verse 28; Peter was always excited to see miracles that Jesus had done and now He is excited to walk on the waves as he sees His master do in verse 29 as Jesus is the Son of God. He walked; He walked on the water because of who He is. So how did this natural man, this fisherman do the same? Walking on the water is impossible for man, but when Peter stepped out of the boat, his focus was not on the water, it was on Jesus.

The same is for us; we can see the impossible done with the sick, with the blind and deaf and with all our fears as long as we focus on Jesus. If not, we find ourselves in the same place as Peter when he turned his eyes to the wind and to the waves and the sea, he became fearful and started sinking into the water. In verse 30 although he was fearful, he knew who would save him, and he cried out to Jesus and Jesus reached out and saved him immediately.

In verses 31 and 32 let us look at this picture, the wind tossing the boat, with men trying to bail out the water; suddenly they see a vision that makes them more fearful than that of the storm. Jesus reassures them that they are in no harm. The storm is still blowing and Peter steps out to meet Jesus and the wind is still blowing. But when Jesus and Peter returned to the boat the storm ceased. Why did the wind still blow all this time that Jesus was out in the water with Peter? Jesus controlled the storm out at sea as well as when He entered the boat. Those in the boat had a fearful night, but for them to know for certain they were not dreaming or imagining something, Jesus had to be with them in the boat. Nature could have taken over and the wind could have turned, and the storm could have ceased. But it didn't, it only ceased when He entered the boat and therefore the disciples understood even better who He was, and they worshiped Him. In verse 33 when they were gone over, they came into the land of Gennesaret.

My title, 'On top of it' is for a very good reason. I read this lovely story of Jesus and His disciples, and I can see my own life experiences the same. Believing myself to be a woman of faith, a woman saved, sanctified through the Blood of Christ, I still have some very childish fears and make some silly mistakes which cause me worry and anguish. When we find ourselves in a storm, in other words with little peace and calm in our lives, we sometimes spend our time bailing out our problems with logic and sense. Faith is not logical or sensible in this world, but we get so concerned with our problems that we forget our Saviour who walks on the waves and calms the storm. While we are sinking, He is 'on top of it.' When we lose control He is in control. We can be like Peter step forward on top of the waves as long as we focus on Jesus. The minute we look the other way we are doomed.

Reference: Luke 2: 30

I hope you have made Jesus the love of your life, as I have and that through faith in Him you are able to stay 'on top of it all.' Amen and amen.

~

OUT OF THE BELLY

Dear reader, I want to start with some verses.

Reference: Mathew 8: 3; 9: 25

As you read in each of these verses Jesus touched the person and healed them. What was so special to me is this all happened before the Cross and Salvation. He sent His disciples out to do the same.

Reference: Luke 9: 1, 2

Before the Pentecost the disciples were healing the sick and Jesus was with them still teaching them and giving them the power to perform miracles. After the Pentecost, when the Holy Spirit fell on 120 followers in the upper room, they all spoke in tongues as their new prayer language. After Paul's salvation he also spoke in tongues.

Reference: 1 Corinthians 14: 18

Paul said we need to pray without ceasing. Naturally we cannot pray 24 hours a day, but the Holy Spirit can, because He is only using our lips not our mind. Paul also says the Holy Spirit has power.

Reference: 1 Thessalonians 1: 5

Do you remember when He said that those that believe in Him would do greater works than he had done on earth?

Reference: John 14: 12

Now we come to this revelation that the Holy Spirit is speaking of. Jesus laid His hands on the sick, prayed and they were healed. James tells us something different.

Reference: James 5: 14

Here we told to pray first then to anoint and touch the person in Jesus Name. I want to give you an example of this.

Reference: Acts 2: 1-4

We know that 120 were baptised in the Holy Spirit and spoke in tongues. I believe tongues are the promise that is given to us that are born-again to trust in the Lord for what we are asking. When Jesus prayed others heard His prayers and knew what He was saying. He said in John 11:42, "I want them to hear what I am saying." When we are given the gift of tongues we can relax about what we are saying or if we are saying the right words. We can rely on the Holy Spirit to say the right words. Then how do we come to a place where the Spirit is praying for the sick?

Reference: John 7: 38, 39

Here is the key to this revelation. Think how the belly's emotions occur. When we are fearful our belly is rigid and our mouth is dry. When we are cheerful our belly is loose, and we feel comfortable with no thirst. Our thirst is being quenched by the Holy Spirit, through our fountain of living water in our belly.

Reference: Acts 9: 40, 41

It is that same living water that Peter had in his belly, flowing though his lips in tongues which gave him the power and the confidence to turn to a dead woman and speak to death. That prayer he spoke on his knees was not in his mind, it was the Holy Spirit speaking that brought life back to the dead woman. After he spoke to the dead woman and she came back, he touched her. Peter was a Jew and respected his heritage, the laws of Moses.

Reference: Proverbs 18: 20, 21

These verses confirm what I have just shared with you. Having the fountain of living water comes with the baptism of the Holy Spirit, speaking in tongues and uttering. The baptism can occur any time after our salvation. Remember Cornelius was visited by Peter and all those in the house were baptised with the Holy Spirit and by water.

Reference: Acts 10: 44-48

Cornelius was a man of prayer, a Gentile believing God and God had more for him and his household, therefore God sent Peter. When we pray, we are praying for more than what we had yesterday or this morning. Cornelius was a rich man; his prayer to God enriched his life, more of God, not more riches. I know we are always in need of material things but let us first ask for the riches of the Spirit in our bellies. God is not through with miracles. All God wants from us is to come forward and ask for His Holy Spirit to flow into our bellies, to be a part of those miracles.

Reference: Revelation 21:6, 7

We need to pray daily for that fountain of living water to flow out of our bellies and we can be a part of God's miracles also. Amen and amen.

PROUD HEART

Reference: 2 Chronicles 26: 1-5

Dear reader, I ask you, "What sixteen year-old is ready to be king and rule a nation?" In verse 2, this teenager not only stared off young, but he also started off big. First, he takes over his father's responsibilities and rebuilds the seaport and the city Eloth; that is on the Red Sea coastline of Judah. How he did all this is in the next sentence and verse 5 "In general, a good king in the Lord's sight." This young king loved God and wanted to serve Him. He grew to be a great king and great leader.

Reference: 2 Chronicles 26: 6-15

In these verses, you have all his great accomplishments. This great king was now grown, perhaps in his thirties. Always loved the Lord and served Him. Therefore, the Lord blessed him, made him famous, wonderful and powerful. He was feared by his enemies and honoured by his people. But something dreadful happened. His prosperity and wealth came to a tragic end. King Uzziah got a 'proud heart.' I know that you have heard the comment, "Pride comes before a fall." I think this story is where the phrase came from. King Uzziah's prosperity came to the point of pride and the Lord punished him.

Reference: 2 Chronicles 26: 16-21

There was nothing as dreadful as a leper in those days, and now the king was one. The Lord had given Uzziah everything a king could wish for, and he overstepped his bounds. Even when he was warned of how angry God could be when such a sin was committed. The priests reminded him of the sons of Aaron that perished for dishonouring the temple. But the King would not listen. His prosperity as a great king had fooled him into a proud and corrupt sinner. The Lord had no more to do with him. He died as a leper isolated from his family and his throne; banished from the temple and his people. He lived many years in isolation, although he was king for fifty-two years, his son had to take the throne and rule the country in his place.

How sad one sinful, proud, and unforgiving act banished the great king's legacy. There are many stories in the Old Testament that tell us of great men that fall into the sinful trap of a 'proud heart.' In the book of Daniel, we have two kings. The first king, Nebuchadnezzar, was the one that conquered Jerusalem and captured Daniel and his friends taking them to Babylonia. After Daniel had proven himself to be a wise man to the king and after interpreting the king's dream the king showed honour to Daniel's God for a short time, then the king was easily persuaded to follow other gods even himself.

Reference: Daniel 2: 45-47

Then we have the story of Shadrach, Meshach, and Abednego in the fiery furnace, again this is about the king's 'proud heart.' The king listened to some of his own advisers who hated the men from Jerusalem. They advised him to make an idol of himself to worship and he did just that, we read it in Daniel 3: 1-7. Once again, the king wants to worship God for a short time. Once again, the king slips back into idol worship with his 'proud heart.' This time when Daniel interprets his dream, it is about him and his future as king. The king writes his own story in the book of Daniel.

Reference: Daniel 4: 1-9

The king had fallen into believing there is more than one Holy Spirit, one Holy God. Wealth, power and prosperity will make the man's heart turn proud. Even in some cases where he worships himself as a god. We see that very thought pattern in the 'New Age' religions worldwide. The results can only be the same in all cases, 'disaster.' The first part of the dream was about his enemies, second part was about him.

Reference: Daniel 4: 19-30

The whole of chapter 4 in Daniel was a testimony from Nebuchadnezzar before the prophecy and after it was fulfilled.

Reference: Daniel 5: 1-4

Daniel served the new king, the son of Nebuchadnezzar. But he was also an idol worshiper. Although, Daniel was still the king's adviser; King Belshazzar was like his father; he dishonoured the temple and ordered the temple furnishings to be brought to him. He drank from the silver cups taken from the temple in Jerusalem and got drunk. His heart was full of pride after inheriting all that his father had and the authority as king.

Reference: Daniel 5: 5-7

The king's advisers were called to interpret the writing; they couldn't and said Daniel was in the place and would be able to interpret it. In these verses you can see what the king did.

Reference: Daniel 5: 8-27

These verses give the interpretation of the dream.

Reference: Daniel 5: 28-31

And now we know what happened as a result of the king's proud heart. I would suggest that you read the complete book of Daniel to understand more of the story of those two kings and their 'proud hearts.' It will also let you know how 'proud hearts' can fashion history.

Reference: James 4: 6-10

There is also a lot in the New Testament about the 'proud heart that is so full of sin. James lists the 'do's and don'ts.' The first one is, "God resist the proud, but giveth grace unto the humble." From the beginning we are told that a 'proud heart' is not acceptable to God.

The second one is, "Humble yourselves in the sight of the Lord and He will lift you up." Throughout the Bible the 'proud heart' displeases God. When we develop a 'proud heart' we are whacked; just like the proud-hearted kings got. "Humble yourselves in the sight of the Lord." Amen and amen.

~

IS IT A RELIGION OR A RELATIONSHIP?

Dear reader, how many times have you heard the phrase, "He or she is very religious?" I have also heard it 100's of times. What does that mean when someone is religious? I am not sure I know what it means. It does not mean that they have given their life to Christ. When someone gives their life to Christ, they start an intimate relationship with Jesus. This intimate relationship is when they trust Jesus completely. They rely upon His judgement, and they honour Him daily. I for one am still on that journey in my relationship with Jesus because 'me, myself and I' gets in the way of fully trusting Him. On the other hand, there is no one else that I have an intimate relationship with that I am closer to as I am with Jesus.

Reference: Genesis 3: 8

I think Adam and Eve must have had a daily, quality time with the Lord every evening in the garden. They had a lot to talk about to the Lord what they were doing during the day in the garden and with the animals. There were only three in this beautiful relationship in Paradise. But like good relationships, people can be so content and happy that someone else will get jealous.

In the garden it was Satan that was jealous; he was not invited to join them in the 'cool of the day.' So, he wanted to break them up and destroy that happy relationship. So that is what he did, tricked Eve to disobey God and Adam also disobeyed God. When we look to these 'religious people' we must observe their actions, it is their actions that define their religion. Are they seeking a relationship with the Lord or are they just acting along with another religious group, perhaps attending a church on Sunday, and forgetting the Ten Commandments, Monday to Saturday? They have no desire to live for the Lord because they are too busy living for themselves.

Religious people believe that their actions are more accountable in their church than an intimate relationship with God. You will see all these religious people serving where they are sure they will be noticed, involved with all the activities in their church and their community. They are working hard for the recognition from the Pastors or elders of their church. Truly religious people also want their families to be recognised when they are all in their pews on Sunday. Those that spread the Gospel and treasure their relationship with Jesus also want to serve, but their goal is to see people saved, not just being religious.

Let me make it clear, I am not the judge of these 'very religious' people. I only want to make it obvious that with all their dedication to their church and denomination, they lack that personal relationship with Jesus. I can explain it like this. Perhaps you like gardening, how close are you to your plant? If you like gardening, then I think you are very close to them and you talk to them. I have now fortunately been able to have some lovely house plants in my screen room. I go out there and speak to my lovely plants every morning and I pet them. Their only response is to lift their leaves to light; I consider it like them worshiping God. Like in the poem, "Trees," it reads, "lifting their leafy arms to pray." Truly a gardener can have a relationship with his garden. Jesus uses this theory in the book of John.

Reference: John 15: 1, 2

We all know how close Jesus is to the Father. In this verse the Father, the gardener disciplines His plants to give fruit. If the branches do not give fruit the gardener prunes them and cuts them off. He prunes the branches and directs them the way He wants them to grow. This garden reminds me of a home, where parents must lovingly prune and direct their children in the way in which they want them to grow. In this home close relationships develop.

Reference: John 15: 5, 6

There are many religious people that serve other gods, prophets, saints, and virgins, none of these idols can do what God can do and has done. In the verse Jesus says, "If," which in this sentence indicates the choice of remaining or retreating. For us to remain in Christ is to meet Him at the Cross, repent for our sins and give Him our life, to get out of a religion and get into a relationship. Before we finish with the Gardener there is two more verses to look at.

Reference: John 15: 7, 8

In this verse we are definitely not speaking of religion. We are definitely speaking of a relationship. Do you remember how the king in the fairy tales would say, "Ask whatever you wish, and it will be yours up to half of my kingdom." But here Jesus is not saying, "Half of my kingdom." He is offering everything, and He is promising everything.

Reference: John 15: 9, 10

In these verses you have the secret of a good relationship. To remain in love with Jesus is to obey Him. Parents often say, "If you love me you will obey me." That is not an original phrase; Jesus said it two thousand years ago. From birth you and your parents have a relationship and if you are born-again, you and Jesus have a relationship. When you disobeyed you hurt your parents feelings, when we disobey Jesus, we hurt Him also. We sometimes rebelled against our parents, perhaps we said something like this, "I want to do my own thing, leave me alone." That is the same thing religious people say also, many times they say to Jesus also. Words can encourage or hurt. The 'power of the tongue' is also a dividing line of religion and relation.

Reference: Luke 11:1, 2

John the Baptist spoke of the coming Messiah, Jesus was the Messiah that John the Baptist was speaking of. Jesus was the teacher to His disciples when they asked, "Lord teach us how to pray?" Jesus was not teaching His disciples a religion He was teaching them relationship. The first sentence was to direct the prayer to the Father in Heaven, not just words about Him. Religions use words to speak about a Saviour. A relationship speaks to the Saviour. Religions will keep you very busy, but a relationship with Jesus will keep you very blessed. Amen and amen.

∼

RELATIONSHIPS
WITHOUT COMPROMISES

This can be a painful subject dear reader. We have many forms of relationships, and as Christians some of these relationships can be hard to deal with. I find when a church begins to compromise with the world, I get upset. On the other hand, I must look at my own life and ask myself, "Am I compromising with the world and if so how?" Who do we have as examples in the Bible of those who compromised and only partly followed God's laws? The answer goes right through the whole Bible. With the examples I have picked out, I hope I have encouraged you to stick to God's laws.

Reference: Genesis 16: 1-4

Now we know that God had told Abram (later renamed Abraham by God) that he was to be the father of nations and yet he and his wife Sarai (later also renamed Sarah) were impatient, they wanted their inheritance quickly, so they took it on themselves to start a family. How sad it must have been for Abram when the Lord tells him that Ishmael is not the child that God had planned for. They must have been confused and disappointed. Then they lose all hope for having children as they get older past the age of conceiving.

What they did was to compromise with God's promise, and now they were too old to have children, they saw no way for it to come to pass. But, in God's timing

He moved into their lives and gave them another child. Abram and Sarai had wasted many years because they had done something that God did not want for them. When we get a word from God, we must also wait for his timing and not try to make compromises, to get what we want done quickly. So, as we do have a relationship with the Lord, we need to be patient and 'let God' move in our lives at His timing. We could say Amen to that.

We can look at other relationships perhaps at work or school or even our home or church. How easy is it to listen to a person, than to listen to God? Our lives are complicated, and it is so easy to find a simple result to our daily problems. A large percentage of those simple results have been our own doing not God's, therefore in time those results backfire on us, and our problems grow larger. If only we had 'let God' have the opportunity to give us a better result. We are tempted by the relationships we have with others to follow their lead. If they are Christian, they would encourage us to 'let God.' Together we can pray and wait for the answer and give thanks that our prayer was heard. I have more examples of people in the Bible that compromise with God's laws. In the book of Judges from chapter 14 through 16 we read the story of Samson, who was chosen by God to be a great Judge for Israel.

Samson really had a problem with his relationships; he was always with the wrong people. Every way Samson turned he was always compromising with God's laws. But like Abraham and Sarah finalising their lives with their chosen son and inheritance from God, Samson also finalised his life by offering his life to destroy the enemies of Israel. He had the opportunity to be a great Israeli leader, but he became a martyr for Israel.

References: 2 Samuel 15: 31; 17: 1-14; 18: 5-15; 19: 4

And then there was Absalom. What a sad story. Absalom had relationships with friends that wanted to get ahead in life. So these friends tried to get Absalom to compromise with them and turn against his own father King David. His friends said he should be king. Absalom listened to his friends and started to want his father's throne and crown. To get them his father the king would have to die. Absalom's hatred for his father caused him to begin a campaign against his father's army and captains. As you read the references of what happened to David's son and how David grieved for him.

Reference: Luke 22: 34, 35

Did you ever think of Peter compromising? He did not compromise because of a wrong relationship. He was afraid when Jesus was arrested and taken before the High Priest.

We know that Jesus healed Peter after His resurrection and Peter became the great disciple, apostle that led the church. Even when we compromise with God's plan for our lives, we can repent and start anew following the Lord and waiting on His word. My question is, "How are your relationships today, are they complying with God's laws or are they compromising with the world? This last reference is very important for us all.

Reference: Romans 12: 2

Amen and amen.

~

RESPECTING AUTHORITY

Dear reader, do you know there are many so-called Christians that do not respect the authority over them? That is from the smallest of things to the greatest; Christian taking the law into their own hands. There was a report about a Christian man murdering a doctor at an abortion clinic. Abortion is murder, but for a man to murder a murderer is breaking the law. I have heard Christians say, "They have no authority over them except God." He is the only one they will answer to. This is wrong, not Christian, and not according to God's Word. After creation how did authority get started? There were many men that did know and respect God, all of them lived before Noah. None of them saw the flood or the judgement of God, Methuselah was the last one to die before the flood. Noah respected God and followed every instruction God gave him to save himself, his family and all the animals.

Reference: Genesis 6: 9, 10

Noah was a family man but unlike Adam he had authority over his family. God told Noah how to build a large Ark. Noah's family respected Noah and his authority, so they all worked to build the Ark. The family believed in God and respected His authority to follow every detail God gave them, for their salvation. I think authority really started with God over Noah and Noah over his family. Staying in the book of Genesis, we have Abraham, Isaac and Jacob the roles God had for them sealed God's plans for His own people and nation. All three of these great patriarchs respected God's authority. At times there were family members who rebelled against their parents' authority, but God never left them on own, they always knew He was there for them. We read about Joseph and the years of being away from his family. He still respected the authority over him even as a slave, he served his masters well. So, after all those years trusting them, he was given authority over his masters. As well, he had authority to save Egypt and Israel. Genesis 50: 20 is a well known verse about Joseph when he faced his brothers.

Reference: Daniel 2: 48, 49

Daniel was captured and taken to another country. This young man was chosen by God to serve as Joseph was chosen. Israelites lads were bound and carried away to a strange land, serving false gods. Daniel and his friends all served the Lord over any false gods or idols. They were all put to incredible tests, but the Lord was with them always and they came through miracles. Some received great rewards from the king.

Reference: 1 Samuel 26: 7-9

Throughout the Old Testament the well-known prophets and patriarchs all lived under authority of powerful kings, but never submitting to their gods and idols. They were servants of the Lord, their lives were in danger, and they were imprisoned unjustly and met horrendous deaths for their faith and loyalty to God. Consider the authority that Saul had over David, who had already been anointed as King of Israel, when he was a shepherd boy.

What a great story about David respecting the authority of King Saul. King Saul was anointed to be King of Israel. Of course, David wanted to be king, but not in such a disrespectful manner. He had a little fun, playing this trick on Saul and all his army we'll see what David did.

Reference: 1 Samuel 26: 12

David waited until morning then called out to Saul. He even poked fun at Abner, the captain of Saul's army, saying, "Where were you while I was robbing the king?" So, for a season there is peace between Saul and David.

Reference: 1 Samuel 21, 25

It is not easy to be unjustly accused by someone that has authority over you. Perhaps you are at work or in school, or even a courtroom, how does a Christian justify themselves against evil accusations? It is now that we go to the New Testament.

Reference: Acts 16: 17, 18

While this young girl was telling everybody the truth about Paul and Silas, they were aware that it was a demon prophesying and challenging them. So they used the authority given them, through the Holy Spirit, in the Name of Jesus, to control and remove it. For doing this, her owners were very angry and had them arrested. They were falsely accused of causing a 'public disturbance.' The question is, "Whose authority was respected?" The answer is, "The Holy Spirit's." And who respected the authority of the Holy Spirit? Paul and Silas did, but they were thrown into jail and beaten, they did not turn on their accusers or guards.

They sang praises to Lord from their cell and were in chains. They trusted in the Lord, and the Lord delivered them. At midnight they were holding a revival meeting with the jailer and all the other prisoners. This is how Jesus taught His disciples true humility.

Reference: Mark 10: 42-45

Reading this verse may burst your balloon of pride as a follower of Jesus. You would think that after all the loyalty to Christ; someone would get a higher position than a servant. Servants are always under their master's authority and have little opportunity to advance. A few do after years of service with one master, but only a few. Not much to look forward to. So how do we servants of Christ gain authority? We have to persevere and work on our humility, increase our faith and respect everyone.

Reference: Mark 11:22-28

The scholars and priests that spent their time in the scriptures did not recognise God's authority or the Messiah's. Jesus was the only one that understood the scriptures and He knew He was on Earth to fulfil them. Jesus spoke and healed with authority.

Reference: Luke 5: 23-26

It was at the Cross that Jesus forgave sins through His word. It was after the Cross that all sins were forgiven through His Blood. Jesus was unjustly arrested and accused, but His only response to them was to acknowledge who He was, the Son of God. We started with respecting authority over us. Now we have come to receive authority, we have authority over all evil in the Name of Jesus as His disciples did.

Reference: Matthew 10: 1

The Holy Spirit that lives in us, and speaks through us, is the greatest authority over us here on earth. He should always be respected, loved, and obeyed. To close we return to those that are in authority, who make the laws and enforce them. Paul has something to say to Timothy about authority.

Reference: 1 Timothy 2: 1-3

Paul says that we must pray for them and give thanks for them, so that they as well as us will be blessed. In verse 3 it says, "For this is good and acceptable in the sight of God our Saviour. " So respecting authority is good for all mankind because it is good for God. Amen and amen.

～

REGRET OR REJOICE

Dear reader, when we are called to go to the hospital to a loved one or friend, we may have mixed emotions. We may be sad or very concerned; we may be relieved that they are now getting help they have needed while they were ill. (How many times can we tell someone they need to see the doctor and they ignore us?) For a Christian our first concern is, "Are they saved?" If they are an unbeliever, we know their salvation is more important than their reason for being in the hospital. As a believer we place the person that is ill in God's hands. Naturally the person that is ill needs our prayers and Christ's salvation.

The believer and the unbeliever can have the same love for the person in the hospital, but the hope of their future is different. The unbeliever is fearful for death, and the believer is praying for salvation before death. If the person in the hospital is saved, then the believer can rejoice for them knowing they will be together in eternity. When, on the hand, the unbeliever can only be sad, thinking of the great separation between life and death and how they will lose a loved one or friend and never see them again. The unbeliever feels life is unfair and they have been cheated by losing someone they love. There can be regret from the unbeliever recalling how they would have liked things to be. Perhaps they have not had enough time together. Time had been wasted and now there was no more time. How sad for an unbeliever facing death; and what about the believer recalling the person as a brother or sister in Christ? The reassurance of their salvation softens the emotion of regret and builds the heart with rejoicing, after death this loved one or friend will see Jesus and Heaven.

Reference: John 14: 1-3

The heart of the unbeliever is very troubled, the reason being because he believes in nothing. Or, he has faith in a false god. The unbeliever does not believe in the Lord God Jehovah and Jesus therefore that is the same as believing in nothing or not believing in anything, which is what makes an unbeliever. Perhaps you are questioning my statement. I have proof in this verse in the book of John.

Reference: John 14: 6

Unbelievers are under the illusion there are other things to believe in. My question to them is, "what is your life worth to you?" We all think our life is worth taking great responsibility for. We want to live, not die. How about the Truth, what is that worth to you? To me the 'Truth' (Jesus) is worth everything contrary to what the world has to offer me. I want the 'Truth' over anything. I don't want lies in my life; my life would be worthless if it was based on lies. How about you? The next thing I want to have is the reassurance that I am on the right path in my life. We all have a very common emotion caused by insecurity. That emotion is fear. If we don't know we are on the right path, then we are fearful of being on the wrong path. All three of these questions are answered in the verse above. Jesus is Life. Jesus is Truth. Jesus is the Way. Anything less than Jesus is not worthy of our belief or faith. How can it be possible to love someone and wish them eternal life and happiness after death?

Reference: Mathew 5: 12

Now there is one more reason why the believer questions the unbeliever. What have these gods and prophets that a large majority of the world worships done for mankind? Are they worshiped out of love or out of fear? When you die and meet these gods and prophets will you not have an answer for your sins? In the first place they have done nothing for mankind except use and abuse mankind.

Reference: John 3: 16

God does not want to use or abuse mankind. He wants to love them. He wants to have a relationship with them like a father and child.

Reference: John 3: 17

God wants you to worship Him and no other god because He loves you. He wants you saved and has promised eternal life with Him in Heaven, because He loves you so much. God had one Son in Heaven, Jesus. In verse 16 we read that God gave His Son Jesus for the salvation of all mankind. Does that sound like a god that wants only to use or abuse you or fear him and the power he has over you? Powerful gods are from evil beings. Man is not good without the love that God has created within our hearts. Although God created man with God's love in our hearts, we still have a choice to choose His love or reject it. Those who worship other gods or no gods have rejected the love of God.

Reference: Romans 10: 9

This verse in Romans directs the believer to the right thing to do when visiting someone in the hospital, to make sure they have confessed their sins and repented to Jesus (the Sinner's Prayer) as well as given Him thanks for their salvation and make sure you have done the same, there is no regret if they die. You can rejoice because they are with the Lord, because of theirs and your salvation, belief and faith in Jesus. Amen and amen.

~

REFRESHING

Dear reader, we all need refreshing. How thirsty we get for that cool water, when we find ourselves in a dry valley or desert area. Our soul is thirsty and our spirit is dry, we are so in need of refreshing God's love and mercy.

References: Psalm 42: 2: Numbers 14: 2

I am thinking of the Israelites after they had gone through the experiences when the Lord sent plagues and even death on the Egyptians then they passed over the Red Sea and saw Pharaoh and his army perish and their enemies being destroyed. After all that they cried out in the desert for water and food believing that Moses had brought them to the desert to die.

Reference: Numbers 20: 7-11

Sometimes the awesome wonder of God strengthens us, but at other times we become weak and empty because of all the greatness that we have witnessed we are astounded and breathless. I think this is what happened to the Israelites. They could not grasp the reality that God is love. They never thought that the great 'I AM' loved them. God's mercy for them was a sign of an Almighty God and they feared Him. God wants us to love Him, not just fear Him. They were tired, hungry, and thirsty and so was Moses after all the pressure that was on him from the people. Moses was ready to have some help with these troublesome people. God wasted no time in answering Moses' request, but he did not listen and obey God's orders. He was too quick to take on the authority of a man and not to rely on the authority of God. In other words, he did not think that speaking to the rock would bring a refreshing stream of cool water, so he smote the rock.

Reference: Numbers 20: 11, 12

The blessing was manifested, but a punishment was also laid on Moses for his rebellion. Although Moses and the people received the refreshing cool water,

Moses was still dry, his soul was parched, and his heart was broken because of his anger. He lost his place in the Promise Land. One slight sign of his lack of obedience, he was out.

Reference: Psalm 42: 2

As I said sometimes, we all need spiritual refreshing.
Do you remember when our Lord Jesus was in the desert and after forty days He needed refreshing and nourishment also

Reference: Matthew 4: 1-10

The Devil tempted Jesus three times to bow down to the evil one, but Jesus rebuked the Devil. He spoke the Word of God in the scriptures and beat the devil down all three times.

Reference: Mathew 4: 11

There in the desert angels came and refreshed Jesus with cool water and sustained Him with food. The enemy in the desert was the same enemy we have, and the refreshing and nourishment Jesus needed is the same refreshing and nourishment we need. The Devil is not dead yet.

Reference: John 7: 38

When Jesus spoke these words, He knew that we too would be found in a dry condition. He was in the desert. Our spirit and our soul can be dry and need refreshing. The 'Living Water' Jesus was speaking of was the pouring out of the Holy Spirit, who is the Comforter that He needed, and we need.

Reference: John 4: 14

The normal method to refresh ourselves is with a cup of cool water; we would take it, swallow it and be refreshed as we are drinking it. In this verse the Lord is saying, "The refreshing of the Holy Spirit is within us and will spring up within us like a fountain of 'Living Water' that will overflow within us with joy, praise, and worship.

Reference: Revelation 21: 5, 6

Our starting verse was in Psalm 42: 2, "My soul thirst for God, for the living God." With these verses in Revelation 21: 5, 6 we have the answer to that prayer from David. Our spirit no longer must be dry and thirsty because Christ has given us all that we need to strengthen and encourage us and to refresh our souls and our lives. Let us give Him thanks, Thank You Jesus. Amen and amen.

REBIRTH

Dear reader, I was thinking of something my friend said to me. Her comment was, "I was not born that way." We were speaking of our childhoods, I said I understood and agreed with her, we were raised differently, but for some reason, her words kept coming back to me. Finally, I asked the Lord to tell me why I was so bothered. He said, "When a baby is in the womb it lives in water. When the 'water breaks' a baby is ready to be born, and there is nothing in my creation more beautiful than a new life coming; a mother giving birth to a child. The child has a mother and father and a country's citizenship. The baby will start on mother's milk then it will begin on solid food to be nourished and to help it grow. It will be called by its own name and will learn a language to be able to communicate. It will also learn to think from listening to its parents and later reading their choice of literature as this baby grows, learns about its environment, it will start to make its own choices. The child will also receive with its family and inheritance of knowledge." This is the natural process of life in our flesh.

Reference: 1 Peter 1: 2-4

Praise the Lord Jesus Christ, in His mercy; He has given us a new birth into living hope through His resurrection from the dead to and into an inheritance that can never perish, spoil or fade and kept in Heaven for us. Amen.

We are all born in the flesh, but as we advance physically and mentally, we develop on our own, we begin to make our desires and choices in life our priorities and daily goals. So that is for the flesh, but we also have a spiritual life that develops as we are growing up. When I was born-again it didn't happen in the flesh, it happened in the spirit. Jesus made it possible from the Cross and through His blood that He poured out for my salvation, and for me to be spiritually born-again. When we are born again we even have a new parent, Father God, a new citizenship to a new country, the Kingdom of God. You even have 'living water' and 'the Bread of life' for your nourishment and to help you grow. You also can have a new language to communicate with the Holy Spirit and you will have a new mind with new thoughts.

Reference: Philippians 2: 5

Your mind will be so full of new things in your thinking, your desires will change, and your environment will change. You will have a new family in Christ and a new inheritance. The day you are born again is not only an extension of the day before, but 'All' things also become new, when you experience the rebirth of your spiritual life, you will gladly tell everyone that you are born-again. The day you were born- again will be the greatest day of your life. Amen and amen.

REBELLION

Dear reader, we all rebel. Oh yes! We all rebel. From children we learn to rebel, and we took that learning with us as we were growing up. It is true; as we were growing up we found that rebelling didn't always get us very far. In most cases those we were rebelling against would win, and we would have to do what they requested in the end.

When I was growing up, I was one of those that rebelled against society. I wanted to surf in Galveston, so I worked as a carhop in Galveston and a model in Dallas, and when I was free, I surfed. I made little money, wore little clothes, lived with my mom in Dallas and in Galveston on the beach, I had little sense in those days until I realised there is more to life when I fell in love with a Norwegian seaman. He wanted a lady, so I became one and married him, moving to Norway. That is my short story about my rebellion to society. Clearly you all have your own short stories. In the Bible we have one short story in the book of Jonah. Jonah, a prophet to serve the Lord, turned out he rebelled against God. It is one thing to rebel against man, but don't be so stupid to rebel against God.

Reference: Jonah 1: 1-3

Now we understand that Jonah had a little setback when the Lord asked him to do so great a task. If he truly knew the Lord that well, he would have known no one can run from Him. The Omnipresent, Omnipotent Almighty; all seeing, all hearing, all knowing great Jehovah. How stupid can anyone be to think they could run away from God? Truth is, Jonah was not thinking straight, if he had been thinking right, he would have packed and started off to Nineveh.

Reference: Jonah 1: 3-4

How about that, he thought that going in the opposite direction would protect him. The darkness that Jonah was now surrounding himself in was a spiritual darkness. He had rebelled against God and was totally disobedient. He went to Joppa; his new direction was Tarshish.

Reference: Jonah 1: 3-6

The Lord was aware where Jonah was, and He was not going to send someone
else to Nineveh, God was not going to call on anyone else to fill the task.
The Lord wanted Jonah for this task. While Jonah was running the Lord was
planning. Jonah just wanted to sleep; he didn't want to think about his future or
his rebellion. Outside the wind was blowing up a gale, the unbelieving sailors
were all praying to their false gods, discarding the cargo that they would lose
money on and would have to pay for, they just wanted to survive the storm.
They were frantically trying to save their lives and the ship. They woke up Jonah
shouting, "Pray to your god that we be saved." Jonah prayed to the Lord, and the
Lord listened to his prayer.

Reference: Jonah 1: 7-14

Jonah knew the storm was his fault, they could all perish because of him, and
yet he would rather drown and die than obey the Lord. This crew knew if Jonah's
god could control the wind, they would sacrifice Jonah to the sea, and not make
his god angrier. They pleaded to Jehovah that they would not be held responsible
for Jonah's death. Jonah was running away from the task of dealing with
unbelievers, and now he was in a ship full of them. They were now believing in
the Lord and praying to their new Almighty God. Jonah was so full of himself;
he was not aware of the revival meeting on that ship.

Reference: Jonah 1: 15-16

Because God turned the disobedience around to repentance, He saved the
captain, his crew and their ship. They all saw the work of the mighty God
Jehovah. There on the ship they built an altar and sacrificed to God and made a
vow to only serve Him. What a miracle meeting that turned out to be, and Jonah
missed it.

Reference: Jonah 1: 17

In other words, the Lord said to the fish, "I want you to be here at this spot at this moment of the day," and the fish answered, "As You wish Lord." Therefore, the fish was there to pick up Jonah and swallow him. We can shout, "Praise the Lord," at this point. By now Jonah was aware of what God was doing with him.

Reference: Jonah 2: 1

There is a song, "Sometimes it takes a mountain, a desert or a raging sea, for God to get a hold of me." I think that Jonah understood what he must do in the belly of the fish.

Reference: Jonah 2: 2-9

Now that Jonah is back, he has a fresh start. God has forgiven him; his rebellion and disobedience are forgotten in the sea. I would imagine Jonah was a sight (bleached) after being in the belly of a fish for three days, and then he was vomited out of the fish onto the beach. He was not good as fish food. I can almost see the Lord smiling when the fish regurgitated a man on the beach.

Reference: Jonah 3: 1-3

Jonah's skin would have been bleached white from the acids in the fish belly. When he arrived in the city, they were wondering, "Where does this guy come from?" He might have looked like an angel or a ghost. It meant no importance what he looked like; it was what he had to say that was important.

Reference: Jonah 3: 4-10

Jonah was feeling very low in verse four, then a change as he is repeating what happened to him, he admits his salvation to be alive. He thinks sitting in the belly of a fish all hope is gone, darkness, no air, not a glimpse of escape. Jonah had nothing but his thoughts, thinking back to his rebellious nature. He didn't know of the revival meeting on the ship; they were all worshiping Jehovah on their way to Joppa. Jonah was repenting and asking God's mercy. Jonah is now promising God his faithfulness, in verse nine.

When Jonah preached the people believed him. From the King to the "shoeshine" boy, everyone in Nineveh believed him and his prophecy. The King even called the animals to repent and worship the Lord. How that worked, I don't know, but animals are God's creatures, why wouldn't they worship Him? They fasted, repented, and worshiped because they wanted to be saved from the wrath of God. Finally, all has gone according to God's plan. Jonah obeyed God, the city repented, and God saved them all.

This short story tells us it does not make any sense to rebel against God. Jonah had taken many steps forward to do so, and then he had to take many steps backward to be saved and repent. When we take steps forward, let us make sure they are in the right direction; we will not have to backtrack on our steps with repentance. In this story we have many miracles, on the ship, in the fish, on the beach and in the city. Jesus used this story also to tell of His miracle of rising from the grave.

Reference: Matthew 12: 38-41

Those they were speaking to were rebellious; always trying to change the way in which God was to be served. They were making worship a business, personal gain. We must make sure when we want to rebel, we are doing it to glorify God. There are a lot of reasons to rebel, but to just have your own way is not one of them.

Reference: Mark 16: 15-16

Any country, person, government, or any church and religion that tries to hinder you from following Jesus' command to preach the gospel, you can gladly rebel against. But never rebel against God. Amen and amen.

∼

HEART CHANGE

Dear reader, sadly we lose blessings that are only for us to take. How this comes about is because we always believe ourselves to be right all the time and in everything. We think if we are not that good, (meaning we are not right all the time) then others do not think well about us or want to be with us, they agree with our boldness, but condemn us for our weakness. We are judged by our intelligence, our wisdom, or our kindness. But others have no right to judge us, for our mistakes or being wrong about a few things. The way others think about us or judge us fills us with fear, anxiety, and lack of confidence. So, all our concepts of how great we are diminish with fear. Therefore, where we may be assigned a blessing from the Lord, we can lose it because of our fear. We can build our confidence, when we pray about any problem that comes up for us or for others, that is the right move. While attending our church we are so quick to question something, or anything said from the pulpit.

Reference: 1 Corinthians 8: 2, 3

We may find we gain a wealth of knowledge from the speaker and therefore we also gain our blessings. The attitude of always being right is the first step in losing our blessings.

Reference: Revelation 2: 16

Reading from the last book in the Bible, we are instructed to change our attitude. That change cannot come about without one more thing, our mind, or our thinking. A stubborn mind has no room for new ideas and blessings. In verse 16, John tells us the Lord will fight against us and our attitudes. He will use a, "Sword of God;" in other words, "the Word of God."

Reference: Isaiah 31: 8

Through the Bible we read of many instances where God has shown His wrath. Isaiah tells us that, "The Word of God," will smite our attitudes. Paul also speaks of the 'sword, Spirit of God' or the 'Word of God' will smite His enemies, in other words our attitude and thinking that does not please God. Our wrong thinking is God's enemy. I am sure we do not want to be God's enemy. Paul speaks in the book of Ephesians.

Reference: Ephesians 4: 23, 24

In this verse Paul says, "Change and better yourself." We all want to better ourselves. The question is, "Do we want to better ourselves by a complete inventory of our minds, what are we thinking?" How do we get our blessings when we don't want to lose them? The answer is resigning to the Holy Spirit and listening to Him, this is our first step in gaining new blessings. The Holy Spirit may convict us, and we may have to go back in our 'mind inventory' selecting something in our attitudes that must be cast out, and then we will grow closer to the Lord.

Three things will bring us closer to the Lord; each one will bring us a blessing. First we need 'conviction' from the Holy Spirit; secondly we need 'correction' from the Holy Spirit; thirdly we need 'change' from the Holy Spirit. Some of our churches are not listening to the Holy Spirit. The congregation in these churches are waiting for their blessings, but there is none. When you are in a church that compromises with the world and has a 'deaf ear' to the Truth, to the Gospel and to the message of the Cross, you will lose what blessings the Lord has for you. Compromising does not always mean that evil is let in the door, but it does mean the Truth has been twisted, so God's laws are bent out of order. Instead of spending all our time trying to prove how right we are, we should open our ears and listen to gain knowledge that will strengthen our life with Christ.

Reference: 1 Peter 4: 10, 11

In verse 10 Peter says, "We need to take all our blessings and pass them on." Our blessings are manifested in our special abilities. Our blessings increase as we share them with others. Our boasting about how right we are, will be changed, Paul tells us, "We will not lose our blessings by sharing them." How many do you have that you can share with others today? Amen and amen.

GOOD LUCK, BAD LUCK, AND NO LUCK

Dear reader, I will start off with, "How lucky are you?" We all have a different idea of what 'luck' really means to us and what it has to do with our lives. I have never thought of myself as 'lucky,' but I have always thought of myself as 'fortunate.' To me luck is something that happens, and fortunate is a state of being. Many times, when things don't go as we hoped they would, we call that, "Bad luck." When things are going very well we call that, "Good luck." The 'luck' can go to some very unhealthy depths. Fortune tellers believe in luck and so do those who practice evil and dark occults. In fact, the TV is full of programs with horoscopes telling you your future, how sad when people believe the lies and direct their lives accordingly. Also, there are advertisements of games and lotteries that catch people's attention, thinking, "Maybe I can be lucky." What about witchcraft with charms and objects that are magical or lucky, that have supernatural powers. Or when you see, "Today's Luck" in the newspaper or magazine, that page is displeasing and dishonouring God.

Reference: Isaiah 47: 13

So just what are you looking for? We all have things in our lives that mean we have to make important decisions, to buy or sell, to open a relationship, to take a new job, or go to a new school, decisions all through our lives and all through our days. The only way to make a good decision is to consult the Lord. No superstitions, horoscopes, or charms, none of these, they are all evil and displeasing to the Lord, they are part of the occult and will only bring you a sad end. We continue in Isaiah with what the Lord says will be the outcome if we displease Him with your faith in evil, superstitious manners of 'luck.'

Reference: Isaiah 47: 14

If you have been playing with any of these superstitions, horoscopes, witchcraft or 'good luck charms;' you had better stop it and cast out all those evil elements out of your life. God knows the best for us; we must trust Him with everything in our life.

Reference: Romans 8: 28

Paul tells us all things, repeating, "All things work together for good, if we love the Lord." God is easy to love, He is our creator, our Father in Heaven. Not only that, "God loves us." You may think that is not possible, not only is it possible, but it is also true. Paul gives us this advice in the book of Romans.

Reference: Romans 8: 24, 25

If we give our life to Christ and believe in Him and the Cross, we can get all we hope for; we may even see our dreams come true. The way is to be born-again at Calvary. Once again Paul speaks.

Reference: Romans 8: 1, 2

When I gave my life to Jesus, I was reborn in the Spirit. I became the fortunate person I am today. My old habit of looking for my good luck and avoiding my bad luck vanished. I need no luck; I have 'My Personal Saviour,' Jesus Christ. Amen and amen.

~

IN HIS NAME

Dear reader, I have always told my lads, "You are only worth your name." I was explaining about their credit and honesty when purchasing or signing a contract. When we go to the Bible, God's Word, we find many well known names. Some are good people and others not so good people. There are hundreds of names in the Old Testament with all the genealogy from Adam to Micah. In Matthew the names are the genealogy Adam to Jesus. The question is, "Where did all these names come from?" That is an advanced Bible study. We'll take it easy and start with Israel's beginning.

Reference: Genesis 13: 1, 2

So in the beginning God did not have a name. He was known as, "the God of Abraham, Isaac, and Jacob." I believe that God's first name came in the burning bush.

Reference: Exodus 3: 14

"I AM" may seem a strange name, but for me when I read the Bible, I believe there was more power in that name than all the other names of God. Later God took other names to lead the Israelites through the wilderness. Some were, "Jehovah, Yahweh, El-Shaddai," there are other names God took that are in the 'Torah,' which are the first five books of the Bible. Sometimes God was called, "God of the Prophets or God of Israel." The enemies of Israel never called God my His mighty name "Yahweh," they called God the "God of Israel," they knew He was a mighty God. The prophet Isaiah tells of a new man coming that will be the highest representative of God.

Reference: Isaiah 7: 14 and 9: 6

This great event arrived 700 years after Isaiah, Jesus was born.

Reference: Matthew 1: 18

So the great event arrives, the birth of Jesus, who is also Christ (Son of God). The first time He was called Christ was with the angels giving the 'Good News' to the shepherds.

Reference: Luke 1: 11

Jesus was with His disciples when Peter made his great confession.

Reference: Mathew 16: 16

In the book of John, Jesus speaks directly of the power that is in His Name.

Reference: John 14: 13, 14

In the New Testament there are many references concerning the Name of Jesus. Here are some I like.

References: Luke 15: 18, Colossians 3: 17, and Philippians 2: 9-11

In Paul's letters we are told that there is power in the Name of Jesus for healing, deliverance, and raising the dead. Also, Paul tells us, "That every knee will bow, and every tongue confess Jesus is Lord."

Reference: Romans 14: 11

We find that, "In the Name of Jesus," is powerful therefore we pray in the Name of Jesus. As a deep study in the Old and New Testaments we find that Christ, the Messiah, the great 'I AM' is always referring to Jesus, born of the Spirit of God, the Holy Spirit. The name Jesus is all power, knowledge and wisdom that we will ever need. The name Jesus has authority over every evil and Satan will flee at the Name of Jesus. It is in 'Jesus name' we have everything. Amen and amen.

~

PROSPERITY

Dear reader, the word 'prosperity' can certainly cover many things. In church we have heard of 'prosperity teaching.' I want more than just teaching to increase my prosperity. I am quite sure you feel the same. We need facts not just opinions. When we read God's Word from the Bible, we get the facts we need. In history and in the Bible the most prosperous man on the face of the earth wrote the Book of Proverbs. I am speaking of King Solomon. He states, "That God's favour, or the foundation of prosperity, begins with understanding."

Reference: Proverbs 3: 3-10

As a rule, we think that our own prosperity comes from our own efforts and understanding. We go to school, and then to college, we get our certificates acknowledging how very smart we are. Then we use our good qualifications to get us into good positions and jobs. We work diligently up the ladder from the first position on the first floor until we get the opportunity to the top floor and top position in our careers. We understand that this must be the true sign of prosperity. The more responsibility we have the more money we earn and the more prosperous we are, isn't that the rule in life? Therefore, we can live a more than average life. We can afford luxuries and comforts that we have no real need of, just a sign of our prosperity. We are always thinking, "Just when I have that, I will be happy." This is the rule in life today. Let's go back to the Bible and King Solomon: He wanted to be a great King and leader of his people Israel as his father King David had been. So, he prayed to the Lord.

Reference: 1 Kings 3: 9, 10

The Lord was pleased with the King's prayer. He had not asked for riches and great prosperity. He had asked for wisdom to rule his nation and his people. He had asked for understanding to be a good judge, honest and fair, knowing good and evil from his throne, he had asked for discernment. After his father King David was dead the nation mourned, could they believe in Solomon the new King, would he be a follower of the Lord or as others had been, serving false gods. Solomon's prayer pleased the Lord, and the new King was greatly blessed. His request for wisdom and discernment to rule his people and his nation was granted, a hundred-fold. Solomon continues writing in Proverbs.

Reference: Proverbs 3: 6

Solomon is teaching his people through the book of Proverbs; see how he teaches them.

1. *In all your way acknowledge God and He will direct thy paths*
2. *Only trust in God, obey Him and stay away from evil*
3. *You will stay healthy and strong following the statues of the Lord*
4. *Honour the Lord with your offerings and tithing*
5. *You follow these rules you and your household will have prosperity*

Solomon covers every need in these rules for his people and for us for our direction, our protection, our health, our giving, and our receiving. So, the question is, "Are you following all these rules or just a few of them?" Solomon took the gift of wisdom and understanding to rule his nation to be more precious than silver or gold. God was so pleased with his humility, that he was enriched with silver and gold more than any man in history. Solomon received the 'abundant life that we all are hoping for.' He never stopped loving the Lord and he saw the Lord in all his scriptures. He wandered a little 'left' when referring to his relationships with women, but we still can thank him through the Holy Spirit for his writing the Book "Song of Songs." Now let us continue with the topic 'prosperity.'

Reference: 1 Chronicles 4: 10

Jabez was a humble farmer, but he was an unwanted child therefore, he was named Jabez meaning, "He was bared in sorrow." Not a very nice name to grow up with! But in verse 9 the Lord saw him more honourable than his brothers. In other words, Jabez honoured the Lord. Therefore, he prayed for three things, in this verse we have the well-known 'prayer of Jabez' that is prayed by Christians today. Number one was for his protection against all evil that could hurt him. That is for protection against anyone that would want to hurt him and against any evil spirit. Number two was to increase his prosperity. Number three was to be blessed by the Lord, in other words to have God's favour on him. Amen. Remember he was not a prophet or king; he was a humble farmer just as his brothers. But he loved the Lord and trusted Him for his blessing, his protection, and his prosperity. He was not favoured with his family, but he was favoured by the Lord. It is such a good prayer and good lesson for us to learn. Jabez knew to have prosperity he had to trust first in the Lord, and then get to his plough. When we look to that prayer, we can pick out our own needs. There are many prayers in the Bible. It is good for us to know them and pray them. Even Moses had a very good prayer in Deuteronomy.

Reference: Deuteronomy 5: 32, 33

I know that we that are born-again Christians will read this prayer differently than an unbeliever. The unbeliever relies strictly on himself or on others for his blessing and prosperity. We that are Christian rely on the Lord and are thankful when He uses us to bless others, that is our prosperity.

Reference: 3 John 2: 2

The unbeliever has not got a clue of what John is saying in this verse, because they are not saved, and their soul is lost. A lost soul cannot be of good health or prosper. That is why it is so important that we must keep up our witness to unbelievers about the Cross and Jesus. What a blessing we have from John, he comes right to the point, Christian prosperity does not begin with material things, but they are where it finalizes, whatever is good comes first from God. I like this favourite verse of mine in Luke.

Reference: Luke 12: 31

The next question, "Are you seeking riches, good health, a good relationship, or perhaps a good job, the list goes on?

The answer is always the same "Seek first the Kingdom of God." Jesus is the Kingdom of God, seek Him first. Salvation and eternal life is truly the only thing we need, so our soul will prosper creating true prosperity. Amen and amen.

∽

LIGHT AND DARKNESS

Dear reader, it is not the size of light that conquers darkness; 'it is light that conquers it.'

Reference: Philippians 2: 12-15

When we look up to the millions of stars on a very starry night, we don't see a large patch of darkness, because these tiny twinkling stars are occupying all the sky. There are a very few planets that light up certain parts of the sky and only one moon. So, the majority of the black sky is covered with small lights in the heavens. This alone confirms my statement, "It is not the size of the light that conquers darkness; it is light."

Reference: Mathew 5: 14

The apostle Paul says, "Keep our salvation with fear and trembling," these words are what strengthens us to keep our lamp lit. In Philippians 2: 14 Paul also refers to tells us, "Remove arguing and complaining and replace them with a blameless and pure Spirit that works for the purpose of the Lord." We have the words of Jesus that confirms what Paul has said, "Let your light so shine."
Have you ever seen the little Jewish lamp? It is like a little clay boat, carried with you as you go round to every room. No one had a bigger one to carry; they were all the same size, little boat, with the same amount of oil in it. In Mathew Jesus also says, "Put it on a stand." He was saying, "Let the light be in the centre of the room, shining outward." That little light will eliminate the darkness in the room and the darkness in the lives of those in the room, that little light is doing a lot of good. Just like the stars that are united in the heavens to produce a beautiful picture in the sky at night-time and take our fears with the small lights (the stars), power to eliminate the darkness of the night. The question is, "What darkness do you have in your life, do you have the light (Jesus) to eliminate that darkness?"

Reference: John 8: 12

There you have the answer dear reader, Jesus is the light you need and can eliminate any darkness in your life. When you believe in Jesus on the Cross at Calvary with all your heart, He will give you a light (which is a part of Him). You will also have the guiding light of the Holy Spirit, the power of the Holy Spirit that will remove all darkness from your life. Amen and amen.

~

PROMISES

Dear reader, we all make promises, but how good are we to keep them? It is not easy to keep a promise; in fact, sometimes something can happen, where we find it impossible to keep our promise. Let's go to the word, to see what it says about 'promises.'

Reference: Numbers 23: 19

So God, because he is not a man, because He is not human, He does not lie. Therefore, when He has made us a promise (8,810times in the Bible, 7,487 times from God's spoken word) He does not lie or has never lied. We know God spoke through the prophets and King David (approx. 300 times) many have been manifested in history up to today, but Glory be to God, there are so many yet to come true.

We are born-again and living in the time that we will see many of God's promises still to come, will come true. Praise the Lord. Although we on the other hand, are too quick to make our promises, we don't make them because we want to be kind to someone; no we make them because we want someone to think better of us. If we want to do something out of kindness (while someone is living), we wouldn't promise, we will do whatever they needed, or wanted. When someone says to me, "Do you promise," I feel as if they don't believe me or trust me. We, unlike God, are always changing our minds or our circumstances. Because of that we can be very unreliable. I like the verse from Peter, where he says, "God is reliable." Read this promise to me.

Reference: 2 Peter 3: 9

Well, we now know the Lord has put a condition on His promises, "Repentance."

Reference: Hebrews 11: 14

God has put that condition on His promises, we must repent. The Lord is a good

Father and very patient, but to see His promises fulfilled, we must repent. Paul tells us in Hebrews, "We must be faithful." As well as repentance we must have faith, faith in the Lord Jesus our Saviour, protector, and provider. In other words, to enjoy and reap the promises of God is to be born-again, and a believer of the Cross at Calvary. God is faithful to what He has promised.

Reference: Hebrews 10: 36

So, God is faithful, and He will keep His promise, when we make Him a promise. We must repent of our past sins and promise to love and obey God's Son Jesus. "After you have done the will of God, you will receive the promise." Amen and amen.

~

PERSEVERANCE

I am going to the book of 2 Kings. The Syrian king went to war against the King of Israel and the Lord gave Elisha a message to the King of Israel how he could save himself and all of Israel. The King of Syria was angry and when he found out that it was Elisha, he sent his army against him to kill him. So we read in 2 Kings.

Reference: 2 Kings 6: 14-17

Oh, dear reader, how many times have we been looking at the enemies' armies as we pray for help? But do we pray for the Lord to open our eyes so that we can see His armies outnumbering and surrounding and ready to consume the enemy with the Lord's horses and chariots of fire? Does our faith reassure us, "They that be with us are more than they that be with them?" The word 'be' indicates, at this very moment and for always. Elisha does not stop at what he sees; he persevered to gain a victory over the Syrians. He continues in prayer that the Syrians be blinded and he leads them to Samaria where the King of Israel is waiting to slay them. This is when the Lord opens their eyes. But what does God want done with Israel's enemy?

Reference: 2 Kings 6: 22

This way the war was over and not a drop of blood was shed. We continue in verse 23.

Reference: 2 Kings 6: 23

Once again, the Lord had brought peace to Israel. From the first morning Elisha had prayed that his servant's eyes would be open to see the Glory of God, but he did not stop there, yes, they are safe, but that is not what Elisha has prayed for. Elisha was a great prophet of Israel and he prayed daily for his nation. Every day he was praying for his country and countrymen, so he perseveres with the Lord. We are safe but what about Israel? What about the victory of Israel? When our eyes are opened to see the Glory of the Lord over our enemy and we feel safe and our prayer is answered, do we just give thanks and go our way praising Him, or do we persevere, asking God for a complete deliverance and victory?

Reference: Ephesians 6: 18

With perseverance we hold out and continue to pray. "Lord let our eyes be opened to see God's army, so that they that be with us, are more than they that be with our enemy, blind and weaken them so they will fall and bow to the Almighty King Jesus and His victory." Amen and amen.

~

PASSED AWAY OR PASSED ON

Today we were saying goodbye to a family member in Christ. Two word phrases are commonly used at a death, "Passed away or passed on." Both are used for the same thing, someone has died. Although they are spoken to mean the same thing, they are definitely not the same thing. First, what happens when a person who is 'passed away' has died? You don't see them or speak to them face to face.

They are not present anymore. Even with all technology you have no means to contact them. No matter how much you want to stay in touch with them it is impossible after death.

Reference: Romans 8: 6

Death is to separate from those you love forever. Death is to be away with no form of communication to stay in touch. Death is the end of life, as we know it on earth. Death is darkness, what all mankind fears is the end of life. Death is carnal.

Reference: Romans 3: 23

If a person is a sinner, they will experience death in sin. In the verse it says, "All have sinned, all are sinners." In the book of Ecclesiastes it is written, "A time to be born, and a time to die." So, does that mean that 'all' must go through death, because of our sins?

Reference: Romans 3:22

First it says, "God shows His righteousness to all that believe," then it says, "To all that have faith in Jesus Christ."

Reference: Romans 5: 17

Adam's sin was a curse (offence) on all mankind to the point of death. "By one man's offence death reigned by one." Jesus paid for that debt of 'offence, sin,' on the Cross at Calvary. Jesus performed the last 'sin offering' that God had asked of mankind. Sin was a debt that was owed to God from mankind; Christ at the Cross paid in full our debt. Death was no longer the final payment for sin. No sinner was any longer required to pay for sin with his life. After the death of Jesus we have this promise, "Much more we will receive abundance of Grace and the Gift of Righteousness and Life through Christ." Man did not need to 'pass away' through death. What man needs is to believe and have faith in Jesus. In other words, there is a second choice. To 'pass on' is a different phase, to go from one place to another place. A destination must be in sight or in our mind if we are to reach it.

Reference: John 5: 24

So the death that we may experience to 'pass away' can be changed to 'pass on' into Life with Christ.

Reference: 1 John 2: 25

Eternal life is surely a destination in which we all want to reach. Reaching that destination comes from having a relationship with Jesus and an unending line of communication with Him called prayer. If we do not stay online with Him, we can lose our way.

Reference: Mathew 7: 14

Why would Jesus say, "That only a few find the right way?" Perhaps the 'wide' way is so obvious, so the majority go there. The 'narrow' way is more discreet, and one must not take their eyes off the path, or they can fall. Watching the exact movements of our life and staying in the footsteps of Jesus in front of us, will bring us to our Heavenly destination.

Reference: 1 John 5: 10-13

The first verse warns, "He that hath not the Son of God hath not life," and will see death. He will 'pass away' and never be seen or spoken to again. Then John says, "He that hath the Son hath life," and will be seen and spoken to again in Heaven. How many do we know that will not believe in Jesus? We pray for those we love that they will receive from the Lord a lasting revelation of salvation, as we keep them in our daily prayers.

Reference: 1 John: 2: 24

To continue with the Son and with the Father is eternal life after death. We all want to 'pass on' in the Light not to 'pass away' in darkness. Dear reader, be the one that tells all your loved ones about Jesus and the Cross, so they will 'pass on' to the same destination where you will see and speak with them again. Amen and amen.

~

NO BARRIER, NO DETOURS

Reference: Matthew 7: 13

Dear reader none of us want to get on the road of destruction, I am afraid a lot of us do get on it and cannot find the way back. Well, if we didn't get on in the first place, if our goal is to come to the narrow gate and stay on that path, we would not have to suffer on that path of destruction. We don't mean to make the wrong turn in our lives. When we are standing at the 'crossroads' in life we look at the easiest road to travel. The little dirt path on the other side of that wooden gate doesn't look too promising. No, we feel more confident passing through that large archway travelling on that wide paved road. Makes more sense, surely the narrow dirt path is going nowhere, but to a dead end. The archway is very pretty and the paved road very comfortable for travelling on, surely it will be a better life and better rewards. My experience with these paved highways is a lot of road works and barriers that slow you down. Also, there are detours that make you lose a lot of your travelling time in life, and you must try to come to your destination from another direction, you can get lost. So, at the end of your life, you find you have made the wrong choice; the easiest choice has taken you to the wrong place, with no rewards.

Reference: Matthew 7: 14

We still have time in our lives to make different choices and change our direction as well as our paths in life. The narrow path is a little more difficult to travel, you may get a little dusty and tired so you will have to take more time, you can rest on green grass and under the shady trees, drink fresh spring water and refresh yourself to continue travelling, you find you are not in so much of a hurry on this path. Also, this narrow path is straight, no barriers, no detours. Every problem you face in life you can go through calmly and slowly on the narrow path. Another good thing about that narrow path is that it leads you to your destination and the rewards you desire and Heaven.

Reference: John 14:6

Jesus says, "He is the way (narrow way), the truth, (no lies, no barriers, no detours)." He says, "If we follow Him, we will have life (an abundant life with many rewards)." So, the question is, what choices are we making? What path are you taking? Are you following your desires to an easy life and on to a paved highway and through a beautiful archway? Or are you choosing the straight and narrow path to travel with Jesus? We can pray this prayer from our heart and make the right choice.

'The Sinner's Prayer.' *(Pray it out loud.)*
"Father God, I come to You, in the Name of Jesus and through the Holy Spirit. I have broken your laws and my sins have separated me from You.

Forgive me Lord Jesus, I am sorry and now I want to turn away from my past and sinful life. Please forgive me.

I believe that, You Lord Jesus, died on the cross for my sin. You rose up from the dead and are alive to hear my prayers.

I invite You Lord Jesus to be the Lord of my life, to rule and reign in my heart forever. Please send Your Holy Spirit to help me obey You.

I want to do Your will for the rest of my life. In the precious Name of Jesus, I pray.

Amen.

Congratulations now you are born-again and saved and can travel with Jesus, on His narrow path and receive His rewards and Heaven. Amen and amen.

~

LOST AND FOUND

Dear reader, I think of myself as an organised person. Some people would agree, and others would not agree with me. Although, I do find myself misplacing things and not being able to put my hands on them quickly. When you live on your own you have nobody to blame when things are not where you believe them to be. No one asks why they are not there. This morning I could not find something very important from the bank. I looked in the usual places and some places that were not so common to put it, but I couldn't find it. So I made plans to contact the bank, and do it all over again.

Reference: Luke 15: 4

When I read this verse it reminds me, that I was the lost sheep (lost sinner) He found in the wilderness, (out there in the world). I was lost and Jesus found me. So, He did find me, He looked for me, because He loves me and He wants to care for me. I am valuable to my shepherd, my Saviour. Jesus tells a story about a woman losing a silver coin.

Reference: Luke 15: 8

I thought about me, I have lost something and done just like the woman, going through the house, looking everywhere, but not finding it. That paper was valuable to me. Therefore, it was important to the Lord also. So, I prayed and told Him, I need the paper, doing it again it would be out of date also. I know He knew where it was. Through the Spirit in prayer I asked, I needed direction to where it was. I started thanking Him for that paper; I sang praise to the Lord and started through the house again saying, "Thank you Jesus for Your love."

Cleaning and dusting again, I came to the top shelf and there was the paper on the top shelf. I quickly put it in my lockup box for safekeeping and continued singing thanksgivings and praises.

Reference: Luke 15: 9

Yes, I too told my testimony of how the Lord helped me find what was lost. Rejoice with me I have found the paper, "that which was lost." Perhaps, you dear reader, feel you are lost, not finding your direction or the right way to live your life. If you are 'lost in sin' and desperately want to be found, Jesus is there for you.

Reference: Luke 15: 4-7

Oh yes, for those who are lost and need to repent, there is Jesus, "Amazing grace, how sweet the sound, that found a wretch like Me, I once was lost and now I'm found, blind but now I see." Amen and amen.

~

REPENT AND RECEIVE

Reference: Deuteronomy 5: 33

There are conditions with this verse written by Moses to the children of Israel. Dear reader, do you think the conditions the Lord gave them are very hard to follow? We want to prosper, we want material things to make life better, we want good relationships to share our lives with. In other words, we want everything that is good, but the conditions are hard. We want to have fun with our families and friends. Perhaps they are not following God, we can't cut them out of our lives because of their sins. In the book of 3 John, he writes of a blessing for us.

Reference: 3 John 1: 2

If we get our priorities right, that is following the commandments of God, not staying on the conditions, just staying on the right path. We have been promised good health, longevity; these are the things we want to have first, except John says, "As our soul prospers." We need to find the answer to how our soul prospers.

Reference: Revelation 2: 5

One thing everyone agrees with is that 'sin' causes illnesses. So, to be with good health we have to be without sin. In this verse to be without sin is repentance. We have to repent to prosper. In Isaiah we have a well known verse, the verse that reminds us of Jesus on the Cross.

Reference: Isaiah 53: 5

For what Jesus did for us, it is to Jesus we ask forgiveness and repent. At the end of the verse it states, "With His stripes we are healed." We repent to ask Him, our Saviour on the Cross, to forgive us all our sins. Repentance takes away sin and restores our soul to have good health and so our soul prospers.

Reference: Isaiah 53: 10

It is time to repent, and time to receive. Repent for your soul to prosper and receive your good health and prosperity. Amen and amen.

~

LONGEVITY IS WHAT WE WISH FOR

Dear reader, the other day I heard a program about the Grey Eagle and how it has a lifespan of 120 years.

Reference: Genesis 6: 3

This bird has the life span as God planned for man. The way he cares for himself is in the way that his nature has taught him to enjoy his longevity of 120 years. He has a process after he is fully grown, he begins the process. This process is one that man would surely benefit from and one that God must have had in mind for a grown man from the very beginning. The 7 year process is fasting for 40 days. Perhaps God meant that for man every year also.

Back to the eagle, he must find a high hiding place in the rocks but still close to water. The process starts as he breaks off his claws, and pulls all his feathers out, and the last thing he does after that suffering, he breaks his beak so he cannot eat. He still can drink and get to the water bathing his sore body daily in the cool water and he sleeps. After this manner he rejuvenates himself and is like a new creature. That is how he lives so long in the wild. Let us look at what God has to say about an eagle, pertaining to man. God shows us how precious we are to Him as He Himself is represented by an eagle.

Reference: Deuteronomy 32: 11

God uses this verse to tell us how much He loves us. There is another verse of encouragement.

Reference: Isaiah 40: 31

In this verse God tells us how he wants us to be healthy and strong and stay that way. God speaks of fasting with the prophet Joel.

Reference: Joel 2: 12, 13

In these verses the Lord speaks of fasting and repentance as one act. An act of obedience; He says to look within our hearts and purify it from all evil. Fasting and prayer can be followed by blessings and favour from the Lord.

Reference: Acts 10:30, 31

Cornelius did not know of Jesus, he worshiped Jehovah, and God was pleased with Cornelius' sincerity, so He blessed him. Because of Cornelius fasting and prayers he and his whole house were truly blessed.

Reference: Acts 10: 44-48

The norm in those days of old that we read in the Old Testament was to fast and pray. The Israelites always came together, as faithful believers, understanding how partial God was to those who truly would fast and pray.

Reference: 2 Chronicles. 20: 2, 3

Now this kind of fasting is done when we need favour from the Lord. Fasting is not starving; it is cleansing the body and mind. We know that Jesus fasted 40 days in the desert. I don't think anyone should try that right off. Start off with a 3 day Daniel fast. This is very wise and very good for you.

Reference: Daniel 1: 12-15

A Daniel fast is mostly eating only fruits and vegetables for a certain amount of time, abstaining from dairy and meat products. Some people use the Daniel fast as a dieting method. This is also very healthy to lose weight. Others use it as their lifestyle and daily diet. I believe whatever your reason this fast is very wise and good for us twice a year. Creatures of nature, like the Grey Eagle follow an instinct that God has placed in them to fast every 7 years to live a long life. Man on the other hand has always had a choice of how to care for himself and how long he wants to live.

Reference: 1 Corinthians 3: 16, 17

Man can decide how long he wants to live.

Reference: Proverbs 3: 1-4

Dear reader, do you remember that when God put man in the Garden of Paradise? He instructed him not to eat one tree in the Garden. All God wanted was that man would respect and obey Him. Adam and Eve could have had an abundant life, but they listened to the tempter, the serpent. All that food and Eve's eyes went elsewhere, the forbidden tree was pleasing to her eyes. How true, we are so guilty, we eat things that are pleasing to our eyes, but are not good for us. We know better, but we don't do better. May I add, we eat more than we need, and that is not good for us. The unhealthy desire for food could easily be given up as Daniel did. This desire of overeating can decrease the length of our days and longevity. We have a God given understanding when we are not respecting Him or our temples. God said, "Yet his days shall be 120 years," we can strive for that, a long and healthy life, just think of the Grey Eagle and the sacrifices he goes through for his longevity.

Reference: Psalms 91: 14-16

David is speaking of Jesus. He is alive. This Psalm reminds me of my Lord and Saviour Jesus. His love for me, and how He died for me, in verse 16 it states, "With long life will I satisfy him and show him my salvation." The Grey Eagle struggles every 7 years for his salvation. We have Jesus and we don't have to struggle. We do have to follow His lead and His Word, and He will give us our longevity before eternity. Amen and amen.

~

IS IT POSSIBLE TO BE A GOOD CHRISTIAN AND NOT GO TO CHURCH?

How many times have you heard dear reader someone comment, "I don't have to go to church to believe in God." I have never said it, but I have heard many times. The reason I have never said it is because of the way I was raised in Christian Science, where church was your salvation. They did not teach salvation at the cross and the blood of Christ. So, what about the churches that do teach salvation through the blood of Christ, do they teach that only church goers get saved and go to Heaven? Some of them do. What is the big deal? If I'm saved and baptised, living a clean life as other Christians I know, what is the big deal about going to church? Today we can watch a good church on the television at home. The big deal is if you are not attending church weekly you are attending 'a lack' of your commitment to God. Paul writes about the church. You will have to have your Bible to follow the references.

Reference: Colossians 3: 16

Paul reminds us how we are to fellowship with one another. That fellowship is what we call 'church.' Paul conducted church in prison, he had a prayer-group, and he preached the Gospel. Paul continues in Ephesians.

Reference: Ephesians 6: 18, 19

The prisoners did not have much choice whether they could stay and listen or go. They stayed, got saved and baptised. Some of them were put to death and some were released to go on preaching the Gospel. So, what about us today if we do not put church at the top of our list of priorities every Sunday?

Reference: Hebrews 2: 1

That does not sound particularly good for a Christian to drift away from Christ. Here in this verse, we are told to "Pay more careful attention." Our attention must be directed to Christ and obey the Word of God. Lack of attendance in church is a form of disobedience. When we got saved, we made a vow; we made Jesus the Lord of our lives, which was also a promise. If we are not showing up in church on Sunday, we are our own lord, making our own rules and not regarding God's laws.

Reference: Hebrews 3: 12

When Adam and Eve made up their own laws instead of following God's laws, look where it got them, look where it got us. To ensure our steadfast position in Christ, is to hear the Word, "To what we have heard, so that we do not drift away," away from our first love of God. So, it is impossible to drift upward, if you are drifting down stream and away, heading for a waterfall and a rocky landing. When you drift away from church, you are drifting toward a dangerous destination; a rocky landing where you will end up hurt and suffer despair. You may be playing games telling yourself, "I am fine, I am saved and a believer that makes me a good Christian." If that is you, this is Paul's reply.

Reference: 1 Corinthians 10: 12

Balancing on a floating log drifting to a 1,000 ft waterfall is not a good place to be. Stop kidding yourself. Why blame the church or the music or the Pastor, why blame anyone but yourself? Are you too lazy to get out of bed or do you have to many things going on to take time for church? Just remember, "Let him that thinketh he standeth take heed lest he fall." You only think you're standing, you are falling. Falling into doubt, yes, doubt lodges in your thoughts and faith is gone as you drift away from church. You find that you start to question God's Word because you are spending more time listening to the world than listening to the Gospel. You are spending more time with unbelievers than with true believers in church. Jesus had a terribly busy life, always travelling from place to place and always spending a lot of time teaching His disciples. But Jesus was never too bus, to attend church.

Reference: Luke 4: 16

What did it say in this verse, "As His custom was, He went into the synagogue (church) on the Sabbath day." In other words, every Sabbath He attended church, because it was His custom. He did not let other things get in the way of going to church. Jesus and His disciples were faithful churchgoers.

Reference: Ephesians 5: 13

So, to close and answer the question 'Is it possible to be a good Christian and not go to church?' No, it is impossible to stay on a Christian walk with Christ and not attend church, "Giving thanks always for all things unto God." If you are living in a country where Christians are not persecuted, then that is your first thanksgiving that you have a church to go to this Sunday. Amen and amen.

~

OUR ADVOCATE

Dear reader I like to watch lawyers at work on TV. When we need a lawyer for some domestic or financial help, down deep in our hearts we hope this lawyer is a real Perry Mason. Alas at times we are disappointed, and the results are not what we hoped for and expected.

I live in Spain now and I have heard of erroneous cases in the Spanish courtrooms. But what about Christians, who will represent us when we come before the Great Judge at the end of our lives?

Reference: 1 John 2: 1 and 1Timothy 2: 5

As we put our faith in our advocate Jesus Christ. He will support us and stand up for. I repeat, He can only represent you, if you have faith in Him and have made Him Lord in your life. In other words, are you saved and born again?

Reference: Hebrews 9: 15

One more thing I would like to bring up is His superiority.

Reference: Hebrews 8: 9

Our advocate Jesus is not confined to a top suite in a high-rise on Main Street.

Reference: 1 John 2: 2

There is nowhere in the whole world, where we that are saved are not represented by our Heavenly Advocate Jesus Christ. Amen and amen.

OLD HABITS DIE HARD

So, my old habits had to go, and I had to concentrate on better speech, when speaking to the church. In our case we Dear reader years ago moved from Spain back to America. My environment had changed completely there in Florida. This revelation of mine is called 'Old Habits Die Hard' because there are a lot of people trying to get rid of old habits, and I am one of them. I had gone to Florida to marry my new husband, Allen known as Pastor Al. One thing he was concerned with was the way I spoke and the comments I made. He was an effective public speaker, and he wanted the same for me as his wife and partner behind the pulpit. On my website I have his tips, what not to say as a public speaker. So, to please him I had some stupid comments and speaking habits that needed to 'die hard.' Good public speakers do not use, "You know" every second sentence, or, "but" with "and da" to pause in their speaking, Allen thought these kinds of public speakers lacked in vocabulary skills and were unprofessional.

We believed in prayer, so we left it to the Lord to help break those old habits. I know that my problem may seem silly compared to the bad habit's others have like swearing, this is at the top of my list, and people just keep on doing it, they do not want to change. We all have friends that have bad habits that we recognised, but they do not. Then on the other hand we have friends that have good habits that we wish we had, and find it had to get into those good habits. Sometimes we make a judgement on others saying, "That is a bad habit, you need to stop that."

I believe most of our habits began when we were children. Most of our habits, good or bad, came from our parents or some we spent time with. Then also our grownups would say, "This is a bad habit, don't you start." I can remember my son always tilting his chair back and forth at the table. I was always afraid of him falling backwards. Well, he is now 30 and became a new father, after a few years he will be saying to his son, "Please don't tilt your chair, you can fall backwards." The boy will say, "but Daddy you it." My son will then learn, after 20 years, that bad habits die hard.

Jesus was born and raised in a country where certain groups of people were not recognised.

Reference: Luke 10: 30-37

In this parable from Jesus, He asks the question about loving your neighbour.

Reference: John 4: 6-9

This woman had the same habit from her parents and from her ethic group. She was accustomed to being shunned by the Jews. Jesus knew when He spoke to her that He was breaking the same habit and ethnic custom between the Samaritans and the Jews. The love of Christ was breaking the habit.

Reference: John 4: 10-14

When the woman heard what Jesus was offering her, she forgot about habits and customs. She knew she want what this Jewish Rabi could give her, and she wanted a relationship with Him.

Reference: John 4: 15-26

How fortunate this woman was, she broke the old habit and custom of her people, and found salvation with Jesus, she left her water pot and ran into the city. In other words, she left what she was doing, and ran to spread good news.

Can it be that some of our bad habits are keeping us from being saved or spreading good news with our friends and family? Perhaps some of your habits keep you from approaching certain groups of people and sharing Jesus with them. Who put their first foot forward at the well? The answer is Jesus. The one that has good news should be the one that makes the first move.

Old habits are hard to remove from our lives. With the Holy Spirit, we can kill off those old habits, that have prevented us from glorifying God. We need to remember; we are the examples of a good Christian. Are you putting off what God is calling you to do, because it is strange for you, and you are not in the habit of doing something strange? I do love this verse.

Reference: Matthew 6: 33

When we put God, His Kingdom, and His righteousness first, we may find many things change for us and our lives.

We have two steps to perform, step one seeks Jesus and, step two is to stand in the gap, where our bad habits have no entry into our new lives with Christ. The bad habits I needed to be free from, to be a better partner with my husband, pastor in the church, faded out of my speaking the more I seek the Holy Spirit. Amen and amen.

~

GOOD EXAMPLE

Dear reader I know you will want to read this, because we all are looking for good examples to follow. All good or bad examples always stand out among groups of people. Some examples we want to learn and some we want to dismiss. Good manners are what most parents try to teach their children. If they are families they live in a public class of society, then there are those who can go to private schools and take private classes for learning good manners. If their children are in public schools the teachings are confined to daytime classes. Then their good manners are expected to be taught to them with the parents. So a good example is good manners, but is that all they are? You will have to take your Bible to follow with the references.

Reference: Leviticus 20: 23

The answer is, "No," good examples do not just start and stop with good manners. He, God, is saying to Israel that He is displeased with the manners of other nations. He says, He does not want Israel to follow or commit themselves to those manners, because they disgust Him. Wow, is that the same for us also today? There are some nations and people that have manners and bad examples that are not good for God's people to follow. In Leviticus God is patiently teaching His people how He wants them to honour Him, in their homes and in the Tabernacle. He wants Israel to be a good example for other nations to follow. The Lord wants to teach His people His laws and statues, to honour Him and be good examples for other nations to follow. He does not want Israel to compromise with strangers or nations, worshipping false gods. The Lord was leading them closer to the 'Promise Land' that He was giving to Israel to be their nation. He knew of the false gods and evil that now lived there. He wanted them to be strong in their faith in Him and not turn away from Him when they encounter these strangers and false gods. Self-discipline was not a high point in the nature of the Israelites or in non- Christians today. Nations are still worshipping false gods and serving the evil of the sinner man. Paul gives us warning on how this can happen to Christians also. By following bad examples we displease God.

Reference: 1 Corinthians 15: 33, 34

Paul says Christians can easily make friends and have communication with those that serve false gods and not the Lord. They are deceived in to thinking they are being kind and good examples with good manners, but the evil and corrupt followers are lying to them and turning Christians away from the Lord. Let me make one example that is very much a part of my way of thinking. I am not pleasant around people that use bad language, cussing. Although I speak occasionally three languages the cussing can be different for the international words, I flinch when I hear them, I do not use or like hearing bad language, which is evil and belongs in hell. God says there is a form of good communication. How do you feel when the Name of the Lord or the Name of Jesus is used in cussing, anger, or humour or slang as well as how do you feel about those speaking such things dishonouring God, Jesus, and anything of the Spiritual realm of Heaven? In the book of Exodus God speaks directly to the Israelites and us.

Reference: Exodus 20: 7

We do not only have to watch our own language, but we must condemn bad language. It is evil and from hell. Now we are the Christians that must show the good examples with a vocabulary of words that please the Lord. And we can prayer for others that they will follow our good examples and watch their tongues. The Lord said that out of our mouths will come that which is in our hearts. When we use the Name of the Lord, we do so with humility and thanksgiving. Always remembering the Cross and Calvary. That is what Paul tells us in Romans. We can call out the Name of Jesus, believing in Him and repenting for our sins, then we will be saved.

Reference: Romans 10: 13

So, our good and best example to follow is Jesus. We should want to be good examples following Him. It is not easy to just hear or read what we should do. No, we need an example to follow, we need Jesus. We also need to be good examples like Him, showing compassion, patience, love and understanding to others. Perhaps we are so set in our bad habits and manners that only a good example, like Christ in His word, will wake us up to acknowledge the wrong example and path we are on.

Reference: John 13: 15, 16

When we look to the life of Christ, we see He is not an average guy in a crowd. How about us are we average men and women in a crowd? When are saved we are saints, ambassadors for Christ, we are not average people! We can be the best examples for those who do not know Jesus. Paul was not average, he was always being pointed out in a crowd, accused of following Christ's teachings. Paul's life was dedicated and committed to following the excellent example of Christ. He wanted the same for the church and for us.

Reference: 1 Corinthians 11: 1

Paul also said that all of us know how to follow his example. He was speaking to the church of Thessalonians.

Reference: 2 Thessalonians 3: 6. 7

Paul's example was how much time he spent, praying, speaking, and proclaiming Christ and the Cross, daily, in the temple, on the street or in prison.

He spoke to the Philippians, how they should be in fellowship and follow his example.

Reference: Philippians 3: 17, 18

Communication with others (unbelievers) was dangerous for the church, and all Christians. He said, "Take note," in other words, be wise who you commune with, and always follow his example and Christ's teachings. Today we Christians are being pointed out in the crowd. Paul's advice for the church is the same today, for us. We are watched and our good manners and good examples represent who we are. Paul also points out the bad examples in the church. He speaks to the Thessalonians. He says, they are idle, lazy, not busy, expect for their (busy bodies) gossip. He knew the comment, "The idle mind is the devil's playground." Paul knew what he was talking about and who he was talking to. Paul continued to say whoever did not follow his instructions, must be spoken to by the Pastor. So now we see the good and bad examples from Paul.

Reference: 2 Thessalonians 3: 11-15; Titus 2: 7, 8

This last reference from Titus is the best example for us to follow as Christians. Show integrity; be serious when sharing the Gospel, use proper language and good vocabulary so no one is offending or insulted. This good example will replace those bad examples that try to condemn Christians and worship false gods. I hope you have got some goodness out of this revelation and can share it with others. Amen and amen.

GET NAKED

Dear reader we're all a little guilty of impertinence and cover up. How we do go out of our way to please others? By speaking, acting, and doing what we think they want from us. We are a little false with our presentations and our representations, we not only use cosmetics to enhance our good features and cover up facial problems to look good, but we also use money, material things and of course the "buttering -up effect" to look good and be accepted in an environment we wish to be a part of. That is a part of presenting ourselves as best as e can. But what about the Lord, none of those pretences work on Him. Open your Bible to follow with these references.

Reference: Psalm 139: 15, 16

God knows us inside and outside.

Reference: Psalm 139: 17

So, we go on trying to please everyone and using our greatest efforts and expensive commercial products to make a good presentation, which I know about as a model when I lived in the States, everything was presentation. Then I met Jesus and He unmasked me and unclothed me, I stood there in tears running down my cheeks asking His forgiveness for my all my sins. Slowly Jesus started putting me back together as He had fashioned me and made me.

Reference: Isaiah 61: 10

So, the Lord wants us to be clothed and robed and decked in jewels and ornaments, but first and foremost He wants that we are to be beautiful for Him. He will present us to others as it pleases Him and where it pleases Him. In other words, if we give our lives to Christ and let Him decide our presentations and our representations, we cannot go wrong.

Reference: Romans 12: 1-3

Well dear reader I do not know about you, but I want to be good and acceptable and perfect in the will of God, so I will 'get naked' and let Him do His handiwork. Amen and amen.

~

BE NOT AFRAID

Dear reader I am not fond of long journeys and now I have been living in Europe 35 years, so returning to America is exciting and a little frightening. I am leaving my home in Malaga and relocating in Tampa with my new husband waiting for me there and travelling this long journey which will take me 15 hours. I have been praying about everything, leaving my home here in Spain, returning to America and getting married, but with all my plans and a little excitement I have forgot to pray about this trip. So, as I was now praying with the Holy Spirit, He reminded me of one of my favourite Psalms the ninety first one.

Reference: Psalm 91: 1-4

I find these verses remind me of a large eagle's nest, placed in a crevasse in the face of a high rock with young eagles nestling under their mother's warm feathers and her enormous wings covering the nest so the rain does not wet the babies. What a picture of safety.

As we have read in verse 4, "His truth shall be my shield and buckler." This verse is so full of God's protection. First, we have the truth. Our Lord said, "Know ye the truth and the truth will set you free." So therefore, I find the truth to be powerful. Second, we have the shield. The shield can protect us as long as we can hold it in front of us or move it from side to side protecting ourselves from getting harmed by the adversary. So long as we are strong, that is with the power of the truth, and the Word of God is our shield, we are fully protected. What about the times we are weak, and slow, unaware of the enemy ready to attack us? That is why we have the buckler or the armour.

Reference: Ephesians 6: 13-17

This armour of God covers us from the top of our head to the tip of our toes and should be put on daily at our prayer and quite time before facing the world. With this amazing armour nothing can harm us for we are fully covered and fully protected.

Reference: Psalm 91: 9-11

These verses tell us that the Lord our God has sent the Lord Jesus Christ to be our refuge, and, "His angels to care for us, in all our ways." When we have Jesus and his angels, "No evil shall befall thee."

Reference: Psalm 27: 1-5

In verse 4 it says, "One thing I have desired of the Lord, that I will seek after." I believe that 'seeking' to be research in the Bible, seeking after the Lord in His Word. This is where I find His refuge and His fortress, and it is there that I no longer have any fear or anxiety.

Dear reader did you know that the phrase, "Be not afraid," is found in the Bible365 times, isn't that comforting to know? In Psalms27: 1 it says, "The Lord is my light and my salvation, whom shall I fear?" We have nothing to fear as long as we stay in His light. In His light we can seek the face of the Lord.

These verses in Psalms are good chapters to dwell on if we are ever fearful. Psalms 27: 14 says, "Wait upon the Lord, be of good courage, and He shall strengthen thine heart, wait, I say unto the Lord." Psalms 51: 1 says, "Have mercy up on me O God, according to Thy loving kindness." Amen and amen.

∾

A HARDENED HEART

We have been studying the book of Exodus in our Bible study this month. The Holy Spirit has brought this comment to my attention.

Reference: Exodus 7: 14

When we first read this verse, we may think that it would be the Devil that had hardened Pharaoh's heart. But, that was not the case. God Himself hardened his heart. What does that really mean? How did that happen to an intelligent leader of a very prosperous nation? What happen is that God withdrew 'the things of God' from his understanding.

Reference: Exodus 9: 12

On Sunday, our Pastor always uses the phase asking halfway through his teaching, "Do you understand the things of God this morning?" God did not only harden Pharaoh's heart, but He also did the same to his servants. Therefore, there was no one in the palace that knew the truth about God, Jehovah the Great I Am, His power, His plan for His people. The Israelites were all in Goshen far away from the palace and the Egyptians where God was going to apply those horrible plagues on them and continue to harden their hearts. Moses warned Pharaoh what was to happen to him and his people, how the wrath of God was to come upon them, but with each warning and plague their hearts were harden even more against Moses and the Israelites. No, their ears were closed to the truth; they would not listen to the man of God. In fact, their hearts were hardening to the point of their own self-destruction. Before Pharaoh would let Moses and all children of Israel go, he let God destroy all the wealth of Egypt. Their land was barren, their cattle perished and their first born were dead. The Egyptian women gave all their wealth to the Israelites so that they would leave and then their men were drowned in the Red Sea. Egypt was desolate. How many times did God give the Egyptians a chance to salvation? Jeremiah explains the same problem Moses had.

Reference: Jeremiah 6: 10

God had visited Egypt so many times from the days of Abraham, Isaac, Jacob and then Jacob's son Joseph, who saved them from starvation as well as Israel. The leaders of Egypt and their inhabitants had seen how God's chosen helped them many times. They could see the blessing of God on his people no matter the tyranny that was put on them, they survived and prospered. The Egyptians could have turned to God and rejected the false idols. God had heard the cries of the Israelites for 400 years; this was long enough as this had fulfilled the prophecy.

Reference: Genesis 15: 13

God did not only want to see his children freed, He wanted to see their enemies destroyed. Therefore, he hardened the hearts of the Egyptians, so they would destroy themselves.

Reference: Exodus 14: 21

How important is our heart over our circumstances? I can tell you our circumstances have no power over us if our hearts are dedicated to God. God is in control.

Reference: Proverbs 4: 23

We can read throughout the Old Testament that God does harden the hearts of the enemies of the Israelites. God was displeased many times with the Israelites, in fact He call them 'hard necks' not hard hearts. They disappointed the Lord constantly, but He never rejected them in all their disobedience and idol worship. He punished them many times, although they always survived because among those that disobeyed God there were those who loved him and obeyed His statutes. Once again, we read in the book of Jeremiah.

Reference: Jeremiah 7: 25, 26

God hardened the hearts of the Egyptians until they were self-destructive. The Israelites hardened their own necks, turning away from the Lord, worshiping idols, and bowing down to false gods. The Jewish people have up to today the hardened necks; they have not yet turned back to God and repented for their father's sins. The sins of the Jews were dealt with over two thousand years ago when they crucified Jesus the Son of God. We know that one day they will repent, and they will bow down the King of Kings, Christ Jesus, the Messiah. The hardened heart is not only a thing of the past. Today many that were raised in the faith or at one time have given their lives to Christ have developed hardened hearts. Jesus was also concerned about the hearts of His disciples. Here we read where He challenges them.

Reference: Mark 8: 14-20

Jesus said, "What is going on?" You just got through feeding five thousand men and now you're worried about us here in the boat with no bread? Jesus was concerned about them losing the sight of God. He wanted His students, His disciples to understand 'the things of God.' Even today new-born Christians, that at one time gave their lives to Christ from their hearts Jesus would ask them, "What is going on, have you hardened your heart toward God and only concerned with your circumstances?" Remember not understanding 'the things of God' is the result of a hardened heart. Your heart does not harden all at once the way that Pharaoh's did. Oh no, first you stop going to your prayer group or Bible study, you have so many other things in your life, so you have not got time for those groups. Then because the family is all at home on Sunday, you can catch a church service on the TV in the morning, while you are still in your PJ's. But watching the church only happens when your family does not want to play golf or go to the beach; you must get up and get dressed early for those Sundays. 'The things of God' are seemingly less important to you every week and then every day. After a few months or a year, you have a hardened heart and no longer understand 'the things of God.'

Reference: Mark 6: 52

Do you have someone that has come to mind as you were reading this or is it
you looking in the mirror? We always have every opportunity to get back into
the fold and with our Good Shepherd, Christ Jesus.

Reference: Romans 10: 9, 10

These verses are the words from Paul, telling the hard hearted or backsliders
how they can come back to Jesus. With these verses in Romans, we find the only
solution to soften a hardened heart is to get back to 'the things of God.' Amen
and amen.

~

EXPECTATIONS

Dear reader, when you get up in the morning what do you expect to meet during
day? If you are a housewife like me you expect to do a daily routine and not
have many surprises throughout the day. If you go to school or work, then you
expect a regular day in the classroom or the office with very little changes during
the day. What if you got up and felt like wow, what a great day and how great it
would be if God moved in my life today? Or what if you got up in expectancy for
God to do something great for you today?

I like the story in the Bible when a man got up to a normal day and found his life
was completely changed in one day. His Name was Zacchaeus. You will have to
open your Bible to follow with these references.

Reference: Luke 19: 1-10

Zacchaeus was very rich, but not too popular with the community, being a chief
publican and tax collector. He had servants and a position of authority. He could
have demanded the soldiers to give him a front position in the crowd following
Jesus. Instead, this rich man stooped to the level of a young boy climbing a tree

to see a parade. Zacchaeus was rich and held an important position, but he was a man of small statue, so in his wealthy rich man's garb, he climbed a sycamore tree to see Jesus pass by. He had a great curiosity to see Jesus, what kind of a man He was, having heard all the good things they were saying about Him. Surely, he never expected Jesus to address him, or call him by name. Jesus even invited Himself to visit Zacchaeus house and to dine there. Zacchaeus must have hoped or expected if he climbed the tree something good could happen and oh, something marvellous happened. Zacchaeus life was completely changed. His attitude was completely changed, he repented of his cheating or stealing, which most tax collectors were known and hated for. He was so joyous when Jesus spoke to him, and came to his house for a meal, that he told Jesus that he would pay back with interest all the money he had stolen as a tax collector, he repented and believed. In verse (9) Jesus said to him, "This day has salvation come to this house, for so much as he also is a son of Abraham." Hallelujah, Zacchaeus was saved. If we expect something good to happen to us, we must also be in the right place at the right time, and to know and to listen to the Holy Spirit and obey. In our prayer time or through God's Word we can hear the Holy Spirit speak to us.

Reference: Joshua 1: 8, 9

The reason I wrote this revelation is because the Holy Spirit spoke to me last night. A brother in the church had asked for prayer for his sister who was having marital problems. He had asked his sister to come to church for prayer, but she denied him and answered, "I will come when things get better." That is when the Holy Spirit reminded me of Zacchaeus, he climbed a tree because in his heart he was hoping for things to get better, and he was expecting something good. Perhaps she is hoping for things to get better, but she was not doing anything in the right direction to get them better, she needed to go church and to read God's Word and pray. It was good that she had some expectation, but only when she moves in the right direction to get closer to Jesus would her expectation be manifested through the Holy Spirit. Her marital problems can be healed. Dear reader, I hope you know Jesus, so when you wake up in the morning, you are expecting something wonderful like a miracle. Amen and amen.

FEAR CAUSES FAILURE

Dear reader, today we are hearing in all the news broadcasts about earthquakes, terrorists and now we have C-19. So, I am writing about fear because I have seen and heard a lot about fearful people with all the tragedy around us. First and foremost, I want to comment on the phase 'an act of God.' I believe they are leaving out something. Let me put it this way, the actions of man against God results in God's acts. But let us not always blame God for the natural movements of our earth or the new epidemic with C-19. I have a sister in the church, she has her family in Japan, and when the tsunami swept through Japan, she was very fearful because there was no connection by phone, and it had been two days with no news of her family. My sister loves the Lord, and she believes He has cared for her family. She believes that as she prays daily for them that Lord has assigned angels to protect them. Although we prayed in the church and with many prayers for her family, my dear sister cried deeply with me and needed comforting and reassurance because she was still fearful. She knew that fear was overcome by faith and she was now giving thanks before she had any news from her family. She was encouraging her faith. We need to know what fear is.

Fear *(noun)*

It is agitation and anxiety. It is disquiet or apprehension or dread.

We can be very emotional and one feeling is fear. The definition is disquiet or apprehension: when we are fearful we are in a state of mind that we find that it is extremely hard to pray or turn our thoughts to the Lord. When I am fearful, I cry to Lord, I get loud and find I have no words of faith. I do not find it easy to show my trust in the Lord, nothing is easy for me. I am fearful and I just want the Lord to comfort me, to embrace me, protect me from whatever is making me fearful. I need Jesus to quieten me down and reassure me that He is there for me and will not leave me. When I am in such a state of mind, I need my faith encouraged, like my sister did by turning to the Lord and giving thanks so her faith overcame her fear. You will have to take your Bible to follow the reference.

Reference: Exodus 15: 16

There are times in our lives, when we are facing impossible, raging water and our enemy is pushing us forward into it. This is when we need to proclaim to the Lord in the same way Moses did in this verse. Although the difference is in this verse, they were all safe on the other side of the Red Sea and Pharaoh and his armies were all drowned in the Red Sea. The verse above is a part of Moses song in Exodus chapter fifteen where he sung to the Lord a song of thanksgiving. This chapter can be also our cry onto the Lord giving Him thanks when we are fearful, after all, we are His children also. Moses was not speaking of the fear of Israel, he was speaking of the fear God placed on the enemy, they would be like stones unable to move full of fear. Moses was saying that fear would come to the enemy at the same time peace would come to Israel. God purchased His people Israel, and Christ purchased us at the cross on Calvary. Therefore, Jesus always greeted over a hundred times in three gospels with a, "Fear not and peace I give unto you."

Reference: Luke 12: 32; John 14: 27

Jesus did not want His apostles and all that believed in Him to fail; He knew what trails they were about to meet in their endeavours to serve Him. The only way they would succeed was through their faith in Him.

So now we know what fear is. Let us look at what faith is:

Faith *(noun)*

A confident belief in the truth, value, or trustworthiness of a person, an idea, or a thing. A belief that does not rest on logical proof or material evidence.

Jesus plan was to build their faith with confident belief in the truth. In fact, the verse on truth confirms that.

Reference: John 8: 32

We may ask free of what? And, the answer is free of fear. If you have confident faith in the truth, how can you fear a lie? Faith even goes for the unseen. We do not have a Moses, David, or Jesus in person here on earth. We have faith that we can believe God, and we can believe in Jesus. We can believe God's Word whether it was written by Moses, David or if it was spoken by Jesus. We have the truth. It is by the truth that we are set free of fear, fear of a person or a situation that we are deeply concerned with. Perhaps it is our health, our finances, or a predicted storm. Whatever is causing our fear it will take us down to a failing position and we will not be able to move.

Reference: Matthew 8: 26

Now we are back to where we started, in a storm. In this storm there was a great wind, have you ever heard the phase, "He is full of hot air?" They are first addressing the Devil with his lies. The Devil does everything he can to deceive us. He blows winds to destroy God's beauty, to make God's children fearful. Here in this verse Jesus spoke to the wind, a stubborn wall of water that resisted and would destroy everything it touched, like the Japan tsunami. Jesus rebuked the storm, and it obeyed His command. The wind became a pleasant breeze that pushed their boat closer to their destination. The sea co-operated by cuddling the boat in smaller waves. The disciples were with Jesus in the boat. It was the storm that caused great despair for them until they turned to their Saviour. That is the same for us when we are facing a storm, whether it be the weather or another impossible situation, to end our fear and encourage our faith, turning to Jesus our Saviour.

Reference: Matthew 10: 28

Our success to follow Christ and serve Him relies on our faith in Him. Our failures occur when we rely on ourselves and the false idols and beliefs that the enemy presents to us just to confuse us and make us doubtful and fearful. Whether it is a great wind or a roaring sea or even a shaking situation when we think our world is fallen apart, we do not have to fail our God or ourselves, because we have Jesus. If we hold fast to our faith, we see our fears will fall away. After my dear sister turned away from her fears that same day, she had a call from her son, all was well with her family, and they were all safe.

Reference: Luke 22: 32

I love this verse where Jesus prays for us. He prays that we will not fail with fear, but we will succeed and be strengthened by our faith in Christ. Amen and amen.

~

EMOTIONS ETC

Dear reader, are you an emotional person? I am under certain circumstances, at times I can 'lose it' as we say. What we need to do is be watchful of our emotions because the Bible tells us that our emotions can be a foothold for the devil to work in our lives. How we determine what emotions are allowed is to name them and ask ourselves, "Is this and emotion that I would have in Heaven?"

Reference: Galatians 5: 19-21

These verses are really a mouthful. First Paul is saying do not give way to wrong emotions and attitudes that can only produce evil. Pornographic websites come under the sexual emotion controlled by lust, which is a dark evil. Fortune telling and horoscopes mess with our emotions and produce an evil lifestyle. Relationships cannot thrive with emotions and attitudes of jealousy or covertness and envy, which can also produce hatred. Hatred is like an open sore that grows and festers as it becomes like gangrene poison, that emotion is so strong that it rots away little by little your good character and you become a slave to that demon of 'hate.' Pride and selfishness are the two emotions that destroy all relationships. Finding fault with everyone and everything is an attitude which develops into an emotion, arrogance, and self-righteousness that brings on confrontation which is directly from the Devil's chamber. With these emotions and attitudes the results can end up with dishonesty, murder, and unnatural sexual desires and all of theses are governed by evil demons straight from hell.

Paul says, "Let me tell you again, as I have before, that anyone living that sort of life (with emotions and attitudes) will not inherit the Kingdom of God." So where do we go to for guidance concerning these emotions and attitudes and the demons that take control of our lives? Dear reader we go to Calvary, to the cross. There at the cross we can unload all this burdensome lifestyle, we need to be free of. We need a new lifestyle; we need to be born again and free of the demons that control in our lives.

Reference: John 3: 3; 1 Peter 22, 23

When we are born again, we move away from wrong emotions and attitudes, in other words we move away from the 'fruits of the flesh.' Our goal is to be filled with the right emotions or in other words the 'fruits of the Spirit.'

Reference: Galatians 5: 22, 23

How could we be in Heaven without love, our strongest emotion? Love is the foundation for all right emotions as well. So, let us go through them as we did the 'fruits of the flesh.' After love Paul has joy and peace. It is God's love that gives us His joy and peace through the Holy Spirit. Patience is an emotion that is a chore that man must work through and cannot successfully achieve without the companionship of the Holy Spirit. Kindness, goodness, and gentleness are fine emotions connected with love, but they only come slowly as we grow in the Spirit and become more faithful to the Lord every day. As we begin to produce these right emotions our whole character changes and we take more self-control over our emotions. Through all this growth in the Spirit our right emotions develop in us, so we become a better person that pleases the Lord.

Reference: Romans 8: 28

Paul puts everything into prospective, so we do not have to doubt our emotions to whether or not they fit into God's plans for us. The Holy Spirit convicts us, so we always know right from wrong. As we watch our emotions and take more charge over them, we share a better relationship with Christ and the plan He has for us.

Now that we have this verse (11) from Paul, we are assured an eternal promise from the Lord. Amen and amen.

~

ECCENTRICS

Dear reader, are you eccentric? That is what a dear friend called me yesterday. Well, I think I would like a clear understanding of what that is before I admit or deny being one.

Eccentric *(adjective)*
1. Departing from a recognised, conventional, or established norm or pattern. Synonym, strange.
2. Especially a person of odd or unconventional behaviour

Wow! That is quite a mouthful, in other words I am defined as 'strange.' As a Christian many times I stand out or stand back when others are indulging in something I do not believe I should join with. My idea as right or wrong perhaps is the reason I was called eccentric or strange. As I have grown from a babe to a more mature person in Christ some things do not appeal to me as they did earlier. I do have a confirmation in God's Word.

Reference: 1 Corinthians 2: 16

Thank you, Paul, for saying we Christians might be a little strange. The real confirmation is not in what we do, but in what we have.

In this verse Paul tells us we have a portion of the mind of Christ, we can think like Him. When we think of a portion, we think of Elisha, he was a student and companion of Elijah.

Reference: 2 Kings 2: 9

That was amazing for Elisha, to have that double portion; that portion he got is the one Paul was speaking of, "Portion of the thoughts and mind of Christ." That same portion he got is the same Holy Spirit we get when we are saved and born again. We can say, "Praise the Lord." Yes, I can rejoice and tell my friend, "Thank you for seeing the difference in me."

There are also the Medieval Latin eccentrics, not having the same centre. I know little about atoms and molecules and all those things. The one thing I do know is, there is a central part that controls the power of the atom. As for a person to be eccentric, they must have a different control centre than others. The power within them as within anything of a material matter must be the centre of their existence. All Christians must also have a centre of control in their lives. This control centre is what evolves through them, giving them power. The centre of the 'norm' is controlled by the environment around them. The centre of an eccentric is controlled from within be it good or evil.

Reference: Revelations 7: 17

The centre of an eccentric Christian is controlled from the throne of God. The Lamb of God (Jesus) is the atom of a Christian. I love that song, "Jesus is the centre." The Lamb of God controls the power of a Christian's life. The more focus the eccentric Christian has on the throne of God the more power the eccentric receives from Christ. An eccentric is also known to be extreme. The more extreme the eccentric is at the throne of God, the more extreme the Lamb of God (Jesus) will control their lives.

Reference: 2 Peter 1: 2-9

When Christ is the centre of your life after you are a new born-again Christian and a new creation, then, you may be considered eccentric, when you build a relationship with Jesus, and you get to know Him better through His Word. As you know Him better, He will give you, through the Holy Spirit, all you need to live a better life. He also shares His glory and goodness with us. The Christian that truly follows in the teachings of Christ and believes that the Bible is the unchanging Word of God, will undoubtedly receive the good life Peter was speaking of in these verses. By the same mighty power of the Holy Spirit that Christ has given us we inherit the 2 wonderful blessings He promised: for instance, the promise to save us from the darkness of the world around us and He will give us His character. There is no doubt that in the days that Jesus was on the earth there were only a remnant of followers that understood Him after the Cross and Calvary. Today those unbelievers that know little of the truth that Christ has taught through His Word, the Bible, are jealous, fearful and hate, eccentric Christians that focus their lives on Christ. There are also people who believe they are Christian's that take their place in the church but have no relationship with Jesus. Dear reader I would like to see all my friends and family have a relationship with Jesus, as born-again, focusing on Him and joining me with all of us that are eccentric Christians. Amen and amen.

∾

DISTORED ANGER

Dear reader how often is your anger justified? Seriously, if you make an account of your little outbursts, will you find 50% or 25% or maybe only 10% of them are justified. I think about 10% is about what we can honestly say is justified. I know you are thinking of others that need to read this. We all need to read it to see what the Holy Spirit must tell us.

Reference: Genesis 4: 4, 5

Was Cain's anger justified? The answer is, "No." I am aware that he worked extremely hard in the fields as he was a farmer not a shepherd like his brother. But he was in the wrong and his anger was distorted. He did not want to ask his brother for a proper offering to the Lord. So, he just harvests in something he thought would be a good enough offering to God. His offering was not good enough, God was not pleased, and Cain was angry. He was angry with God and his brother. He was jealous that his brother's offering was pleasing to Lord. He could have also offered a blood offering to please the Lord, but he did not, and he was not obedient to God's rules. The entire problem Cain had was he wanted to do things his way and not God's way.

Do you find that if things are not done your way you get angry? You do not think about how others may consider things differently than you? Oh no, you want it done your way, and when you think it is the best time for you. If it is not pleasing to you, you get angry. That is the human nature or in the Bible it is call the sin nature, the flesh. So how did God approach Cain when he was angry?

Reference: Genesis 4: 6, 7

God spoke kindly to Cain, but He also gave him a severe warning, "Sin lieth at the door." All Cain had to do was sincerely say he was sorry and repent and ask God for forgiveness. But not Cain, he was angry. He was not calm, he did not repent, and he felt rejected because of what he had done. God warned him, but Cain did not listen. Cain let the devil, the sin nature, enter his heart and his life. Cain was not justified for his anger; it was distorted and destroyed him.

On the other hand, there is a story in the Bible about Jesus getting angry. When Jesus got angry with moneychangers disgracing the 'House of the Lord,' His anger was justified.

Reference: Matthew 21: 10-13

Jesus did not make an unpleasant discussion with the moneychangers. He made one statement to justify His anger. When you are angry how long does it go on? Jesus' anger was not sinful; His actions demolished the sin in the temple that was dishonouring God. Jesus made it noticeably clear why He was angry.

Anger is allowed with self-control to rebuke sin or the flesh. We, as Christians, are justified to be angry with evil and sin, but to rebuke it and not entertain it.

Now we have a new story about distorted anger, the story of Jonah.

Reference: Jonah 4: 1-4

Jonah did not want to obey God. So, he ran away. He did not think the city of Nineveh was worthy of salvation. But God thought it was. At last, he did what God called him to do and the whole city of Nineveh repented and was saved. Jonah was angry with himself for all he had gone through for this city he didn't like. Why had God been so merciful with the people in Nineveh, and not with him? He forgot he had been disobedient and still he was alive from being in the belly of a whale. He was just angry about everything. So, he sat in the shade the Lord provided for him to sit and sulk. We only have one book of Jonah and this is how it ends.

Reference: Jonah 4: 4-11

In verse (4) the Lord asks Jonah if he is happy being angry? What silly question! How can anybody be happy and angry at the same time? The Lord asked that silly question for Jonah to see how silly he was in his emotion of distorted anger. As we continue with this story in verse (5) Jonah goes outside the city and sulks some more. Jonah was hoping that the city would finish with their worshiping in church and go back to their sinful behaviour. That way Jonah would be right, and God would have been wrong. Then in verse (6) once again God has mercy on Jonah and protected from the heat of the sun. Jonah was happy for the gourd, so he could rest. But in verse (7) God sent a worm to eat the plant and it withered. The coolness, the comfort and protection he had had the day before was gone. When you read the rest of the verses to the end of the book Jonah's anger was distorted. First, he was angry with himself for being foolish and having to repent in the belly of a whale, and then he was angry at God for saving Nineveh and all the people after they had repented. Then he was angry with the worm that took away his comfort. God had mercy on Jonah, but he was not merciful with himself or the people on the city. We have no more stories or books about Jonah, just his amazing experience, three days in the belly of a fish that was mentioned by Jesus when He told of what will happen to Him, three days in the tomb.

Reference: Matthew 12: 40

Jonah is never more spoke of as a servant or prophet; he must have stayed in the city or gone back home. There is no account of his repentance or his changing his attitude. As the book ends Jonah is still angry and feeling sorry for himself. I guess God just left him there sulking and in his distorted anger. God had mercy on Jonah, but Jonah was angry and therefore had to intention to have a good relationship with God. This story of Jonah is a good story for anyone that is always angry, spoiling fellowships and feeling sorry for themselves. A good reminder for all of us is that only 10% of anger is justified. In other words, 90% or the times someone is angry that is distorted anger. We can ask ourselves that silly question from the Lord, "Doest thou well to be angry?" Remember you cannot be happy and angry at the same time. Amen and amen.

~

MOLECH THE FALSE GOD

Dear reader I am so sad about these disgusting laws concerning abortion. I know that it is an act against the Lord and His Word. I have never written anything about abortion until now, when the Holy Spirit spoke to me last night. Enough is enough. Now I have started to read the commentaries connecting to today's abortions and the barbaric acts of idol worshipers in the Old Testament.

Reference: Leviticus 18: 21

So here are the spoken words of God to Moses. We know the Israelites were very weak and immoral in their worship; they were willing to follow the easy way with rituals as they saw with the Egyptians. The Egyptians had no morals, sin, sex, and human sacrifice was common in their rituals of worshipping their false gods. Even after leaving Egypt they met other idol worshipers and found their rituals inviting and entertaining. None of these false gods needed to be obeyed and respected as the Israelite's God Jehovah did, for that reason it was easier to follow the false gods.

Reference: Leviticus 20: 2, 3, 4

In the first verse God has said very clearly, that the burnt sacrifice to the god Molech was a "seed" a child. When we follow the agenda of abortions today, it is the "unwanted seed" or child that is their reason for the barbaric act of abortion. God is the creator of all life; human sacrifice is an abomination against God. It is sin against His Sanctuary and profanity against His Holy Name. He tells Moses that anyone of His people that partakes in such rituals should be put to death by stoning. This is His first warning. The Lord also says that He would turn away and cut off the Molech worshipper. Moses is told that this person or persons are to be stoned, that means the camp is to take them and stone them to death. The Lord continues, if they know of a person or persons that are worshipping Molech and do not expose them, they too will be cut off as well as their family. Now the warning is getting stronger, because not only the idol worshipper is to die, but anyone related or protecting the idol worshipper is to die. With these verses and warnings from God how can anyone recommend abortions? God was not just warning the people, He was ordering that stoning was the punishment for idol worship.

Reference: Deuteronomy 12:31, 32

I am bringing to the forefront the comparison of the Old Testament sacrifices and modern abortions. When the gods were being worshiped, the worshipers would burn up on their alters up to two hundred children. That is about the same number of abortions in a day at these legal abortion clinics in America.

Reference: Deuteronomy 12: 31

Once again God is saying that He knows all the abominations that are done publicly. These sacrifices are for all to see and for all to take part of. So who is He speaking to?

You remember that the Israeli men were all circumcised. That was a painful and physical act that God Himself commanded of them, to acknowledge that birthright as a Jewish nation. So God was speaking to those who had already declared that their God Jehovah was the God of Abraham, Isaac and Jacob. If so, what were they doing with this false god in the nation? What are we doing with false gods in our nation? "For even their sons and their daughters they have burnt in the fire of their gods." So here we are in our country sacrificing our sons and daughters our "unwanted child" because they are a burden or responsibility we do not want to have in the future. 1) Too many children in a family, (mostly daughters) was a good reason to sacrifice one to Molech, the same reason for many abortions today. 2) The child is deformed or has a problem that the parent does not want to care about so sacrifice it to Molech, the same reason for doing away with them in an abortion today. 3) The child was conceived in whoredom, it must be sacrificed to Molech, as well as the secret of its mother. Oh yes, this one is the best reason for an abortion in an abortion clinic which are thriving and getting rich, because of the "unwanted child" today.

Reference: Deuteronomy 12: 32

The Lord has made His commands very clear. He has instructed the people that they must observe His commands. The leaders in America and European countries have not observed God's commands; they have made their own laws and banished God's laws.

Reference: Deuteronomy 12: 30

We have no excuse, why we are letting the leaders of our nations lead us into sinful abominations against God. When we elect a leader, we need to acknowledge that they are God-fearing believers, and would not bow down to a false god. We have the responsibility to vote them into office. God said, "Take heed to thyself that you be not snared by following them." We need to find a way to banish abortion clinics. We need to have the right leaders to banish them.

Reference: Deuteronomy 11: 26-28

These three verses are very well known with Christians. Although, the false god worshippers are increasing and getting stronger each day believers are getting weaker, they are not standing up for their faith, they are moving back behind the crowd. The believers no longer believe, the intercessors, no longer intercede, the gospel is no longer preached from the pulpit and the children are no longer taught God's commandments in their homes or in their schools. Now what did God say? He gives us a choice; do we want His blessing or cursing? Well we have little chance for His blessing, with the leaders that do not honour or obey God. That goes for the churches as well. God has been taken out of the government, the community, the home, the schools, the workplace and some churches. Do you love God? To love God is to obey Him. If you love Him you want to serve Him and be bold and strong for Him. The nations need to repent, they need to close abortion clinics and stop abortions. "Go PROLIFE."

Reference: Jeremiah 26: 13

With this verse I close. Amen and amen.

~

ANTICIPATION

Dear reader some people might think that we Christians are a little nuts, when we say, "We have no fear of death." They might think we are trying to be tough. The world does not understand that once a person is saved in Christ, they are saved from fear of death. Perhaps this is very confusing for a non-believer. We do not say it because we fear death. Why do happy, joyful Christians always talk about dying? We do not talk about it because we fear death? No, in a way we welcome it. That sounds a little crazy, but we welcome it with anticipation.

Reference: John 14: 2

This verse in John confirms our hope in the future with Christ. We know that to live with Jesus is to live forever. That is a part of the reason for our anticipation, our expectant hearts. The other reason is for the first part of the verse, "In my Father's house there are many mansions." Not many Christians here on earth live in mansions. Most of us have an average income or pension and live in a two-bedroom apartment or house. Mansions are for the wealthy. So, after death new-born Christians are saved and go to Heaven, the Kingdom of God, to live forever with Jesus and His wealth is ours.

Reference: John 3: 16, 17, 18

This verse is the most well-known verse in the New Testament, by Christians, and non-believers who do not take it seriously. What makes people believe that God loves mankind, but they do not believe that He judges mankind? Even so it is in His Word, verse 17 we read very clearly how serious it is to God to see mankind saved, so serious that He sent Jesus, His Son to pay the ultimate price on the cross at Calvary, for mankind's salvation. In verse 18 we are condemned for not believing in the Name of the only begotten Son of God. Can it be so simple? Can our very life and death situation, our living in light or darkness be dependent on Jesus Name? How important is His Name? Jesus gave His disciples a prayer; we call the "Lord's Prayer." First in the introduction is, "Our Father," then what? Yes, it speaks of His Name, "Hallowed be Thy Name." At the same time Jesus speaks of His Father's Name, the Father speaks of His Son's Name, they are one. Jesus is our Saviour and Lord and we have the privilege to speak His Name. The reason I say it is a privilege is because we know that the Israelites would not call God by His Name, Jehovah, they feared His wrath.

References John 16: 26 and Matthew 18:20

Right there in your lazy chair you can be with Jesus, and He will take your every request to God Jehovah. That makes me feel like a true diplomat in the presence of a King. As commoners we need that anticipation of being in the presence of King Jesus. Although Paul tells us we are more to Him than commoners, we are His heirs.

Reference: Romans 8: 14-17

With John we read, "In my Father's house." Now we repeat it with new information we have from Paul. As adopted children of God, we now call 'the great creator of Heaven and earth and all mankind' our "Father Abba." When people casually repeat the "Lord's Prayer" are they aware of whom they are addressing? With great anticipation we know we are going to meet our Heavenly Father when we leave this world. In other words when we die, or maybe not, Jesus has something to say about this also.

Reference: Luke 17: 34-36

Jesus said that while we were doing our daily chores or sleeping in our beds that something of a miracle may happen to us, if not to us it will happen to others. "One shall be taken, and another shall be left behind." Paul explains this clearer for us.

Reference: 1 Corinthians 15: 51-53

Pauls tells us that we, "the elect," will be changed with the process of death or with the process of what we call "the rapture." When I speak of "the elect" I am speaking of whom the Holy Spirit has called to give their life to Christ. Those that are saved through the Blood of Christ on the cross and have confessed to be so. Knowing that this miracle, "the rapture," could happen at any time in our lifetime is so exciting. Our anticipation for the great event to come is accompanied with our joy of getting up every morning and getting on with our faithful lives. Wow, dear reader waiting and anticipating for that day "when my Jesus I foresee." Past, present, and future all of it is in the Word of God. All of it is in the Bible. One of my favourite verses in 1 John is like a "cherry on top." These verses top it all and fires up our anticipation for the future after death.

Reference: 1 John 3: 1-3 and Revelations 22: 20

And we wait His coming with anticipation. Amen and amen.

BREATHING IN AND BREATHING OUT

Dear reader, I would like to talk about a subject that is more comfortable when others do it with us. Forgiveness is a thing we find hard to do, but we always want it from others. We get angry because someone hurts us or is dishonest with us; perhaps there is an immoral or a criminal act that makes us incredibly angry. We then have the duty to forgive. Instead, we hold our breath with the anger in us and when we breathe out it has turned to bitterness. We breathe in anger and breathe out bitterness.

Reference: Ecclesiastes 7: 9 and Ephesians 4: 31, 32

We read here in these verses that forgiveness can be given from the mind and that is the way the world forgives; a decision is made to forgive, and the thought is a good one, to approach the person and ask their forgiveness. In most cases it is accepted, and a friendship or casual relationship is mended. The problem is with this type of forgiveness in the mind, the mind does not forget.

Therefore, the forgiveness does not last; the mind remembers why you were so angry and bitter. The forgiveness resigns, and you are back where you started, except the other person does not know what you are thinking. So, you have more of a problem, you are unhappy and try to cover it up, so they will not find out you were not sincere. Of course, you were sincere when you said, "Forgive me" but it went right out of your mind.

What is lacking in this kind of forgiveness is your sincerity from the heart which bypasses your mind. That is the supernatural forgiveness of Christ that is built from the foundation of God's Love. How could Christ forgive those accusers, tormentors that hurt Him so horribly, how could He forgive the associates that were killing Him on the cross, how could He forgive them? With every difficult breath Jesus took while hanging on the cross He could have breathed in anger and breathed out the hate and bitterness, but He did not.

Reference: Luke 23: 32, 33

There He was being mocked and tortured then murdered in excoriating pain, breathing in the pain, and breathing out forgiveness. This kind of forgiveness can only be manifested from the heart, the heart of God. When you, dear reader, become "born -again" that same heart will replace your old one.

Reference: Psalm 51: 10

The heart of God's Spirit replaces the heart of flesh, and you too can forgive as Christ forgave. And that sincere forgiveness will last in your heart forever. Amen and amen.

~

GOOD, BAD AND THE UGLY

Dear reader, I hope I do not have an attitude that makes others uncomfortable to be around me. This concerns me very much because I get incredibly stressed with people and their attitudes. I must search for myself in this area. I am now at that age where even if my loved ones, my family will come to me or speak to me and they have an attitude that upsets me. I must contain myself; pray through it so I do not afflict the same attitude on them. How about this prayer, "Please Lord do not let me do the same to other people as they are doing to me. Amen." I am sure these unpleasant attitudes abide in us, like an evil spirit. That doesn't mean those with an attitude are evil. Although it does mean that they or I have allowed the spirit to be a part of our being, our character. This can be an extremely sensitive theme to talk about.

The only place to acquire the right information about attitudes whether they are good, bad, or ugly is from the Bible.

Quoted from Questions.com
"An attitude is a hypothetical construct that represents an individual's degree of like or dislike for something. Attitudes are generally positive or negative views

of a person, place, thing, or event- this is often referred to as the attitude object. People can also be conflicted or ambivalent toward an object, meaning that they simultaneously possess both positive and negative attitudes toward the idem in question."

Reference: 1 John 4: 1

Beloved, do not believe every spirit, (hypothetical construct) but test the spirits (that represents an individual's degree) to see whether they are from God (of like or dislike for something). I would like with all respect to change a few words from John's verse. We are speaking of attitudes which I have already written above can be an evil spirit. John wrote, "Do not believe them," and I will add this "do not receive them." The question is, "Did God create man with an attitude?" Did God create man with an hypothetical construct?

Reference: 1 John 4: 8

Yes, He did create man with an attitude of love, that is how He placed the (hypothetical construct) and He gave man (an individual degree of love) so to have the attitude of love that God created in us is to (represent the degree of His love in our individuality).

Reference: Genesis 31: 2

Laban was jealous of the success that God had given Jacob. The enemy was Laban's jealousy. Therefore, the love Laban had for his son-in-law, Jacob, had changed. Remember the only attitude that God created in man was love. So, the evil attitude of jealousy caused Laban to lose his relationship with Jacob, his daughters, and grandchildren. This kind of a bad attitude is easily developed when the spirit is not tested as to where it comes from. If Laban had tested this spirit of jealousy and rebuked the evil attitude, he and Jacob's good relationship would have continued.

Reference: Daniel 3: 19

Once again, an attitude of a person that had a good relationship is turned to hatred against their friends. How did this happen? The same way, as with Laban, listening to an evil spirit, the evil attitude that was based on jealousy. The governors of the king were jealous of God's faithful children and the favour the king had for them. So, by being weak and not testing the spirit of where this information has come from, the king turned his love attitude to hate and anger. As Laban had developed a bad attitude against Jacob, so too the king became furious, he had an ugly attitude against God's faithful children to the point wanting them burned up.

Paul writes to two different parties in the book of Ephesians chapter 4. He is speaking to the believers and the unbelievers, in others words to those with a good attitude and those with a bad attitude which can also be an ugly attitude. We can go to the fourth chapter of Ephesians, where all three are mentioned. Paul begins with the unbelievers, their bad or ugly attitudes.

Reference: Ephesians 4: 17-22

Starting with verse 17 the first party is the Gentiles, the unbelievers, they are the ones with a bad or ugly attitude. Paul says their thinking is based on themselves and all they can gain from their own endeavours. In other words, an evil spirit of selfishness and pride is behind their attitudes. In verse 18, Paul continues with the evil attitudes of the Gentiles. Their evil spirit controls them and has changed their hearts to stone. God created them to love Him first, but they have no love for God. They live in darkness with only the desires of the flesh, but there is hope as we now come to the second party which Paul was writing to. Verse 20 is where there is hope. Hope for the Gentiles; hope to change their evil hearts and attitudes. Hope for their salvation, which will bring them out of darkness into a life with Christ and a good attitude in themselves.

Reference: Ephesians 4: 22-24

Paul needs Christians to witness to the Gentiles. He needs them to understand that it is from hearing the Gospel that their lives and attitudes would all be changed. The evil spirit that was always interfering with their good attitudes would now be out of their lives and hearts, because the Christ like attitude will take control. They will be new creatures in Christ. Their thoughts will no longer be on just themselves, now they will be focused on Jesus. They would be new creations, righteous and holy. Only with a Christian's good attitude on Jesus, could they bring the light of salvation into the darkness of the Gentiles. This was Paul's goal and what he wanted to teach them. Paul exhorted the church to develop six attitudes to be better Christians and witnesses of the Gospel.

Reference: Romans 12: 1

1. Put God first. Paul wants his brethren to develop these six attitudes, because he himself has suffered, and know what they may have to face in the future.

Reference: Romans 12: 3

2. Humble yourself. To be humble does not mean to be weak. Paul wants his brethren to be strong, but also humble, not show themselves to be proud. What have they to be proud of? They did not go to the cross at Calvary, and they did not die there. Only through their humble hearts can they be good witnesses for Christ.

Reference: Romans 12: 20, 21

3. Bless your enemies. How difficult it was for Paul in prison for so many years, and yet he did just that. His prison guards and others in authority were blessed by his presence. His life in prison brought him to his greatest witness in Rome, that was his goal and he reached it.

Reference: Romans 13: 1

4. Submit to Authority. Paul made it clear to his brethren that the law was to be respected and those positions of authority were to be respected.

Those sitting in authorial positions were to be included in their prayers. This was and is a difficult area for all of us, even today we struggle with our leaders in our nations and in the world.

Reference: Galatians 5: 16

5. Live in the Spirit. As the Holy Spirit called us to Christ and took up lodgings in our hearts, our minds, and our lives, that same Spirit we walk with daily. That Spirit entered our lives replacing the evil spirit that had been in control of us. The Holy Spirit is what changed our ugly, bad attitude into a loving, caring, good attitude. The problem we have is to keep that good attitude. The solution is walking daily with Christ and refreshing our spirit with Him. I too want to have a good attitude that I believe can develop in me and in us. With these six attitudes we can surely bring glory to God and be a strong wittiness for Christ. These six attitudes can change our lives.

Reference: Philippians 4: 4-6

6. Be filled with joy. To be filled with joy is also difficult attitude to have all the time. But to help us in this area is to remember our Saviour Jesus, the Cross, and what He did at Calvary for us. Then it will not be difficult because our thankful hearts will also be filled with joy and a good attitude. Amen and amen.

∽

KEEPING THINGS IN ORDER
IS NOT AN EASY TASK

How hard dear reader do you find keeping things in order in your home, office, or even in your life? Personally, I find it hard in all these areas. The reason is I see the cloudier not only the dust. I want everything neatly in drawers and cupboards, where I can find anything I need blind folded. Living alone that should be no problem, but I still have a problem to have things in order. Order starts with God, looking at His creation everything is in order .

Reference: Isaiah 38: 1-7

If the Lord had spoken to me to get my house in order because my time on earth is ending, where would I start? I would think how can I change His mind? Have I done something to displease the Lord? How can I repent and change His mind? I would check all my cupboards and drawers to see if there could be anything in my home or office that would be displeasing to Him? What is going on in my life, friendships or social life that could displease the Lord? I know there is no one that has order like God. Everything about God is order.

Reference: 1 Corinthians 14: 33

If we have any knowledge of the universe, we have a slight idea of God's order. The sun in the centre and nine planets revolve around it. What would happen if God took a day off and one of the plants did also? If that did happen there would be chaos and discord in Heaven and earth. As well as something like that would reduce God to be like man. Oh! No, God is perfect, all He does is perfect and all He has is perfect. Keeping His universe in order glorifies Him.

Now what about us? The story of Hezekiah, God was telling him to prepare for his death. He was on his death bed, but he did not want to die, so he approached God to change His mind. The reason he believed he could change God's mind, is because he knew he had been obedient and did not deserve to die so young.

Although God had said to him, "Get your house in order." Hezekiah had already done that, he repented, he worshipped the Lord and he loved the Lord. When you read the story, you will like the way he approaches God and God does change His mind.

Reference: Isaiah chapters 38 & 39

After reading those two chapters how would you respond to God's message to Hezekiah? Seriously discord and disorder is a form of death. What joy derives from such things? What peace and contentment can exist in disorder?

Reference: 1 Corinthians 14: 40

I have hobbies and I have difficulty keeping those things in order, always trying to put things back in their proper places. Sometimes things get piled up, and I do not know where I am in the middle of it all. I believe that there are people who experience the same thing in their lives. They are in so many tasks that they never finish one correctly. Perhaps they are a wife, mother or husband, father, having so many responsibilities they fear the outcome. That would be a particularly good time to ask grace from the Lord. A good way to acquire order in your life is to read a verse from the Bible and pray. These should be number one on your list of 'to do's.' I always had a 'to do' list when I had a family, in fact my boys would always say every Saturday, "Mama, hope the list's not too long, we want to go out this morning." Praise God they always knew, number one was morning Bible reading.

Children have a lot to keep in order in their lives today, other than studies; they have sports, and other activities that press their lives into discord. Too much of a good thing is not good. When parents find time in the morning, before going to work or sending the children to school, to read a daily verse and have prayer, their children's schoolwork goes smoother, and the day runs more peaceful for the whole family.

Reference: 1 Corinthians 14: 33

It should not be only God that Paul is referring to, it should be us. Keeping order in our lives is like a game board, you begin with the fist move on start. That square is named "Daily Reading & Prayer." Then the day or game gets interesting. Let us start the game. What is it you have been looking for and still have not found? You remember seeing it somewhere in a drawer or in the closet. Why not get your house in order, God knows where it is, ask Him? How are your finances? Do you have order in your finances; are you a good steward with them and a good tither? God knows what you need ask Him. This is a good game as you follow the rules you will always be a winner and have that joy and peace in your life. Amen and amen.

~

MARRIAGE A HOLY COVENANT

Dear reader I do not like the expression 'partnership' referring to married couple. Where in the Bible was a married man and woman referred to partners? They were called husband and wife in Holy Matrimony. Paul speaks of a partnership with Titus.

Reference: 1 Corinthians 8: 23, 24

Two brothers in Christ or sisters in Christ are the partnerships God wants for His disciples. When there is marriage between a man and woman He wants and expects a different relationship to evolve. As I was growing up, I cannot remember my mother or my father calling the other a 'good partner.' The first time I had heard that terminology used was when I moved to Spain and met an English couple in church. I believed they were a married couple, they resided in the same house and their conversation and actions indicated that they were married, to my surprise they informed me they were partners. Therefore, in my little 'pea brain' I thought they were in business together. They lived together many years and had children, to make their family. Now partnership takes the place of Holy Matrimony.

Reference: Genesis 5: 2

Boy meets girl they are blessed. To begin we must let God be the matchmaker, we must trust Him to make the right choice for us. The Lord wants us to be content and fruitful, be satisfied in our homes with all our needs met. Conducting our lives to be dependent on Christ will be reward spiritually, physically, and materially. Paul had to answer so many questions from the church concerning marriage.

Reference: 1 Corinthians 7: 1, 2

Paul wanted the brethren to live pure lives in the church. It would be good if we were as concerned about purity in our churches today, as Paul was in his day. He also wanted the church to understand the spiritual area of marriage. In those days, a Jewish man could divorce his wife because she burned his breakfast, or not give him children, if she were getting too old and not pleasing to him any longer, he could divorce her. His vows meant nothing, there was no holiness in their marriage, no sacrament between them. Paul wanted the church to know how Christ wanted married couples to be wholly committed to one another, for life.

Reference: 1 Corinthians 7: 3, 4

The first part of verse 4, "the wife hath not power of her own body, but the husband" was exactly what Jewish men wanted to hear. But Paul continued, "and likewise also the husband hath not power of own body, but the wife." Men want to be kings in their castles, and they should be, by the way they treat their wives as queens. The church thought that Paul was making it difficult for a man to live according to God's rules in marriage. He wanted the church to be stricter, more disciplined with married couples. Those same rules apply to our church today also. Paul gives us a list of rules to control a holy family.

Reference: Ephesians 5: 20-25

The reason I included verse 20 is a little reminder of giving thanks to God and your spouse. Then the serious verse 21 is about submission. Submission to each other and to God. Submit to your spouse as well as to God. Through your love for God, you are filled with love for your spouse. Verse 23 is the verse that is hard for men to understand, how can they act like Christ? Personally, I do believe that my husband is the head of our household because I want it that way. I believe a man should handle the business in his home, if he is capable. As well at the same time he should not do anything concerning his home without informing his wife, no secrets. The man needs to be strong so his family can rely on him. When a woman gives her hand to her husband, she too will have to learn to be the wife that submits herself to her husband in all matters in their home. Marriage according to God's rules is only possible with Christ as the head of their lives.

Reference: Proverbs 31: 23, 28

How lovely this verse is, her husband is so respect among the elders, because they know, how he runs his household. This verse is written for a happy wife. She supports him at home, at his work and his ministry. When the elders come to visit, they are aware of the love and spiritual environment in this home with a happy wife. Now we come to the last verse in the reference in Ephesians 5: verse 25. Christ gave His life for the church, are husbands to give their lives to their wives? Yes, that is what the verse is saying, that is the Holy Covenant of marriage to give your life to your spouse. Now we will go a little deeper into marriage. There is such a thing as a 'broken marriage' which happens when there is a strong disagreement. Paul has something to say about that also.

Reference: Ephesians 4: 31, 32

Paul goes right to the point of what could be the cause of a broken marriage. Why would a beautiful Son of God put Himself through Calvary and the cross to build a relationship with us? The same way we want to build a strong relationship with Christ daily, the married couple must be building a strong relationship with their spouse. Christ forgave us our many sins; we must forgive others their many sins. The Holy Matrimony is built on man and wife that love each other as Christ loves the church. Man and wife that love Christ can complete God's plan for the Holy marriage. I hope that if you are in a 'Partnership' you will repent and turn your life around, to follow God's plan for man and woman, God's plan for Holy marriage. Amen and amen.

~

BELEIVERS IN BONDAGE

Dear reader I want to start with a Bible verse.

Reference: John 8: 32, 33

Jesus was speaking to His followers; they were all believers. In fact, here you see they believed themselves free. Well maybe they were not looking at all the Roman soldiers on the streets listening to every word to condemn some one of tannery against Caesars house. They had forgotten about the bondage of 400 years in Egypt or in Babylonia. "Abraham's seed were never in bondage to any man."

Believers believe themselves free because they are saved. But what is happening in their churches? The truth is not being taught in some of the churches, so these believers cannot be free because they are not getting the truth in their churches. Therefore no one that is not hearing the truth can be free. Believers saved by the Blood of Christ and reading their Bible but attending a church that is not teaching the truth from God's Word are not free.

There are teachers and holy priests that did nothing but study the prophets and Torah. Yet they could not teach the truth, because they had the truth in the temple every day at three o'clock, but they could not accept the truth. Like philosophers the Priests, Pharisees, and Sadducees all taught the people, but they never taught them the truth.

Reference: Luke 18: 10-13

Now let us look at these two men. The Pharisee is truly trying to convince God that he was telling the truth. The publican also is praying to God, but he is speaking the truth. Well of these two men who do you think is free? Oh! Yes, the publican was free. The Pharisee was bound to his convictions to God. The publican was bound to God. That was right when the Pharisee said to God that he was not like the publican. The Pharisee loved himself and all that he was able to do to enlarge his position in the temple and the city. The publican loved God. The Pharisee was a believer and a hypocrite; the publican was a believer and redeemed.

Reference: Romans 8: 14, 15

It is true, dear reader, the root of bondage for a believer is fear. When Jesus came to the disciple's house, He always greeted them with these words, "Fear not." Jesus knew that fear would hold them in bondage, physically, emotionally, and spiritually. The heart is where fear takes root. From there blossoms jealousy, deceit, suspicion, dishonesty, and how much more all because of fear in one's heart.

Reference: Romans 8: 15-17

As little children we are no longer fearful in the arms of our Heavenly Father. I love to share this with you. My boys were very small when their father was offered to sit in a small airplane flying over our community. At the time we were staying in our cabin on the island for summer. He said he would love to go but he wanted to take his two young boys with him. His friend said, "Yes, there will be just enough in the back seats." So off they went home afterwards my neighbour asked them if they were afraid up there? "Oh no!" My five and four year old replied, "We were with papa." That dear reader is the kind of relationship our Heavenly Father wants us to have with Him.

Reference: Galatians 5: 1

As a believer we should not be in bondage, we should not be fearful, we should be free. As we break the chains of bondage, we grasp hold of our freedom through Christ Jesus.

Reference: John 14: 6

There you have the truth now, the truth that sets us free. Amen and amen.

~

CONTROLLING SPIRIT

Dear Reader, to start this we will go direct to a reference.

Reference: Galatians 5: 1

A controlling spirit is found in Christians who want things done according to their concept of what is right and wrong. A person under the manipulation of another person that has a controlling spirit can be in two mind sets, first rebellion, and second subjection. In both cases the controlling spirited person slowly wears down the other person or persons to a state of frustration and depression. Paul describes this as a 'yoke of slavery.' A person with a controlling spirit can get angry and terribly upset if they do not see everything going their way. In fact, they believe 'my way or no way;' they are not open to suggestions that any other way would work. They must be in control to be comfortable.

Reference: Romans 1: 17

The controlling spirited Christian takes so strong a control over another person that this person struggles with 'faith.' When both are Christians and close to each other as in marriage or in a relationship and they attend church together and pray together the controller will always manipulate the environment, so that the weaker of the two will believe that revealing their desires are selfish and self-centred. The weaker person will be subject to the control of the controller, believing they are respecting them as a Spirit filled leader. Their faith falters from God to the person in control and leading. Therefore, to regain their faith only in the Lord, they need to be separated for a season, if possible, whether they are family, married or their church leader. The separation needs to be an agreement not an argument. Both parties need to search their spirits and hearts to uncover their faults. They need to put more trust in the Lord and confidence in their faith with Him only.

Reference: Genesis 25: 29-34

Jacob had the opportunity to share his meal with his brother. He took that opportunity for his own benefit and his own gain. He did not offer his brother food because he was hungry; he offered him stew as a tool to make a deal. Controllers are always looking for a deal. They have little to offer others without seeing something for themselves in return. This is how a controlling spirit enters another person life with a deal. A controlling spirited person has few friends and is quite lonely; therefore they are in need of a relationship, a close relationship such as marriage. In such a Christian marriage the controller is the man or the woman after a time in the marriage other loses their independence being solely dependent on her other, in the belief they are honouring them in this manner. Families can also be manipulated my other family members and workers by their bosses. In any case the Christian controller will believe they are following God's will for themselves and others in lives. They will believe that their dealings with others in which they always benefit from, are blessings from the Lord, instead of their own selfish control.

Reference: 1 Corinthians 13: 5, 6

In this verse Paul is referring to Love. A Christian controller honestly believes he or she love others. But they have little affection shown to others. Physical contact is a seldom event or unfortunate event with a controlling spirited person. Christian controllers find they are more content with themselves and the Lord than with other Christians around them. It is extremely hard to share with them at any time. Although they are Christian, they are easily angered. They find little time to reward what others are doing right, but they find a lot of their time to pick out wrong things which they record for future references.

Reference: 1 John 4: 18

Controllers find it extremely hard to be disciplined or corrected even out of love. Their desires overtake their wisdom, and, in many cases, they make big mistakes. They expect gratification for all the energy they use controlling their homes, work, relationships and their church. It is awfully hard for a controller to be denied or told, "No." It is extremely hard for a person who wants to be an independent thinker to overcome fear of a controller; this fear is the punishment John was speaking of, and to Christians.

Controllers do not find it easy to socialize, but they like attention from others. On the other hand, they are unsure of the attention they get. Perhaps the attention is based on fear, guilt, dependency, and they will put love on at the end of the list.

The Christian controller is always isolated and at the same time afraid to be isolated and lonely, not fully understanding the reason for their feelings. Controllers are aggressive and yet intuitive, they can make great progress in arts, science, education, and ministry. They advance quickly and usually become leaders.

Reference: Genesis 32: 22-24

Jacob was a strong leader; he was a rich man, with wives, sons and many possessions that made him a rich man. He had always been in control, he had always been an aggressor, but now he was fearful and about to meet his match.

Reference: Genesis 32: 24, 25

Jacob was alone and still wrestling with the Lord, until the Lord made him a cripple. When a controller is broken God can use him. Jacob now was broken and ready for his blessing. Jacob was now a broken leader and ready to lead a nation, given a new name Israel. In other words, controllers have a future with God when He is the only one in control.

Christian controllers are not to be judged by other Christians. But they can be changed. When one person is being manipulated by a controller they are under attack and believe themselves to be facing an army, with no weapons to fight them. After years of fear and under control of their enemy, the Israelites turn to the Lord. After years of a controlling spirit in the family or work, in your marriage or in church, prayer is the answer to be free. The controller needs deliverance from a demonic spirit, perhaps God will break them, heal them, or separate.

The Israelites had to admit, "We don't know what to do?" To admit and rebuke the spirit of a controlling person is the first step to freedom and deliverance. Only keeping your eyes on the Lord and not the controller will you overcome them and still have them in your prayers.

Reference: Psalm 118: 23, 24

Praying for something to change in a relationship, both persons have things to do; the controller to repent and the other person to forgive, these two processes may take years of prayer. Although these two people love each other the demonic spirit of the controller must be cast out with full deliverance so love can rule. They can rejoice feeling the chains falling away and giving them both freedom and a new life in the way God first planned for them. Amen and amen.

LOVE YOUR NEIGHBOUR AS YOURSELF

Dear reader, for half of my life I did not love myself, and then I met Jesus. I committed my life to Him, everything changed, and I was baptised and became a member of a wonderful fellowship. Everybody was so nice and always had a pleasant smile as well as a comforting word.

My whole family found a better and more joyful lifestyle within the Church. My lads were in Sunday School and my husband and I were within the Church services three times a week. How we looked forward to going to church. At the end of the year, we were helping in the church and moved into the apartment upstairs over the church. "Wow," you say, how fortunate you were. Oh yes, I agree we loved doing what we were doing. Although I always had an inferiority complex, it's not normal for a model from Houston. But it is true; I did not love myself and found things wrong with me all the time.

I was in a new country, with a new language, so I was always looking at the other wives and mothers; I was trying to follow their examples, thinking they were better than me, at everything. A new-born Christian telling everyone how Jesus had died on the cross and His blood had washed away all my filthy sins, yet when I looked in the mirror I had a problem, I did not like what I saw. Jesus loved me, but I did not love me. When I got saved, I loved everybody, I couldn't do enough for anybody, I thought I was obeying the Golden Rule.

Reference: Luke 10: 25-28

How can I love the Lord with all my heart, soul, and mind, and still think He made a mistake with me? To love me is to agree with God, to honour His perfection, His creation and imagination. It does not make any difference what I see in the mirror, I belong to the Lord, I am His, if I do not love me, I do not love Him. A model is very self-conscious of her looks. Now I have hit the big sixty, I am still self-conscious, but not of my looks, now I am conscious of my relationship with God. God loves me, I love me, and that is why I take good care of myself now, so I can do more for God. Now I know how to love my neighbour with the same measure of love I have for myself.

Thank You Lord that I am who I am. Amen and amen.

~

MICAH'S HOUSE

Dear reader I have just finished reading about a man named Micah in my Bible Study. As you know some of the judges that governed Israel were not all worshiping the Lord. Some of them worshiped idols. Micah was also an idol worshiper, although he knew the commandments and Moses' laws. It was his mother that took costly coins of silver and fashioned the idol and placed them in a sanctuary in their home.

Reference: Judges 17: 3-5

Sometimes it may be easier to make an idol and bow down to it, than it is to be obedient unto God. So that is what his mother did, and he just follows along with her receiving idols, rejecting the Lord.

Reference: Judges 17:6

From the verse above it sounds like the country we are living in. Our government takes no heed to following the Ten Commandments or God statues.

Reference: Judges 17: 7, 8

Micah was an Israelite; he knew that Levites were the chosen tribe of Priesthood. Therefore, he thought that he would have more success as a leader, if he had a Levite priest serving in his sanctuary.

Reference: Judges 17: 9-13

Do you see what Micah was trying to do? He was trying to trick God, by bringing this Levite priest into his house, God would be pleased. Foolish man, deceitful man, disobedient man, thinking he can cover his sin, by halfway being a good Israelite. Micah states, "Now know I that the Lord will do me good, seeing I have a Levite to my priest." This makes me shiver, when I think how many churches there are saying these very words, "We know God is going to bless us, because we are trying to be obedient most of the time." And, "We are going to try to keep the Ten Commandments, most of the time." Sorry, but none of these churches will impress God at all. Remember, He is a jealous God, He wants all our attention, all our time, all our obedience and all our love, and with it He offers us nothing, not even half of something, got that? We are finished with this foolish man Micah.

Reference: Judges 18: 17-20

Here we have another foolish attempt to correct a miserable situation. The Levite priest, who has been getting food and lodging with Micah is now being offered a better deal, he now can be a priest to Israel as he was born to be. The Danites only robbed Micah's sanctuary of all the idols and other precious objects to set up in their own sanctuary at Shiloh, and now the Levite priest was serving them as he had served Micah before.

Reference: Judges 17: 6

When I visit a new church, I want to know what their doctrine is, what they teach, what they believe, and what they live by, and if the congregation agrees. My concern is about a Levite priest but not the publican prayer warrior. The church I want to attend is built on the teaching of the Cross and a foundation of prayer. Micah's house was filled with costly things that surely were appealing to those that wanted to worship them. Micah's Levite priest made his sanctuary complete.

There are many churches that use a great deal of money, to make the sanctuary appealing to their congregation. These churches also believe that a Levite priest, or in others words, a leader that has an office full of Certificates of Achievement from well-known Bible College. They make the same statement of Micah, "Now I know that the Lord will do me good, seeing I have a Levite to be my priest." Moving on to another group of deceitful churches such as the one Paul speaks of in 1 Corinthians.

Reference: 1 Corinthians 6: 9, 10

The church that allows homosexual as members of their church and practise this immoral lifestyle has no regard for God's plan of creation, man, and women joined in holy matrimony as man and wife. Sadly, these evil gatherings, group together in the so-called United Church. They are like the idol worship in Micah's house. Micah worships graven images and the United Church worships the flesh and their sins. These churches are now growing by the thousands. They carry a Bible, sing traditional hymns, and preach a sermon in their fellowship. They are devoted to the flesh and their evil lifestyle as Micah was devoted to his idols. Micah thought some good would come to him, if he brought a Levite into his house of idols. The United Church thinks some good will come to them if they make a house to cover their sins. We must be watchful for the Micah houses to come into our communities and countries. How watchful are we, when these appealing buildings come into our neighbourhood, welcoming all lifestyle and beliefs? Watch and pray. Amen and amen.

~

MATCHMAKER

Dear reader, are you still looking for the right match, and you have not yet met the right person. Well, I can tell you that the Lord is the best matchmaker on earth, because His work starts in Heaven. When Abraham was old, he asked his servant Eliezer to go back to Abraham's homeland Mesopotamia to the city of Nabor, and to take with him many gifts, so from there he would come back with a wife for Isaac. So now the Lord was preparing the marriage of Rebekah and Isaac. That is a beautiful story and example of how the Lord matches couples and make marriages. Eliezer had a long journey and the Lord protected him on the way. When he arrived in Nabor he prayed to the Lord there at the city well, that of all the young girls that were taking water from the well, one would offer him and his camels' water, then he would know that she is the right one.

Reference: Genesis 24: 63-67

God sent the right person, to the right place, at the right time. God started His matchmaking in Heaven and manifested it for Isaac and Rebekah on earth. There are many matches made in the Bible, done by the Lord. Reading about the different marriages that were made in Heaven, brings me to my marriage. When we read the story of Ruth and Boaz in the book of Ruth, we may think nothing like that can happen to me. Not true. Marriages like the ones in the Bible happen every day, to those who ask God to be their matchmaker. Ruth and Boaz's marriage extended to bless others; Naomi was cared for the rest of her life after they were married. All that Naomi had lost from her husband's death was returned to her. When God wants to bless two, He extends His love to many more in their family.

My husband and I both told the Lord exactly the kind of mate we would like to have forever, and He heard us, our requests, and our prayers, so He started His matchmaking in Heaven and had us meet on internet Christian Café.
My wish is to see everyone with someone that the Lord has matched them up with. When you go to the Lord and ask for your match, who you have been seeking in your heart, He will listen. Be patient and wait on the Lord to do His handiwork. "Matchmaker, Matchmaker, make me a match, catch me a catch," so we will be happily attached forever. Amen and amen.

~

ANGER IS LIKE AN ALLERGY

Wow, what a subject dear reader. Anger is a part of life we like to forget. They were angry, we were angry, I was angry. All these phases are the ones we want to forget when we begin a new day. Anger in most cases comes quickly and hurts one or more people by something said or done. Anger can also be extended over a long period of time with sad results.

Reference: Proverbs 15: 18

In this verse we read that man can be slow to anger. In other words, he has the ability to control his anger. Anger is an emotion that takes hold of the hold man. His thoughts (mind) his mouth (heart) and his body (spirit). So man's mind, heart, and spirit can be under the power of the emotion called anger. How sad.

Reference: Proverbs 16: 32

Controlling anger gives man more power. Have you ever watched boxing? The advantage of a small guy against the bigger guy is anger. Anger makes the bigger guy unaware. He loses by leaving himself open for the fatal punch. The last time I got angry was with my friend when we were shopping. She was driving and started rambling about something about my church and me being a Christian. Finally, I had heard enough, and I blurted out, "Be quite I don't want to hear another word on the subject, or you can let me out and I will take a bus home." She froze and after the cold air warmed up a little, she started talking about something else. The subject never came up again. That was constructive anger as we read about in this verse.

Reference: Matthew 21: 12, 13

Anger is like an allergy. It comes and goes. This is an allergy that can be healed. How many people do you know that have allergies and think nothing of them? They just live with them and can always blame the weather, the plants, animals, or food for the reason they have them. Those who are always angry blame others for their anger. Anger comes from an evil spirit in most cases, it also can be demonic. Anger can be cured through the love of Christ.

Reference: John 5: 2-6

Perhaps you have been angry many years like the man in our scripture. Anger can separate us from loved ones in family and friends. Anger causes unforgiveness to be a part of our very being. Anger after a long period of time becomes hate.

Reference: John 5: 7

After 38 years of lying there, I believe I would have wiggled myself to the side of the pool and gotten healed or drowned. That man after 38 years was given the opportunity through the power of Christ to change his lifestyle; instead, he blamed others for his constant condition.

Reference: John 5: 8, 9

The man was healed by the grace of God. The same grace can change your lifestyle. The same grace can remove anger from your mind, heart, and spirit. Forgiveness is also the key.

Reference: Matthew 6: 12

We want Jesus to forgive us, but are we sure we will be happy with the same measure of forgiveness we have forgiven others with? If you are a person that lashes out at others and regrets later your action and your words, you can be healed of your anger, it does not have to be like an allergy one lives with, it can be healed.

Do you suffer with a fallen relationship, which now is full of hate? Hate is an emotion of anger that can be healed.

Reference: Ephesians 4: 31, 32

Let us read that verse 32 again, give thanks and pray. Amen and amen.

∽

IT DOES NOT HELP TO COMPLAIN

Dear reader, I am reading Habakkuk, not a very pleasant reading. He reminds me of myself, like, "Lord, I love You, I worship and adore You but?" Or, "Lord, I want to thank You but?" etc... I was not being nice with the "buts" adding my complaints. Habakkuk, a man of God, a prophet, and a complainer. He could praise the Lord and complain or criticize someone all in one breath, and that reminds me of me at times. Habakkuk chapter one starts off saying, "How long must I call upon the Lord and He has not listened?" Was that a man of faith speaking? God did reply to him, "Look and see what I AM is about to do." Habakkuk did not have faith, he did not believe the Lord, he continued complaining with great anxiety, "You Lord are everlasting and Holy, but we are going to die, and You go on tolerating the injustice to us and do nothing."

Reference: Habakkuk 2: 2, 3 & 14

Now this time he changes his tune, now he believes the Lord. Why did Habakkuk now believe the Lord, was it because the Lord said He heard his cries? No, he believed because, the Lord said, "Write it down." When God's word was written down, He would come and not delay, Habakkuk believed. Habakkuk was stubborn, it was not enough for him to hear God's word, and he had to have it in writing. Habakkuk and Israel had suffered violence, injustice, and death, but now he has the word of God in writing to spread throughout Israel, so the people would know God had heard their cries and He has answered, then He will help them. God had been patient with Habakkuk's complaining and doubt. Habakkuk repented and worshiped the Lord.

How does this story apply to us? How often do we doubt the Lord? We too, like Habakkuk, must repent; we can do that daily, asking forgiveness for our lack of faith. Our Heavenly Father is so patient with us, He loves us. We do have the opportunity to do His work without complaints. We can spread the gospel, "The knowledge of the Lord over the face of the earth, as the waters cover the sea." Our faith is not to be a hidden candle; no we should be a shining light and a sounding trumpet. When we overcome our doubt we increase our faith, "So the earth will be filled with the Glory of God, as the waters cover the sea." Amen and amen.

KING OF KINGS "WAS FIRST A SEED"

Today I planted a seed for a charity. Praise the Lord. Daystar said they would double my seed. Then is prayer and thanksgiving a seed? I was telling the Lord how much I loved Him and how I am believing Him to give me the request that I had placed on my seed. Opps, I had to backtrack myself and say, "Lord I am not saying that I love You because I believe You will give me my harvest for my seed. Father You have given me everything a child needs, most of all You have given me Jesus my Saviour. God in the flesh, Jesus, sacrificed on a wooden cross, for the sins of mankind.

Not one of us could ever be worthy of His sacrifice on the cross at Calvary. We know of one human's life for another, that happens in the hospital all the time, or dying for a good cause as a martyr. Jesus was not a martyr; He was a willing sacrifice, out of love on the cross for the sins of all men.

Reference: 1 John 3: 16

That kind of love, like the love that Jesus had for mankind, the agape love. So great a love is hard to imagine or understand that it all started as a seed. God passed Himself as a seed in a young girl's womb. That was Mary and became the mother of the Messiah, Jesus.

Reference: Luke 1: 35

Jesus tried to tell people why He was here on earth. He even tried to make it easy to understand with stories and parables. Jesus wanted to teach them in a simple way, like parents want to teach their children. He was so gentle and so patient, He tried for three years to explain the Kingdom, but very few understood the teaching. Jesus tried to explain who He was, our Saviour and King. He wanted us to understand that we are also "children of God." I am giving thanks for this revelation, so I now have a better understanding of the "seed."

Reference: Exodus 16: 4,31,33,34

The "coriander corn "was manna. The manna had to be beaten and thrashed and must be changed from a kernel to a powder. Then salt and water must be added, rolled and kneaded into a tough dough then formed into a cake. The cake was on a griddle over a fire or baked in a stone oven. When it was ready it was eaten, and it nourished the body every day. That manna was the bread of life for the Israelites out in the desert.

The Lord Jesus is the "bread of Life" for us. The Word of the Lord nourishes us daily and that is Jesus: on the way to Calvary and Cross, He was beaten and thrashed by the Roman soldiers, He was changed from a strong young man to a lifeless corpse. In the tomb, with the power of the Holy Spirit His lifeless body was brought back to life. The "Risen Christ came forth on Easter morning. The King of Kings, the bread of Life was raised, and we celebrate His resurrection from the dead and the tomb. We celebrate eternal life that started with a seed. Amen and amen.

~

LOSE YOUR TEMPER

Dear reader I do not think of God having a temper or of Jesus having one, although they can be angry.

God is slow to anger; He does not have a temper. Man has a temper that flares up quickly, that is not like God.

Reference: Genesis 6: 11-13

In these verses we are talking about some hundred years from when God created the earth. God is so patient, all these years man had been sinning and filling the earth with evil and God sat back sadly watching it happen. God has His righteous nature and there comes a time when God says. "Enough is enough." Here in verse 13, He tells Noah that His time has come to make right what has been made wrong on earth. If God flared up with a temper like we do, He would not have been concerned with the animals and the beauty of the animal world. God had a plan of survival for Noah's family and all the animals. There was no place for a 'hot temper' in God's plan. If God gets angry, His wrath is patient, perfectly performed.

Reference: Genesis 18: 20, 21

God loved Noah and his family, and He also loved Abraham and his family. God always had a plan first to Noah and his survival then to Abraham to save his nephew Lot and his family. God and Abraham were friends, an amazing friendship between them. Before God moved on the evil cities, He consulted Abraham for his thoughts about God's plan. God gave Abraham the opportunity to save his family, and that is what Abraham did by consulting God, and asking for survival of his family. God created the earth and man offended Him with evil ways and unbelief. Therefore, He flooded the earth, only saving believers and innocent lives; once again He will do away with evil and unbelief.

Reference: Mathew 21: 12, 13

In these verses we find Jesus in His Father's house. Evil men were using the temple as a marketplace. People were purchasing animals and birds for sacrifice for their sins. Also, these evil marketeers were exchanging currencies from other countries, they were called "moneychangers," but they were thieves. Jesus came into the temple angry and offended to see what was happening in the Lord's house. Jesus walked in and threw the tables of money over and rebuked them all. Jesus did not flare up with a temper He was angry and bold with the authority He alone had as the Messiah, Son of God. He was righteous and just, therefore His anger was justified.

As we know Jesus never did anything with consulting His Heavenly Father first, so what He did was God's will. Temper is the opposite of tolerance. It is an action with words that appear in an instant. Tolerance is intelligent thinking before any action or words appear. We need to practise tolerance to rebuke our temper.

We should never instantly flare up or shout at another person. If we are angry, then we must think before approaching them. We can speak with authority and justice without doing or saying something we may later regret. Temper is a time bomb that almost always causes regret in the future.

Reference: Romans 5: 3-5

Paul tells us when we do run into problems, we should rejoice, because it is those problems that develop strength of character in us. When we lose our temper for good, let it stay lost for good. When we discover that tolerance is a better way, we also discover that patience is even better and is truly a blessing from Father God for His children. Amen and amen.

~

IS YOUR DESIRE TO OBEY GOD?

Dear reader when we are little children we do not want to obey our parents, we want to go our own way from the day we arrived on this planet. We begin to rebel as soon as we are weaned from the bottle. We begin to make our own decisions as soon as we refuse to eat what our mother gives us. We laugh when the baby spits the spinach back, but it is not funny, incidentally it is the first sign of disobedience and rebellion.

The first time we find this in the Bible is in Genesis. Genesis means 'beginning.' In this book we find many beginnings including rebellion and disobedience. When our parents try to feed and care for us they have good intentions. It is the same with God. First as little children, then students and adults. We think our lives would be better without so many rules and discipline. We are wrong. God has always known what is best for us, and He still knows. All He asks of us is our obedience. He has never wanted anything but a good relationship with mankind. Good relationships are usually spoiled with a third party. That is exactly what happened with our relationship with God.

Reference: Genesis 3: 1-5

There you have it; the third party that spoiled Adam's relationship with God was a serpent, the Devil. The Devil enticed the woman to disobey God and she invited her husband to disobey also. Adam and Eve had one rule from God, and they disobeyed it. I repeat, God had one rule for them, and they blew it. The woman was tempted by her desire of something better than she had at the time. The tempter won her alliance and she obeyed him instead of God. Disobeying one rule allowed sin into the world. Mankind has been struggling with sin ever since.

Reference: Genesis 3: 6

Her desire was not to please her creator but to please herself. She was not thankful for Paradise in the Garden, no she wanted more. Remember she did not want more until the serpent suggested the possibility she could have more. You noticed that the serpent did not refer to her creator as her God: he referred to other gods. This was the comment on idolatry and pagan gods. The only thing God wanted to do was to enjoy His creations. Like a child playing with a teddy-bear, talking, and hugging and loving their playmate. I think this is what God wanted when He created man and placed him in a beautiful place called Paradise, he wanted to have a loving fellowship with them.

Reference: Genesis 3: 8

Well, it did not work out the way God desired. Man fell, so great was his fall that all mankind were condemned to death because of sin. We read through the Old Testament how mankind was up and down with God before Jesus. With the prophets and all the blessing God bestowed on His children the Israelites; He never really got through to them how important it was for them to turn from their sinful ways. He could never convince them His desire was for them to overcome death and receive eternal life in His Kingdom. Even today there are so many that do not understand the following scripture.

Reference: John 3: 16

Jesus had to come and settle the score between God and man.

Reference: 1 Timothy 2: 5-6

A third party brought sin into the world and for hundreds of years there was no one as an intercessor for man. Man needed another third party to intervene into the lost relationship between God and himself. Jesus was and is that third party. For once man had a helper and not a tempter. Oh, how true it is that man was so unworthy of a saviour. We will never be worthy for such a Saviour as the Son of God. Jesus' only desire was to obey God His Father. He was not like us wanting to have gain and our own way. Jesus loved God the same way we need to love Him. That same desire can only be ours as we grow closer to Jesus and learn to love the Father more each day.

Reference: Acts 5: 29

Here the disciples were on their own. They were facing all the obstacles that Jesus had warned them of. Their only strength and courage came from their faith and love for Jesus and a reoccurring desire in their hearts to obey God. They met each day like 'a morning glory' blossoming with anticipation. What will this day bring? How will we serve our Saviour this day?

Reference: Psalm 1: 1-2

To be blessed is our desire. We always want a blessing. David is making a point that man's delight should be in the law of the Lord. My point is that the word 'delight' could be exchanged for the word 'desire,' and the word 'Lord' could be exchanged for 'God's Word.' Reading, "His desire is the law of the Word of God." In closing this revelation I would like to leave you with the comfort of Jesus' words regarding obedience.

Reference: John 15: 9-11

So now we go back to the title, "Is it your desire to obey God?" I hope your answer is, "Yes." Amen and amen.

DELIVERANCE

Dear reader have you heard the phrase, "Accident prone." Perhaps you have this problem or have a loved one or friend that suffers from this problem. Believe me it is a problem, and it can be a very costly problem. I have a loved one that when growing up had this problem. I have been calling it a problem, but to be exact, it is a demon that is controlling the person's movements. In many cases a person that possesses this 'accident' demon can be accused of being clumsy, stupid, or negligent.

My loved one was one of my sons, always having accidents and costing us money for repairs and compensations. When he was studying in Madrid to become a flight steward for Spain Air, he was doing very well and the day of his exam I was praying for him. He was driving a rented car and on his way to his exam the car spun out of control and turned over 3 times, he walked away and told the police where he needed to be, so the police took him there and waited until he had finished his exam. He filled out some papers with the police, and then he called me.

We gave the Lord the glory and our thanksgiving for everything. His exam was good, and he was appointed his job and moved to Mallorca the same day. I spoke to him about this problem and told him I was going to take it to the church which I did on Sunday.

Reference: Psalm 107: 13-15

This is what we did on the Sunday, we called that demon, that accident demon, and we called him out in Jesus name and cast him out of my son, so the demon could no longer abide in him. I have noted in my Bible 'released.' My son was being held in a shadow of death, 30,000 ft in the air, one accident could have caused a death, but praise the Lord, Jesus is our Deliverer, and our demons must flee at the mention of His Name. Hallelujah. We must be aware of the demons existence and what name it is called and so we call it by name and rebuke it 'In Jesus Name' with prayer for complete deliverance. That is what we did on

Sunday in 2002 and no accidents.

Reference: Ephesians 1: 19-23 and Psalm 107: 1, 2

Dear reader I hope this lovely testimony has encouraged you to study more of God's Word on deliverance. Amen and amen.

~

DIETING

This subject, dear readers, is very unpopular with me and a lot of other people. I have been very naughty because I do not watch my appetite. I have let it get out of control, so now I find my zipper is only going halfway up, my buttons and holes are not meeting, my drawstrings are shorter, and my elastic is tighter. So, you understand I need to go on a diet. My husband loves to cook, and I love to eat. Our daily schedule is full most of the time so our fellowship together eating our meals is very important.

I have tried Weight Watchers, but I was not very good at that. I guess I am putting the blame more on my husband for my lack of control of what I am eating and drinking. It is not his fault it is mine. I have decided to bring my problem to the Lord and pray about it. I should have done this a long time ago. Why do we always come to Him after all our trials and failures? I know with my prayer I must also go to the Word.

Reference: Psalm 139: 14

My first step in losing weight is my attitude. It is so easy to look into the mirror and be disappointed with what I see. In Psalms David says, "I am fearfully and wonderfully made." I am fearfully made tells me that God, when he designed me to look as I am, He did it out of respect for me His creation. And He made me wonderful. When I count my abilities, talents and how I function, I am an amazing creation.

Reference: Genesis 1: 26, 27

God the Almighty, our awesome God wants that I should be like Him. So now after reading these two verses in Psalms and Genesis I am getting a more positive attitude. Then for more encouragement I can also go to Paul's letters.

Reference: 1 Corinthians 3: 16, 19-20

When Paul tells us we are temples of the Holy Spirit to glorify the Lord, I can look in the mirror with a more positive attitude. In other words, I can look at my body as a vessel for the Lord. So, then I must take particularly good care of it. Taking good care of my body, the temple of the Holy Spirit is my first step of good stewardship. My attitude is improving, and I am more encouraged to start my diet. It is Holy Spirit who encourages me to take better care of my body. I do not have to eat a lot of things because they taste good. I can with self- control enjoy what taste good at a minimum quantity. So, step one to glorify my Creator is to take better care of His creation, me. Take better care of Holy Spirit's temple, me.

Reference: Romans 12: 1-3

When we read these verses, we learn that attitude and humility play a big part in my ambition concerning my diet, "But be ye transformed by the renewing of your mind, that ye may prove what is that good, and acceptable and perfect, will of God." In other words, 'do it for God, and do it with God.' I am particularly fond of verse 1 which suggests that it may be good for my husband and I to diet together. It is always easier to have someone with you when you diet. We would be showing better stewardship of our bodies and pleasing the Lord with our respect to Holy Spirit's temple. Since my husband and I are ministers we can be good examples for others in our church. As we both start our new diet, I pray by the grace of God, He will help us become more humble, holy, and acceptable to serve Him. Amen and amen.

~

THANK YOU

*I hope you have had your own revelations and references ,
encouraged by my book. Listening to Holy Spirit in our earthly
life, brings us closer to our eternal life with Jesus and that is all
I have done to write this book. Bless you dear reader.
Shalom in His Name.
REVBON*

Rev. Bonnie A. Nygaard

~